OUT SOU RCED

DR. LISA DUNNE

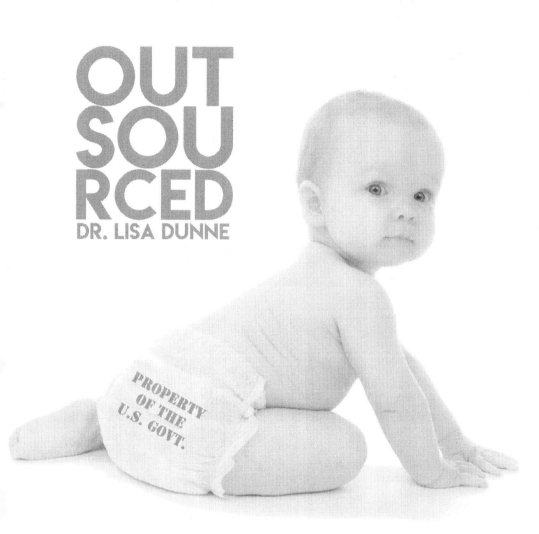

PROPERTY OF THE U.S. GOVT.

WHY AMERICA'S KIDS NEED AN EDUCATION REVOLUTION

The Impact of Outsourced

"My friend Dr. Lisa Dunne has provided a compelling, comprehensive, and convicting book that strikes at the core of human experience. This book is a clarion call for parents to recover our Deuteronomy 6 responsibility as teachers. Written with compassion, extensive research, and speaking from experience in her own and thousands of families, Lisa provides a roadmap of hope for your family. Parents, the day of Outsourcing is over! Rise up and receive your inheritance!"

- *Dr. John Jackson, President of William Jessup University and Author of Books on Leadership and Transformation*

"In the decade that I have known Dr. Lisa Dunne, she has always been a mover and a shaker in the field of education. Her book *Outsourced* is certain to awaken parents to a cultural movement that will not only help restore the socio-academic trajectory and spiritual health of our nation's youth but will assist in turning the hearts of the next generation back to their parents."

- *Dr. Jim Garlow, CEO of Well Versed and Author of 21 books on Worldview, Leadership, and Biblical Governance*

"We only get one opportunity to educate our kids. I have personally trusted Dr. Lisa Dunne with the strategies for educating my own children because of her robust knowledge, proven track record, and biblical strategies. *Outsourced* will serve as a wakeup call to parents who have blindly put their faith in a public school system that does not have their children's flourishing at heart. Dr. Dunne is shifting the paradigm of what it looks like to educate our children and we are fortunate to have such a pioneer in our midst!"

- *Dr. Mike Yeager, Structural Engineer and Campus Pastor at Awaken Church*

"Dr. Dunne's decades of applied acumen is a lightning rod of wisdom that cuts directly to the core that students need *relationship* and are not simply a number in a mind-numbing transactional outsourced machine with an agenda to extract life. Her undeniable God-given passion for the cause of homeschooling breathes exponential and transformative life into today's children while inspiring parents and teachers to reach new heights of meaning and prosperous success. She not only pinpoints problems, but offers tangible, refreshing and inspiring solutions that equip any person willing to learn. This resource and Dr. Dunne's other

2

resources are guaranteed to positively impact you and those you lead for long-term sustained growth."

> -   *David Baldwin, Husband, Father, Leadership Consultant to the Fortune 100, Co-Founder of AbundantLifeEducation.com*

"Dr. Lisa Dunne is a voice crying out for a generation in need of rescue. Her wisdom and insight is the byproduct of years on the frontline of education. As the stewards of our children's development, we are in dire need of such a herald. She understands the battle for our children's minds and it's with compassionate clarity and fearless honesty that she is equipping us to understand how to meet their needs. As an attachment specialist and clinician, I have never seen an educator who so deeply understands the needs of both heart and mind, and how to create the conditions our children need to thrive emotionally, socially and academically!"

> *- Brian Reiswig, Marriage and Family Counselor*

"Dr. Dunne's jaw-dropping truth bombs of how public education has failed our children ignites parents to take the reins back so we can restore what was lost. *Outsourced* highlights an obvious and urgent need for parents and churches to become education mentors to the next generation. Through bonds of community and the resources in this book, it is possible to create a balanced, fruitful home-based learning plan."

> *- Christine Gail, Best-Selling Author of Unleash Your Rising*

"I count Dr. Lisa Dunne among my heroes for having the courage and conviction to write such a powerful and unapologetically honest diagnosis of our current educational and spiritual crisis in America. It's an absolute must-read for any parent, pastor, or marketplace leader. In *Outsourced* Dr. Lisa Dunne expertly weaves in extensive research, personal experience, and biblical principles that conclusively shut the door on the idea that public and private education are salvageable. We absolutely need an education revolution, and this book must be in the hands of every parent embarking on the brave journey of home-schooling and discipling their children."

> *-Ebey Sorenson, M.Ed., Homeschooling Parent, Former Teacher and Behavior Interventionist*

"So many at the tip of the spear for their respective *quests for change,* either lead emotionally with their heart or robotically recall data to support their position. Dr. Lisa guides us to understanding *and* appropriate action with *both.* She leverages the quality, relevant data with a tenacious passion. She is intent on upending a long broken cornerstone of our society—a rebel yell for parents to rally for school at home. She did it for her own children and continues to charge forward for us and ours—for the generations to come."

- David Ewing, Lead Teacher: Awaken Academy San Diego,
Owner & Creative at Heave Ho! Creative

"Dr. Lisa Dunne is making a way for the next generation of parents to have clarity and be equipped for wholehearted, Biblical parenting. Her words are both comforting and convicting, serving to encourage and inform parents who are seeking wisdom in raising children. *Outsourced* is the perfect balance of her real life experience and thorough research, poised to launch every reader to their full parenting potential."

- Corie Di Matteo, Homeschooling Parent and Mentor

"Dr. Lisa Dunne is a trailblazer in the field of homeschooled education. She has created a space unlike anything I've ever seen. Under her exceptional leadership, parents and students can simultaneously thrive. Dr. Lisa is a much-needed advocate and voice for the next generation."

- Brittni De La Mora, Pastor, Author, and Founder
of LoveAlwaysMinistries.com

"Yes, America's kids need an education revolution. Dr. Lisa makes that apparent. She carefully explains how we as a society got where we are today and outlines in a clear and compassionate way what parents can do to fix it. Let me give you a hint. The answer isn't found inside the four walls of a public school classroom. This message is timely and needed. Dr. Lisa's message is a clarion call for all of us. Read this book and join the rescue mission."

- Rebecca Kocsis, Lifelong Homeschooling Parent and General
Manager of the Christian Home Educators Association of California

First copyright 2022. All rights reserved.
Published by CVCU Press, Chula Visa, CA.
ISBN: 978-1-951797-80-5

CVCU Publishing is dedicated to furthering the messages of innovators,
visionaries, and culture-shapers. Bulk discounts of this book, as well as study
guides and online resources, are available at Chula Vista Christian University
through the CVCU.us contact page.

Title: Outsourced: Why America's Kids Need an Education Revolution
Author: Dr. Lisa Dunne

Printed in the United States of America

Book design by Adrian Dunne

SOCIAL SCIENCE / PSYCHOLOGY / RELIGION / EDUCATION

Dedication:

Over the past 20 years, I've had the privilege of watching the gradual light of revelation flood across the faces of parents who are being transformed through home education. Of the many impassioned conversations I've been privy to, one in particular stands out to me as the socio-cultural core of this book. Fresh into detoxing her family from traditional academia, a parent stopped me in a church hallway to share an epiphany that had suddenly registered in her conscious mind. "Dr. Dunne," she began, as tears of that profound mixture of regret and gratitude glazed over her eyes, "I've just realized that my whole life, I've been outsourcing my children." Like the thousands of parents who have so recently rescued their offspring from the grip of our nation's failed scholastic model, this mom recounted the moments, the years, and the milestones she had missed in her children's lives. As she stepped out of the methodological rat race and into the freedom of educational discipleship, she saw with great and tragic clarity that for most of her life, her children had been sold out to the lowest bidder, America's public school system. She knew it was time to turn the tide. This book is written for the courageous parents who stand ready to reclaim their rights to the educational discipleship of the next generation. The devastation is real. The harvest is ready. It's time for an education revolution.

OUT SOU RCED
DR. LISA DUNNE

TABLE OF CONTENTS

Foreword

There is supposedly an ancient Chinese curse: "May you live in interesting times." Although there is no clear evidence that this is either ancient or Chinese, it is a wry statement we can relate to. Every generation has lived during "interesting times," a euphemism for challenges or troubles, but there are a few paradoxes that make these times particularly "interesting."

One of them is this: Almost everyone in our country—and the world—is better off today than almost everyone was a hundred—or even fifty—years ago, in terms of comfort, convenience, and security, along with access to information, medical care, food, and certainly entertainment. It is truly an embarrassment of riches because so few realize how fortunate we are. Instead, people—especially young people—believe themselves more miserable than any generation before, more even than those who lived through real hardships such as war and famine. Currently suicide is the third leading cause of death among teenagers, and the number of young people medicated for depression rises continuously.

Parents of teens don't know what to do, and many of them feel the same hopelessness. And it doesn't make sense. Given the relative comfort and ease with which we have been blessed, we and our children should be the happiest and most grateful people ever to live on the planet. But we are not, and we don't know why. The cognitive dissonance creates stress and angst to the point that many are unhappy because they don't know why they are unhappy, and feeling subconscious guilt on top of that. A deep dissatisfaction pervades our almost unbelievable comfort. In part, it's because we don't know history. Movies may show suffering or heroism, but they aren't real to us. We don't compare our lot with the people of the past; we compare our level of wealth with the "rich and famous" who, for the most part, are the most miserable of all. Perspective is missing.

But that's just the symptom. The causes are more

disconcerting. In *The Coddling of the American Mind: How Good Intentions and Bad Ideas are Setting Up a Generation for Failure* (2019), Lukianoff and Haidt posit that university students are being taught three "great untruths" both in classrooms and through campus culture. Students are coming to believe 1) Exposure to adversity or discomfort is inherently damaging, i.e., the snowflake syndrome, 2) Trust your feelings—and correspondingly disdain logic and reason, and 3) Everyone is either good or bad, thus denying that there is good and bad in everyone, including ourselves. Haidt and Lukianoff have no religious or political agenda, which has allowed them some credibility in the debate about what higher education should be, though it seems they have remained largely ignored by the institutions themselves.

However, that college students are falling for these three lies is not surprising to anyone who has looked closely at what schools have been teaching—and failing to teach—children for the past several decades. Many of us grew up in public (or private) schools in the 1970s era, and we can easily think, "It wasn't so bad. I turned out okay." I would counter that we grew up with a modicum of faith and reason intact not because of the schools but in spite of them. Now, the anti-Truth curriculum is fully entrenched, and there are very few children who escape an indoctrination which leads so often to despair and hopelessness.

In these pages, Dr. Lisa Dunne brings clarity to the core of the problem of relativism by providing not only the history of how schools came to be the way they are, but the twelve "toxic traits" we must be aware of if we want to purge the poisons from the minds of our children and restore mental and spiritual health. Perhaps you have avoided the worst of these; if so you have been both diligent and fortunate. But no one in today's culture can avoid all of them. It is urgent that we detoxify our minds and hearts, our families, churches, and communities. The medicine is not easy, but it is time-tested. Repentance. We must turn our hearts toward our Creator and Savior, who gives us the words of life. Repentance isn't pleasant, either personally or communally, but it is vital. As schools have canceled God and replaced His truth with the lies of relativism, children have become victims of soulless education.

Yes, 2020 and the consequent shutdown of schools was a wake-up call for parents, who may have had for the first time an awareness of what the schools are really teaching. Many have realized that "outsourcing" education has not—and will not—provide the foundation in skills, knowledge, and faith with which they hope to equip their children, and they are looking for alternatives. Thankfully, there are energetic visionaries like Dr. Lisa who work tirelessly against the enemies of family and faith. Her insights will strengthen your resolve and equip you to assist others to make choices toward education with better outcomes. Our future depends on it.

Andrew Pudewa
Founder of the Institute for Excellence in Writing

CHAPTER ONE

Systemic Failure: The Public School Model

Like any good student, I vividly remember many of my childhood teachers. The finality of their words imprinted on my heart, but more than that, their evaluations took root in my soul. At my sprawling brick elementary school in Belleville, Illinois, my kindergarten teacher, Mrs. Burns, taught me how the adult world functioned. She showed me that the teacher's words were the final words; her thoughts were the most important thoughts flooding the classroom airwaves. I was the pail. She was the expert, the filler of the pail. And I was never, ever to question a teacher's expertise, motive, or meaning.

She taught me that I must never leave her sterile, lifeless classroom at the same time as a classmate, for children were never to be trusted alone together in the hallway. If I needed to get a drink or use the restroom, I must raise my hand and wait like an obedient little student. As the expert in all things, the teacher knew better than I the precise timing for a student's individual needs and wellbeing. Mrs. Burns said I must always stand up and project my voice in class, despite a painful shyness that made me want to disappear when anyone called my name. Once, in a moment of quiet rebellion, I learned that if I held in my sneezes, no one would say, "God bless you" to the shy girl in the back: I could remain invisible, at least for the moment. And Mrs. Burns taught me about the stars. No, not the celestial lights hanging overhead in the night sky—she taught me about the coveted gold stars of the classroom. I learned that if I could anticipate what Mrs. Burns wanted me to say, if I could read her teacher-mind and articulate exactly what she was thinking, I would be rewarded with a gold star, the public certification of her approval.

By the time I graduated to third grade in 1976, my family was in turmoil. My mom, who had gotten pregnant with me in high school, was starting to feel the predictable effects of domestic abuse so common in unwed pregnancies. She felt lost, alone, afraid. The vehement yelling between two parents filtered down the stairwell as a constant refrain, like the hum of a motorboat or a continuous stream of freeway traffic outside your bedroom window. You just got used to it. And one day, before school, my mom came downstairs with a suitcase in hand and announced dryly that she was leaving for work. She walked out the door that morning and never came back.

As I sank into my seat at school the next day, the uncertainly hung over me like an ominous cloud. Mrs. Reuter, my third grade math teacher, had watched me slump slowly up the steps to the portable building the served as our mathematics classroom at Dewey Elementary School. But she didn't know me. She didn't know the weight of fear and worry and confusion that was swirling violently inside my 8-year-old heart. When I was dull and non-responsive in class, she took it as her pedantic duty to make sure other eager-to-please students did not sink to my level of disinterest and disengagement. She looked directly at me: "Where is your homework?" Silence.

"What is the answer to number 15?" she demanded, her tone growing more aggressive as she peered down at me through her horn-rimmed glasses. I sat in silence. She asked again. "What is the answer?"

"I don't know," I whispered, barely audible, lest my esteemed third-grade peers notice that I was unprepared for class. "Where is your homework?" she countered, teetering on a decades-old pent-up frustration that seeped in, flooding her mind with hundreds of memories of previous students who had refused to cower in her presence. "I don't know," I whispered again.

Her subsequent rant began in full view of the whole class. "You, young lady, will never be good at math. Never. Now, put on the dunce cap and go stand in the corner." I obeyed, dutifully. And, standing there in the corner with the dunce cap on my head, the label of my mathematical deficiencies stamped forever on my childhood psyche, I vowed that I would never, every displease a teacher again.

The next week, I was whisked away to a new scholastic training ground, an impoverished school in neighboring Alton, where my mother's grandparents owned a grocery store and a two-story house, making them some of the wealthiest people in the barefoot, arid little country town. I was the new girl, and there was a swell of popularity that moderated the emptiness I felt. But there was something else, another skill that emerged, a latent characteristic previously unrecognized by my other teachers. Apparently, I was a good reader. When I was called on to read aloud in class, even though my heart pounded so audibly I was certain every student could hear it, I read. I read aloud. And the room was suddenly quiet. I felt the class—and more importantly, the teacher—listening intently as I read, impressed with my emotive linguistic skills.

Halfway through the school year, I was sent to

another school four states away to live with my aunt while my parents navigated the first of their seven divorces. I was the only blonde student in a sea of classmates from Cuba, and I wasn't sure if my classmates liked me due to my novelty or if they despised me because I stood out from the crowd—a crucial social error for young schoolgirls. But there in that room, next to the hurricane windows and dark-haired children, I was called upon to read aloud again. And just as before, the room fell silent. The teacher affirmed me. A warm swell of what I imagined must be pride swept over me. Another gold star was mine.

Outside the classroom, I was faced with myself again, the cold, harsh reality of my brokenness. I began to imagine significant defects in my appearance. As I stood in the bathroom at Flamingo Elementary School in Hialeah, Florida looking in the mirror, my ordinary nose suddenly looked gargantuan, too monstrously large to suit my face. I imagined that my tiny, pre-pubescent frame was burgeoning with fat, and the seeds of self-abuse began burrowing into my soul. Certainly, many of the physical defects I was imagining were part of the painful process children go through when parents divorce: the self abasement, the ruminating, wondering what words or deeds the child was responsible for that would have caused a parent to abandon the family. There's a reason, after all, that Malachi 2:16 says God hates divorce. Social science research tells us that the sting of divorce leaves a deeper wound than the death of a parent. Why? The divorced parent remains alive, possessing the agency to make a difference, and yet chooses to reject the home, the child, the family, whatever the object of previous affection.

But in that moment at Hialeah Elementary, the sting of rejection was buried beneath a new and secret pathway out of the present pain. It seemed so innocent, so benign, so perfect. My daily scholastic lessons in the world of traditional education taught me not only reading, writing, and arithmetic; they taught me a worldview, a lens, a way of seeing the universe, others, and myself. I learned to be performer, a gold-star student, driven by the smiling feedback of my teacher. I learned to live for the approval of others.

E.B. White says that when we allow our minds to fall into the groove of memory, thoughts and feelings can come rushing back, and we can suddenly recall with great clarity moments that we thought may have been lost in the recesses of our minds. It's vital for our healing that we remember our history, that we develop a "coherent narrative" about our lives, our strengths, our weaknesses, our blind spots, our motivations.

As I was writing the first chapter of this book, the street names of my early childhood homes, now buried 48 years in my memory, came flooding back, and I had the sudden impulse to look them up on Google Earth. For some reason, I expected the houses to have been burned down, leveled, with another city built on top of them, like some forgotten, ancient ruin. But there they both were, still standing, still looming large next to the forest and the cemetery I recall so vividly, both now housing someone else's future memories.

Like me, most people reading this book went to public school. So what's the big deal? We survived, right? Today's public schools have changed, though not as much in the last 50 years as you may have thought (we'll get to that). But public schools are only part of today's multifaceted crisis. Public schools, churches, and parents have all contributed to the breakdown of the American psyche, to the fragmentation that causes us to drift anchorlessly through life. It's not simply a one-dimensional impact, of course, but the influence from the public school system is so intense, so directly correlative of modern social behavior, that I believe it is a vital starting point for the conversation. If we can leverage significant changes in education in partnership with the family and the local church, I am fully confident that we will positively and powerfully shift the trajectory for the next generation.

In his most recent published study, George Barna says that the youngest generation is "largely the product of the unaddressed dysfunctions of the generations that came before them—the generations that raised the Millennials to become who they are today." In other words, their problem is our problem. Barna reminds us that the natural response to a research project that analyzes the brokenness of a generation is to point a finger, to "scour the data in order to identify the perceived shortcomings of the subject population and criticize those alleged failings," he says. "But all that does is stretch the culture gap a bit wider and harden the protective shields the cultural combatants have seized." The younger generation is pressed between a rock and a hard place. They have "inherited a cultural war zone," as Barna puts it, "but not the tools to bring peace to that war."

Yes, the content of the public school classroom has grown more fiercely wicked over the last decade, and the bullying and aggressive politicizing are paramount. We'll talk more about this in the chapters to come. But these essential elements of identity confusion, of trust and mistrust, of knowing and being known, of pail and filler, expert and fool, has, I believe, created the fundamental rift in the neural development of America's children, of America's families, and that's just the beginning.

GenZ emotional distinctives are sobering. They are anxious, depressed, overwhelmed, suicidal, self-injurious, STD-ridden, and more likely to cohabitate than any other previous generation. Tragically, they are the most atheist generation in the history of our nation. The two main areas of disbelief are as follows: They can't believe a loving God would allow evil, and they don't believe that science and the Bible are compatible. This "knowledge base" is easily traced to its source: public school indoctrination, where on our watch, science has been pitted against Scripture, and the Great Commission has literally been outlawed in every public sphere of American culture.

While I was completing my doctorate in human development (happily accompanied by many gold stars), I began noticing distinctive patterns of behavior across generations. And I was shocked by the fallout. As I worked with parents across the nation, these striking patterns began emerging, distilling, offering clarity into the cause and effect of the cultural crisis. The assessment of patterns is vital to the social scientist, for patterns help us see cause and effect. They help us unravel how small decisions, daily habits, can take root in the heart of a generation. Most importantly, they help us see where the ship needs to be turned if we are to make incremental, positive changes for the future.

One day ten years ago, rather serendipitously, I stumbled across an overt generational shift. I had just written my first book, *Emerge,* and I was speaking to audiences in northern California about some of the main findings and principles coming out of the research. When I asked audiences over the age of 35 how many of them knew someone who was cutting or burning themselves on purpose, hardly a hand would be raised in the entire auditorium. But when I asked their 18 to 25-year-old children the exact same question, virtually every single person in the audience knew someone who had engaged in self-injurious behavior. I couldn't believe my eyes. I tried the experiment over and over with every adult audience, comparing the findings again with every college classroom. That pattern of response underscored a generational shift that had taken place on our watch. Something had changed, dramatically, in just 15 years.

Certainly, every generation has trauma. The survivors of the Great Depression have behavioral markers that govern their thoughts on scarcity, lack, provision, fear. But as neuroscience shows us, it isn't the existence of trauma that creates the wound; it's the lack of processing, of unpacking, the lack of an adult human being who can unpack the experience and and make sense of the trauma in the format of genuine, caring, healing conversation. Today, we have an entire generation of students who have grown up in an eerily similar void to GenXers, a vacuum of presence, of support. Though my own parents were physically absent, the parents of this generation are absent in a different way: emotionally absent, distracted, detached. Parents don't trust their instincts, their parenting ability (they've been taught to leave that to the "experts"), and many of them tell me they don't feel the natural depth of emotional connection with their children known as attachment. Lack of trust in themselves and others keeps them from deep relationships.

So as we contemplate the question, "what's wrong with public schools," I invite you to reflect, to remember, to recognize yourself in this picture. One of the great lessons that we learned about the adult world as children was that we ourselves were never to be trusted. Only the adult, the classroom authority figure, knew everything. Only the teacher knew the correct answer from the stupid answer, the smart question from the stupid question, the dunce from the genius. Only the teacher held the power and the gold stars. A pervasive lack of confidence has led us to deny our own testimonies, to eschew our own wisdom, to cling to the label of follower instead of leader of our lives, our own families.

As a child, and even as a young adult, I was out of

touch with the most basic core of who I was, what I knew, whose I was. I was numb. But something shifted when I became a mother. My poetry began to overflow with hope. I marveled at the life that was sprouting inside my womb, and a new sense of purpose arose in me, something greater than me, more powerful than me, something archaic and yet new, something that gripped me at the core of my being and literally shook me back to life. When my first child was born, I had a spiritual awakening, an overwhelming sense of God's unconditional love for me, his daughter. There was no perfect performance or gold star needed for the affection of a child (or, as I saw so clearly in that moment, our creator). I was suddenly both loved and lovable. This is one of the many reasons Psalm 127:3 tells us that children are an inheritance of the Lord, a gift, a reward, and that our children will contend with our enemies at the gate. Our children give us an exponential surge of power. I believe this same parent-child connection will be the turning point for our nation, the rising up of the Deborahs, the Esthers, the Jaels of the modern era, women who have witnessed the attack on their children and are ready to let go of fear, to step up to the battle line, and to fight back for the freedoms of the youngest generation.

We often think of child abuse in solely physical terms, but the reality is that many children in American culture, though perhaps well-fed in the physical, are malnourished in the spirit. They have been withering away in public school environments devoid of hope and encouragement, devoid of the spirit of the living God. Souls crushed, they try in vain to push upward through the din, past the discouraging voices, past the naysayers. But for the vast majority of them, the pressure is too great, the negativity and cynicism too intense. They succumb to the hopelessness; they embrace the darkness. The light of joy that once brightened their youthful countenance grows dim, and despite their parents' naively optimistic goal of sending their 6-year-olds out "to be salt and light," the child becomes a product of the ungodly environment into which he has been planted.

Plato once said that the two most important questions every culture must ask are, "Who teaches the children, and what are they being taught?" Since the introduction of the Values Clarification Movement in the public education system in 1964, and the removal of the Bible in 1963, the United States has seen a steady decline of the moral output of its youngest citizens. The collateral damage of secular education is tangible. Today, 51 million kids sit in public school environments across the country for 6-7 hours a day, 180 days a year, where they are overtly indoctrinated in gender fluidity, revisionist history, macro evolution, critical race theory, and overt promiscuity. Today's K -12 curricula is more about serving a political agenda than meeting the true academic needs of the next generation.

In his 1931 novel *Brave New World*, Aldous Huxley predicts a future where children will be indoctrinated against traditional values through a cradle-to-grave education system. It's the subversive framework we see all around us right now, cultivating, indoctrinating, training up an entire generation of children. Years ago, former Focus on the Family President Dr. Dobson stated in no uncertain terms that the public schools are "indoctrinating students" in "a godless, anti-Christian agenda disguised in progressive curricula." Christians, he said, must "flee" public schools. Some parents listened, but many, most, chose to believe schools would change. They didn't. They haven't. They won't. Lieutenant Colonel Ray Moore, founder of the Exodus Mandate, adds, "If we don't change the way we do education, we will lose our country."

When I contrast my scholastic upbringing with that of

my homeschooled children, the comparison is striking. Their daily schedules consisted of reading classic literature and holding engaging discussions around the dinner table (and the breakfast table, and the lunch table) with their parents, two parents, who have now been married 31 years. They explored the great outdoors. They took field trips to see and feel and taste the world that exists outside the classroom, the world that houses our greatest life lessons, the laboratory of reality. They were told daily that they were valuable, loved, that they had unique and wonderful talents to be discovered and pursued. From this secure base, their sense of confidence and curiosity, motivation and determination, has emerged. They are confident, strong, independent, compassionate. Their ability to think deeply and critically not only astounds me, it outpaces me.

In the dim reflections of teachers like Mrs. Burns and Mrs. Reuter, I remember another teacher, a teacher very important to my timeline. Mrs. Donna Bollier was not only my English teacher (who no doubt appreciated my read-aloud prowess), but she was also my next-door neighbor. She was willing to risk professionalism and safety to step into my world and throw me a lifeline. Walking through the front door of my childhood home, she would open the kitchen cabinets, and, seeing that the only edible ingredients in the kitchen were Saltine crackers and Busch beer, she would invite me to her home for dinner, to show me "what a real family looked like," as she once put it. I asked her many years later what motivated her to walk so boldly into my house, open the empty kitchen cabinets, shudder in disgust at the neglect, and then bring me to her own home to feed and care for me. My dad, an undercover police officer, carried a gun. She had to know that. In response to my reflective question decades later, she told me that her own safety wasn't her focus. In fact, it wasn't even on her radar. She had one goal and only one goal in mind: me. I was the object of her rescue mission. Maya Angelou described a similar mentor in her life, Sister Flowers, as the "measure of all a human being could be," the person who threw her the first lifeline.

Like Mrs. Bollier standing at the front door of my childhood home, we too, as adults, are poised at a similar moment in history. As we cross the threshold of the front door and enter the living rooms of the American family, we see a resounding and vacuous disconnect between parents and children, between siblings, between generations. We see a dramatic peer orientation that has made friends more influential than parents. We see a culture of "experts" in the classroom and on the screen who are vying for the hearts and souls of our children. We see a generation labeled by anxiety, fear, depression, hopelessness, atheism. But if we look closer, we can see a light seeping through a crack beneath the front door, its ray of hope spreading out across the floor like a thin layer of gold. And it is on that light we must focus. The agency is ours. The time is now.

Let hope arise.

If we are to reclaim the next generation, radical education reform is required.

CHAPTER TWO

Rescue Mission:
Why We Need an Education Revolution

In the classic story the Emperor's New Clothes, an entire village is deluded into a rather conspicuous conformity. Playing on the vanity of the emperor and the people's fear of looking foolish, two swindlers convince the leader that they can weave him beautiful clothing that will be invisible to anyone lacking wisdom. Though deep down the villagers know the truth, they don't trust their own opinions enough or feel confident or courageous enough to be the truth-teller, the culture-shaper, the lone voice of truth that will break everyone free of the deceptive mindset. They've been culturally conditioned to fear the perceived stigma of the whistle-blower label.

There is a reason the story has been translated into 100 languages: It resonates with the human condition. It's the ultimate example of groupthink, and it's never been so powerfully evidenced in America as in the present day. From overt indoctrination to radical racism to Marxist movements, our nation is outplaying a collective theatrical production of the Emperor's New Clothes. Many know (or at least suspect) the truth, but their fear of man and desperate need for approval keep them from speaking up, from delivering the truth that would set others free. And one of the grand arenas where we see this farce playing out today is the field of education.

As I have stood in classrooms with the youngest generations over the last 20 years, as I have scoured over the research, and I have witnessed the tragic fallout, I am possessed with a compelling sense of urgency to alert parents to the causes and effects of this generational numbness. As I've stood across from teens that parents have asked me to pray for—icy hearted teens with deadened eyes and dark language—I feel necessary obliged to warn parents to stop the train and leap off before it's too late, before the worldview has formed, before the attachments have fractured, before the family system has reach the relational point of no return.

As I've studied modern students and their fragmented families, I have noted an emergence of twelve toxic traits that have been cultivated in their lives as a result of traditional education. These fruits are evidenced in the generational beliefs and behaviors of the youngest students. The seeds that have been planted in the public school classroom are sprouting their tragic fruit across the landscape of an entire generation. I've outlined the twelve toxic traits of the public school systems that we will be addressing throughout this book, but by way of a summary, when we look at the tragic stats of GenerationZ, the middle generation between Millennials and Alphas, we see a generation characterized by anxiety, depression, and suicide ideation. We see the highest rate of atheism in the history of our nation. We see a generation that feels more hopeful about socialism than capitalism. They are historically illiterate, biblically illiterate, relationally illiterate.

We see a generation that spends 65% of their social time on screens, a demographic that now flounders when it comes to authentic communication. They prefer ghosting to authentic responses. When pressed, they just disappear from the conversation. We see a generation that pushes the commitments of adulthood further and further out into the periphery, living as what Postman called the "childified adult," or as more modern researchers have termed it, the "perpetual adolescent." They lack trust. They lack motivation. They lack direction. They lack hope. They lack (but crave) a deep sense of meaning.

I outlined some of these sobering trends in the book *The Science of Social Influence* in 2009. Tragically, they have not changed for the better. A full twelve years later, the numbers have not improved. The roots have grown deeper, and the fruit is now more visible than ever before, in the actions, the carriage, the lifestyles of the youngest generations. They deal with an extraordinary level of interpersonal and interpersonal violence: The Center for Disease Control says that the US is a world leader in youth homicide, the second leading cause of death for 12-19 year olds in America and the leading cause of death for Black and Hispanic youth in America. Cornell University has shown that 17% of US high school students have made at least one plan to take their own lives, and 1/5 of the students in our nation's top schools are cutting or burning themselves on purpose in an attempt to relieve emotional pain.

Hypersexuality and general promiscuity has become the nomenclature of the "hook-up" culture. According to Indiana University School of Medicine, 64% of US residents age 14 and over have at least one sexually transmitted disease. In 2013, 8,000 US teens contracted an STD, with three million teens becoming infected in one year. However, in 2016, the Center for Disease Control released an even more shocking report:50% of the 20 million (!) sexually transmitted diseases in the US every year are represented in the 15-24 year-old population. This means that over 10 million teens and young adults are engaged in promiscuous lifestyles that are resulting in STDs. Over 50% of the young adult population sees cohabiting, living together in a sexual relationship, believing this arrangement to be a viable option to the institution of marriage, despite the research that demonstrates that cohabitation leads to a greater likelihood of abuse, fatherlessness, and relational insecurity, among other challenges. As a result of the high level of promiscuity, the US leads the developed world in teen pregnancy. According to the Heritage Foundation, this number is 3-10 times higher than other developed nations. Social scientist David Blankenhorn calls the fatherlessness of today's generation "our most urgent social crisis."

The growth of atheism in the youngest generation is unprecedented: youth are walking away from the Christian faith in droves. According to research by Josh McDowell and Ken Ham, 85% of students who grow up in Christian homes but attend public school walk away from the faith by 12th grade, with the vast majority abandoning their beliefs by the end of junior high. Any semblance of Christian home life (a minuscule percentage overall, with only 10% of families investing spiritual into their children on a regular basis) is being polluted by the indoctrination of the secular school environment, and students find themselves unable to rationalize the existence of the God of the Bible. Not surprisingly, the youngest generation has the highest rate of anxiety, depression, suicide ideation, and atheism in the history of our nation.

And if the emotional and mental health issues weren't enough to convince us something is terribly wrong, we could look to the reports outlining the youngest generation's less-than-stellar academic performance. A 2017 Pew Research study showed that academic achievement in the United States lags behind many other developed countries. An NAEP study ranked 40% of 12th graders as performing "below basic" levels in science, and a 2015 Pew report showed that 46% were below average in science, technology, engineering, and mathematics (STEM). In comparison, 23 other countries outperform the US in science and reading, and 38 countries outperform the US in math. According to a 2013 study by the US Department of Education and the National Institute of Illiteracy, 32 million adults in the United States can't read, and another 21% read below the

5th grade level. Today, 19% of high school graduates are illiterate. Now, this is after going to school 7 hours a day and struggling through another 2-3 hours of homework at night! The system is a failure, and the parallel trajectory is clear: Once God was removed from the educational sector, the acceptance of sin skyrocketed, and the tragic fruit of secular humanism was harvested in the lives of our nation's children. Proverbs 9:10 says, "The fear of the Lord is the beginning of wisdom, and knowledge of the Holy one is understanding." Without the fear of the Lord, we cannot fully and accurately explore or understand the universe he has created. "He is before all things," says Colossians 1:17, "and by him all things consist." Dissecting the God of the universe out of the educational sphere has impacted the next generation of children academically, socially, and morally—creating a spiritual bankruptcy unknown to previous generations in America.

In the 1980s, well-known leaders like James Dobson, former president of Focus on the Family, began warning parents of the dangers of a godless educational system and instead began promoting the values of home education. Parents responded. The modern homeschool movement was birthed out of the desire to provide the next generation with a faith-based system of education, one that refuses to sever God's name from the studies of the universe He created. Today, we see the fruit of millions of children who have been told by public school teachers and celebrities that their life has no purpose, no destiny. They have been given no reason for faith or joy or goodness or integrity. Romans 1:20 tells us that God's nature is evidenced in the created realm—that we can learn of God's character and qualities through studying his world. "The fear of the Lord is the beginning of wisdom," Proverbs 9:10 reminds us yet again. But most students have not been taught this foundational idea. Instead, they have been forced to sip from the fount of folly, of frail human philosophies, rather than being permitted to drink freely from the fount of wisdom. And thus, their growth is stunted. Their capacity is limited. Their ceiling of maturity and responsibility is a long elevator ride down from where it could be, where it should be.

We need only to look to the philosophical man-in-the-mirror to discover the foundations of these shortcomings. In 2007, George Barna surveyed students between the ages of eight and twelve. In his book *Revolutionary Parenting*, he detailed the striking results: less than half said that their faith was important in their lives, only 19% believed they had a responsibility to evangelize their peers, and only 1/3 believed that the Bible is accurate. Thirteen years later, these impressionable students are now young adults. Their worldview then is magnified in their actions now.

Our worldview, the lens through which we see and filter every event we are confronted with, is largely established by age 13. This, by the way, is one of the reasons it's against the law to evangelize anyone under the age of 18 in China. Instead, Chinese youth must instead be indoctrinated by the state system. Sound familiar? As many wise researchers have demonstrated, when students learn from mature adults rather than immature peers—as was the predominate system of education throughout much of human history—they are smarter. Why? Because, as King Solomon put it, we become like the company we keep. Drs. Nabor and Mate, two French doctors who have studied peer-driven versus parent-driven environments for decades, distill the point in their highly recommended book, *Hold On to Your Kids*, where they demonstrate the value of parent mentorship, discipleship, over peer influence.

It probably comes as no surprise to learn that the government school system teaches anti-faith, anti-family, anti-America doctrine. It's probably not a shock to hear that students are taught political agendas that mirror the Marxist philosophies of the 1970s, because, of course, the students who sat through those same lectures in school 40 years ago have been teaching the classes your kids take. They've been training the up teachers who will replace them when they retire. They've been running the school boards and teachers unions' that make all the decisions for your local "public" school, a true misnomer if ever there was one. The steady stream of humanistic discipleship in the government school system trickles down year after year, training teachers in public colleges who will train students in public high schools who will become teachers who train teachers and so on, ad infinitum.

I felt the shards of this rocky systemic trail up close and personal when my oldest child was five. We had just moved to California from the Bible Belt, and because I grew up in public school, and many of my relatives were either public school teachers, principals, superintendents, or professors, I had never considered academic options outside the public school environment. But our church in Florida had been courageous enough to break out of the public school stronghold (more on that later), and as I started reading about the state we would be moving to, I saw some significant red flags surrounding the school system. Given the stats, I thought it best to enroll our 5 year old in a "faith-based" alternative, an expensive private Christian school.

Something felt askew when I dropped my son off and stood at the door of the kindergarten classroom with all the other moms. It didn't feel right to leave him in the care of someone else, a stranger, but since I was trained in school not to trust my instincts, I decided instead to trust the authority, the school system, the experts, who must certainly know what is best for my child. I figured I was probably overreacting, just worrying for no reason. This is normal, right? We give our kids to someone else to train them, to encourage them, to pour into them, to cheer them on as they reach their academic and personal milestones. That's giving them the best, right? We outsource them to a coach or teacher or Sunday school worker who will teach them right from wrong, safe from dangerous, wise from foolish, right?

But very quickly, I saw the red flags. My firstborn, who normally loved reading and learning, was suddenly coming home discouraged because he was "always" getting in trouble. The teacher took his watch and made him stay inside for recess. She moved him to another seat so he wouldn't talk. She corrected him for behavior he said he didn't engage in, mistakes he said he didn't make. If you know my firstborn, you know this teacher's account bears no resemblance whatsoever to his scholarship, his obedience, or his personal discipline. It was almost like she was talking about someone I'd never met before. Short of handing him a dunce cap, she had relabeled and redefined the once-curious, studious kindergartner with the vocabulary and reading skills of a 12th grader, questioning his ability, his motive, and his academic capacity. Suffice it to say, there were gold stars decorating this classroom. So I set up a meeting with her to find out what I was missing.

In the first breath of the conversation, I realized immediately that there were two uniquely individual planes of experience defining the moment. My educational ambitions were different from hers. Our educational methodologies and philosophies were different. Her goals were not my goals. Her understanding of human development was not my understanding. Her knowledge of androgens, neural rest states, and the difference in learning styles for boys and girls was based on very little real world application: As a 23-year-old non-parent fresh out of college, she didn't have the same level of wisdom and experience to draw from as a parent would. And how could she, even practically, differentiate and individualize lessons and experiences for a class of 25 students under the age of six? The class size and the absence of parental support made the process nearly impossible. Most importantly, though, it was clear that her teacher training at the big public university down the street was not at all in line with my values, my beliefs, my goals. Our family quickly realized that the private school model was simply a carbon copy of the public school methodology masquerading as Christian education. It was little more than a secular textbook sporting an "I love Jesus" bumper sticker slapped on the front cover.

Parents, it's our responsibility to stand at the gate, to feel the pulse, to observe the fruit of the harvest. "Guard what has been entrusted to you," 1 Timothy 6:20 tells us, "avoiding worldly and empty chatter and the opposing arguments of what is falsely called knowledge." I later learned that the pricey private school where I had sent my firstborn for six months was itself struggling with the offshoots of rebellion that are so common in today's educational arenas, mainly promiscuity and illicit drug abuse. The absence of parental involvement, and the managing of Christian classrooms by those who lack a biblical worldview, has created an army of secular humanists singing hymns. They have heard little snippets of the Bible, but it hasn't been activated, made alive. It's never made the ten-inch journey from the brain to the heart. Needless to say, we recognized that there had to be a better way to educate our children. We pulled the plug on private "school."

Ken Ham writes in his book *Already Gone* that the youngest generations are growing up in a culture where church buildings have been emptied of their congregational contents and filled up instead with clubs, restaurants, and kitschy hotels. In the same way, the vast majority of schools that call themselves Christian by name actually bear very little resemblance to Christian teaching, training, or discipleship. In his equally stinging book about Christian colleges, *Already Compromised*, Ham describes this alarming trend in higher education. Less than 15% of the colleges in America that describe themselves as Christian actually teach from a biblical worldview (or even hire professors who profess a biblical worldview). Dr. Rick Green, constitutional expert and founder of Patriot Academy, puts that number much lower, at a mere handful across the nation. As parents, we have to look first at the values, the outcomes. If an institution doesn't share the same desired outcomes as the parents or constituents it serves, one side or the other is bound to be unfulfilled by the results of the educational experiment.

We've all heard the term "outcome" as an educational buzzword. Program outcomes, what we used to call programmatic or institutional objectives, are the tools by which educators measure the success of an academic system. This idea naturally assumes the possession of a shared goal, something we all agree is important, in order for an outcome to be effective and meaningful. When parents ask me about the implications of this term, what they are really asking is related to a much deeper question, a socialized question. What is the outcome of said educational system? Let's unpack that from both an experiential and a scholastic perspective.

Most modern educational institutions anchor around this idea of measurable outcomes, a specific and measurable goal they want their students to demonstrate by the end of the class, the year, or the program. The challenge is that the institution's goal is not always the same as the parent's goal, or, more importantly, God's goal. What the institution wants to see accomplished in your student might not be what you want to see accomplished in your student. This was evidenced most clearly to me when I was working with secular accrediting agencies at the university level, and oftentimes they had difficulty understanding why a Christian institution would "waste" so much time studying Scripture or spending resources on scripturally sound curricula. Their narrow, frustrated gaze said it all: Dispense with the spiritual stuff and focus on what's "really" important. The few truly Bible-based colleges left in America won't likely hold to programmatic objectives that line up with the reasoning of the secular humanists driving the accreditation engine (though many continue to bow their knee to this education form of the approval of man). In the same way, as parents, we have to know and hold to our end goal.

As victims of the expert culture, today's parents have been duped into thinking that a child's scholastic experience is all about academic achievement, measurable goals, and educational outcomes. And yes, of course we want our children to reach their full scholastic potential. I'm obviously not anti-education; I've earned five college degrees and taught for 20 years in the college classroom. But as Christians, our measurable outcomes are not simply academic. They are social. They are spiritual. They are relational. If we raise really smart kids who go to Harvard and earn a Nobel Peace Prize but they walk away from God, what have we gained? Nothing. "What does it profit a man," Mark 8:36 asks, "if he gains the whole world but loses his own soul?"

The traditional system is failing America, from values clarification to Marxism to the lack of critical thinking and the eradication of the arts and creativity. Instead of a determined effort to discover and develop individual potential, the focus for the last 50 years has been on creating these ridiculous measurable outcomes, a system designed to create a product, something predicable. Measurable. What parent wants to raise a predictable child? In the traditional system, students are taught what to think but not how to think. The school system desires rigidity, predictability, control over human behavior, and this is antithetical to the true heart of education. The traditional school system is a social construct with the singular goal of producing an outcome, a product.

Margaret Thatcher once said, "Consensus is the process of abandoning all beliefs, principles, values and policies in search of something in which no one believes...what great cause could have been fought and won under the battle phrase "I stand for consensus?" We don't make our decisions on the broad basis of public opinion. "Broad is the way that leads to destruction," Matthew 7:13 says, "and many will enter in." The broad road is what has led us to the place we are now, saddled with the highest rate of anxiety, depression, and atheism in the history of our nation. And the type of product being manufactured by government monopoly schools, as Gatto calls them, is subpar at best.

In assessing the traditional model of education, legendary educational prophet Neil Postman says there is a distinct difference between school and education. He once published a study on questions in the traditional environment that assessed the types of inquiries students make in school. To no one's surprise, the vast majority of the questions that students asked (93%) were what Postman called "administrative" questions: "How do I hold my pencil? How do I say this word? How many questions can I get wrong and still pass?" And, equally unsurprising, the kinds of questions teachers asked students were deductive (what I am thinking?) rather than inductive (what are you thinking?). These formats are a far cry from learning that is built on critical thinking, on the question of why, not just what, how, or how fast. There is no exchange of real information, no training, no inspiration, no critical thinking here. Like my childhood kindergarten teacher, these teachers were seeking a measurable outcome: students must read their teachers' minds to gain their approval. The gold star goes to the conformist, the leader of the groupthink parade. He must go along to get along.

As parents, our goal, our measurable outcome, should be creativity over conformity. This should be evidenced in our structure as well as our style of education. For example, the military and prison systems use uniforms to create conformists, as do many private schools and even some public schools. The systems and behavioral limitations we put in place institutionally are designed to foster a specific outcome. If our absolute goal is to create critical thinkers, world changers, and industry disruptors, then our classrooms should be active, not passive. Our students should be encouraged to ask questions. Our models of education should be built on dialogue rather than lecture, on participation rather than spectatorship.

At CVCU, it was important to me to hire professors who understand what it means to function as a "guide on the side" rather than a "sage on the stage." Why? Because we are training up critical thinkers. In the traditional sector, "why" questions are squelched. Good behavior is defined as sitting quietly with hands in laps, getting along with others, conforming to the behavioral norms and the teacher's preferences. This format is antithetical to creative analysis and critical thinking and industry disruption. Like its Industrial Era intention, the pail-filling method creates cogs in the machine. In fact, Gatto notes that American education teaches by its methodology that humans are machines.

Let's contrast that method with how Jesus taught. Why did Jesus speak in parables? Why did he ask questions? Here are a few of his many inquiries:

> "Who do you say that I am?"
> "Why are you afraid?"
> "Why did you doubt?"
> "Do you still not understand?"
> "What does scripture say?"
> "Who touched me?"

Now, Jesus could have easily and readily given the answer to any of these questions. He could have imparted his teachings through city-wide lectures as his main point of contact and influence. He could have stood at arms-length to the crowds, positioning himself as a distant, wise sage, but instead he chose the path of healing, touching, and walking next to them as a guide, a model, a disciple-maker. Think about it. Ultimately, instead of choosing only lecture to the masses, he chose relationship with the twelve. He used instructional methods of riddles and inquiry that would cause his followers to think, to reason, and to return to him.

Postman says that we can't keep brilliant people locked up in classrooms for 7 hours a day. We need to get them out using their gifts in the community so that schooling and educating can, for the first time in modern history, be united as one concept, with a multigenerational model of the older students teaching the younger students. When we look at the stats on private Christian schools who have made academic outcomes their god, predictably, we see the same fruit of the public school systems arising in the midst of the private school systems. What we focus on continually, day in and day out, becomes our goal, our overarching drive, our vision, our god. What kind of a generation do we want to raise up? A local teacher of the year shared his story with me recently. Like many of us, after graduate school, he realized that the K to 12 system was broken, and he came back to his high school classroom with a gleam of hope in his eye. He began applying the inquiry-based method and, in just a few weeks, he had already turned some of the most disinterested back-row dwellers into semi-conscious human beings. He was energized by the work. But then, no surprise, he suddenly got a call from the principal, who admonished him for this "non-traditional" methodology. He was told to stop teaching his students in this method or resign from his position. He chose the latter. If we want to raise up a generation of world changers and culture shapers, students who care enough to ask why, then we need to utilize a different methodology than the one traditional schools are peddling.

The data shows that the best return on investment comes from educational formats that have parents in the mix, what we call an "involved parent." In fact, Harvard's Family Involved Network of Educators found in a longitudinal study that the number one predicator of a child's socio-academic success from kindergarten through college is actually an involved parent. When we add to that mix the support of the local church, we create a cooperative model that provides the resources and opportunity for sharpening and benchmarking. We create a model for educational discipleship that simultaneously restores the church to the center point of culture and the parent to the center of healthy relational orientation, elevating the most important measurable outcomes and insuring the transmission of the faith from one generation to the next.

Many parents tell me that they have somehow absorbed the mindset from prevailing culture that their kids only need them in the early years, and then once they are potty trained, we must turn them over to "experts" to do the real work. As a case in point, the public school system in Chicago once banned "the brown bag lunch" because they said parents didn't know how to pack the right lunch for their children, and parents were better off leaving it to the "experts." How incredibly insulting. This mindset is a disservice to parents everywhere! There is no one more qualified to love or care for your child than you, Mom and Dad. My friend Denise Mira writes in her book *No Ordinary Child* that many Christian parents spend years waiting for God to open their womb and then when that child finally reaches her first independent milestone, they check the box and hand her off to someone else to train her up. The child who was prayed for, fasted over, the child for whom the parents pounded the gates of heaven suddenly becomes someone else's responsibility. As Mira puts it, this baby that mom desperately prayed for is now just a forgotten picture cluttering the office desk. Parents, it's more than just potty training. Our kids need our influence from K to college.

Radical education reform is required here, friends. We delude ourselves if we think that sanitized, secular, soul-less education programs can teach true wisdom or godly character. Again, at the end of the day, what will it profit a man if he gains the world, yet loses his own soul? If our children are academic legends or sports superstars but they walk away from God, it doesn't matter how many trophies grace their bookshelves; simply put, we didn't do our job as parents. As Josh McDowell once noted, "This is the first generation to be more influenced by things outside of the home than by things inside of the home." It's time to reverse that trend. The parent-directed education model can be a powerful and effective tool for rebuilding the faulty foundations that play such a significant role in most of our modern social ills.

As you can probably tell by now, I'm passionate about the transformative power of Christian education, the primacy of the local church, and the stable family as the cornerstone of healthy culture, and I knew there had to be a way to bring these entities together to shift the tide for the next generation. After spending two decades in the college classroom, I grew increasingly concerned with the burgeoning rates of anxiety, depression, and atheism in the next generation. I envisioned an academic model that would counter the common struggles in American higher education: crippling student loan debt, sweeping secularization, and ineffective educational methodology. As I began surveying students and talking with parents, building a support system for them, I saw many of the same comments and questions emerging in the data.

I knew there had to be a way to create a unique model of educational discipleship that would equip the next generation with biblical literacy, relational resilience, and academic success. I knew there had to be a widespread method for reclaiming the secular government's cradle-to-grave indoctrination with a Kingdom education. In talking with parents, I found that many of them had never been given the freedom to think fully for themselves in realms like education, and so it was difficult for them to imagine the possibilities that might exist on the other side of that freedom. The vast majority of American parents have been told their whole lives what books their kids must read, what assignments they must complete, even when and where and with whom they need to complete them. When they would find themselves in conversations with people walking in freedom, they felt unsure of themselves, and the pull to anchor down in Egypt was, for some, overpowering.

But then, 2020 happened. Parents got a rare glimpse behind the iron curtain of the public school system, and they started to connect the high rates of anxiety, depression, and suicide ideation to the atheistic, Marxist teachings of their children's 40-hour-a-week indoctrination center, the public school classroom. Parents began to recognize that the foundations our children form in childhood are subconsciously guiding them in the way they think, the way they act and interact, in the way they work, in the way they vote. Remember, Luke 6:40 tells us that the student will become like the teacher. We will become like the company we keep. If the company our children keep for the vast majority of the week is immature six-year-old classmates (or equally immature 60-year-old atheist teachers), the influence will be visible in the long run.

As they awakened to the harsh reality of this trajectory, some parents felt a sense of despair, fearing that it was too late to make a difference. One mom, distraught over her teen's iciness, verbally recounted her parenting process for me. Like many other parents I talk with, she told me that her child had been raised in church but, in retrospect, she realized the child had never really discipled at home. They were a nice family, an intact family, but there had never been an intentional transference of the faith from parent to child. They didn't read and discuss the Bible together. Their homes and lifestyles weren't built on the word of God. They attended church and went through all the motions with the best of intentions, but the end result was tragic: A child who once stretched up her tiny arms for her parents to hold her, a child who at one time wanted to love and be loved by her parents, had gone the way of the world. Her heart was cold. The daily separation from parent, the unnatural clinging to peers, and lack of discipleship in the home drew her further and further away from this connection until it completely dissolved. It's a haunting image. This is a conversation I have with many parents today, parents who thought they were doing enough, only to look in the rearview mirror and recognize, often after the child's worldview has been formed, that they failed to disciple their children. And sadly, this view often becomes clear to them at the end of the parenting journey, when their teens are icy-hearted toward the church, toward God, and toward their parents.

I began my teaching career in a Christian high school, went on to teach in community college, and then taught in universities for many years before becoming a university president. Through my graduate studies, my classroom work, and my doctoral research, I began to see very clearly the brokenness of the modern American education system and its impact on the family and the larger culture. Because of these findings, my husband Adrian and I not only educated our own children at home K to college, but 15 years ago, we began founding homeschool support academies across the state that were designed to help parents grow and learn together in the context of community. More on that topic in a minute. For now, let me take you back to the start of one of my favorite years in American history (next to 1776, of course), the year 2020.

On January 9, 2020, Pastor Jurgen Matthessius, a courageous global influencer and the lead pastor of our church, invited me to share with the pastoral team in great detail what was happening in the public school system and, most importantly, what we as a church could do in response. We talked about the sobering stats on hypersexuality, critical race theory, socialism, Marxism, atheism, macro-evolution, early childhood "education," the Values Clarification Movement, and the resultant rise in anxiety, depression, atheism, and suicide ideation plaguing in the next generation. At the end of that meeting, our pastor prayed Mathew 18:6, that God would bring down the walls of any institution in our county that was leading children astray. Just a few short weeks later, every school district in our county was closed down. School doors and windows were shuttered. Students were sent home, and parents suddenly became aware of the troubling trends that had been permeating the classroom culture of their neighborhood schools. It was a moment of awakening for an entire generation of parents.

Call me crazy if you want to, but I firmly believe that just like Elijah prayed for rain, and Joshua prayed for the sun to stand still, a modern day pastor's prayer of faith and frustration helped to bring down the walls of an ungodly system and gave us a window of opportunity to rescue the next generation. In fact, several pastors in our county have now told me they were praying the same prayer! Little did we know it at the moment, but the Church collective was uniting in prayerful preparation for the harvest that was about to come. When the schools closed their physical doors, parents walked into the living room and heard teachers on Zoom calls telling parents they weren't welcome in the room. Don't miss the palpable irony here—not only were parents shooed out of the rooms they themselves paid for, but their excommunications were assigned by teachers whose paychecks are funded by the parents' tax dollars! That's worthy of a laughing emoji right there. And, thankfully, as parents listened in despite the threats, they heard and saw the classroom content: lies masquerading as truth, myths masquerading as science, fiction masquerading as fact. Many parents heard with their own ears, some for the first time, the socio-political agenda targeting their children in their own homes through the computer screen, which had become the gateway of the public school classroom. They suddenly realized that, as noted earlier, today's K-12 curricula is more about serving a political agenda than meeting the true academic needs of the next generation.

What happened to families as a result of the shutdown was beyond remarkable. Many had been conditioned to think that public school was a safe, healthy, happy environment where their children would ingest the necessary academic nutrients to grow up big and strong with successful. But then they heard what their children were learning (and not learning). Parents hovered outside the bedroom door as teachers used words like gender fluidity, telling them that their "old-fashioned" parents would probably not understand the importance of diverse pronoun choices. They listened in as children were taught that the color of their skin made them either a victim or an oppressor. And they were told to stay out, to step back, to leave the room. Parents, if a teacher doesn't want you to know what he's teaching your children, he's not someone who should be working with children in the first place. That person is the moral equivalent of a creepy man in a white van driving around the public parks offering kids candy. We're supposed to teach kids to flee from people like these.

Most importantly, 2020 opened parents' eyes to the very real battle over the belief and behavior of their children, that the school system they thought they could trust was not their friend; it was, sadly, their enemy. And parents recognized that they themselves would be the ones responsible for turning the hearts of the children back to the family, retraining their children to think, to dream, to believe, to hope again. They recognized that radical education reform would be required.

In the midst of all the deception and confusion swirling in our midst today, I am heartened by a movement making its way across America at the time of this book's publication. The movement is known as the Great Resignation. Having experienced the freedom of working from home, parents are checking out of the rat race. A 2021 study by Monster found that over 95% of employees are currently pondering changing their jobs. Another 4 million quit this jobs in April 2021, the launching point of the Great Resignation. An article in the *Harvard Business Review* explains that the market has switched from an employer's market to an employee's market, and employees are reluctant to return to the drudgery of a 9-5 office job after having tasted freedom.

As adults were called back into the workforce after being home with their families for months as a result of the shutdowns, their hearts began to thaw. They realized that they actually like their homes. And they liked working from their homes. And they wanted to spend more time in their home and their family than with their clients and their office. And something shifted. A new priority emerged. A full 40% of employees surveyed across America told their employers that they don't want to go back. They want to work from their home base. According to the US Labor Department's Job Opening and Labor Turnover Survey (literally, JOLTS), the "quits rate," which measures the number of employees voluntarily leaving their jobs, is now at an all-time, historic high of 4.4 million employees. I find this incredibly heartening, a great awakening, a new prioritization of family, of work-life balance, of meaningful career pursuits.

Can you feel it rising? Can you sense the ground shaking beneath our feet? Change is breaking out across the landscape of our nation. There is a sense of empowerment piercing through the pedantic dysfunction of Marxism's bourgeoisie and proletariat teachings, now cleverly disguised in the public school classroom as victim versus oppressor, labels for life. Hope is rising. People are thinking, prioritizing, weighting their life choices.

"Time is the coin of our lives," American poet Carl Sandburg once observed, "so we must beware how we spend it." Parents have begun to see that they were going to have to dig deep to help their children unlearn the vast majority of the anti-family, anti-Christian, anti-America philosophies that had been indelibly written on the hearts of their children. The longer the child was a product of the government school system, the deeper the roots had grown, and the more insidiously those roots were wound around the child's sense of identity, confidence, wonder, faith, and zest for life. As Jack Hayford once said, it's easier to build a man than to rebuild him. Though it may not be a panacea, parent-directed education can be a powerful and effective tool for rebuilding the faulty foundations that play such a significant role in most of our modern social ills. When done well, this system can connect the hearts of parents and children in a wounded world. It can teach, train, and transform a generation through a Christian worldview, and it can help parents invest wholeheartedly in family discipleship.

When I met my husband in England, I was struck by the prevalence and positioning of churches. No matter where you stood in a city, you could see a church. This was intentional positioning; the church was once the center of culture. Now, as Ken Ham writes, those churches have become museums, devoid of the life and joy of God; they are no more than buildings fulfilling a perfunctory historical role in an increasingly atheistic culture. America is in danger of this same decline unless we begin to restore the local church to the center point of culture, unless we begin to restore the local church to the center of growth-oriented activities, drawing families back into the heart of church culture.

As Christians, we are responsible for weighing out our specific realm of impact and influence. We are responsible for determining our educational and spiritual outcomes. We can improve family life and limit social media, of course, but until we change the trajectory of K-12 education, the next generation, and thus our nation, will continue to fall further and further away from truth of God's word. Even if we are un-indoctrinating our children for an hour a day every day, the preponderance of influence still falls on the system that has the biggest time investment, the public school. This is why the first step in the rescue mission is to break off the alliance with the government school system. Sever the tie.

In Luke 1:17 the angel Gabriel tells Zechariah that his son John would come in the spirit and power of Elijah to turn the hearts of the fathers to their children. That's a heart cry for this generation. True, Bible-based educational discipleship connects the hearts and minds of children and parents, establishing a model that dethrones the spirit of peer orientation and replaces it with the healthy model of parent orientation. Deuteronomy 6:6-9 instructs parents to impress God's laws upon the hearts of their children, to talk about them as they travel on the highways and the byways. In the traditional system, most students go to class for 7 hours and then have another two to three hours of homework each night, which can significantly limit the opportunities for family discipleship. Again, Luke 6:40 says that when he is fully trained, the student will become like the teacher. Who is doing the teaching? What is the content of that teaching? And what is the generational fallout? As we re-assess Plato's admonition, we have to ask ourselves if we are seeing the harvest of righteousness in the next generation. Bad company corrupts good character. It's time to rescue our students from the soul-less, godless education system of state indoctrination.   Through the establishment of the parent-directed model of education, we can train up K to 12 students to love God, country, and one another, changing the world for the kingdom one student at a time.

Over the next few chapters, I'll be sharing a model that is built on years of research in GenZ education methodology, a model that, when correctly appropriated, creates a love of learning and a curiosity that fuels research and inquiry. It enhances academic performance and awakens vital character traits in the next generation such as their commitment to volunteerism, their social maturity, and their real-world experience. When a child is solely surrounded with other children his age, his ceilings, the limitations over his life, are his age-group peers. The new format gives students the opportunity to see possibilities beyond themselves, to be trained up by those outside their generational lens and maturity.

Through this system, we can increase intergenerational connectivity, providing a rich framework of relational discipleship and mentoring, provide young women with hope and encouragement, provide young men with the training they need to carry the mantle of manhood. Through this system, we can restore the local church the center of spiritual formation and community, providing a holistic approach to family discipleship and the fulfillment of the Great Commission. When it's done well, parent-directed education creates a love of learning and a curiosity that fuels research and inquiry. Most importantly is a purposeful and powerful methodology for ensuring the transmission of the faith from one generation to the next, helping to reverse some of the grim statistics relating to modern American discipleship and biblical literacy.

As I said in the dedication to this book, of the hundreds of conversations I've had with parents and students over the last year, the one in particular that stands out to me most is a parent who stopped me in the church hallway to share her revelation. Looking out over her life, she saw the coaches, the teachers, the daily dropoffs, the endless chauffeuring, and it suddenly became clear: Her home was running on a business model. Like many modern parents, she was outsourcing her children.

Over the next few chapters together, we will look at data from the fields of education, human development, sociology, neuroscience, and theology that will help you locate yourself on the parenting map, on the mentoring map, the leadership map— on the map of every sphere of influence—and get you equipped and encouraged for the road ahead. There is too much at stake for us to sit back and allow the secular government to erode the foundations of our nation. We can't just twiddle our thumbs and watch passively as our country falls apart at the seams. As Martin Luther King said, we can either curse the darkness or light a candle. Parents, it's our time to shine. Let's roll up our sleeves and get to work.

It's time for an education revolution.

CHAPTER THREE

How Did We Get Here? The Tragic Timeline

From the highly secularized environments of the public school system, where the Great Commission has literally been outlawed on our watch, to the ineffective educational methodology that's dumbing America down, the next generation is caught in an undertow of anxiety, depression, hopelessness, and atheism. It wasn't always this way, was it? No. Many of us grew up in schools where the teachers and administrators at least partly supported the values of the community, where the vast majority of the subjects and textbooks and extracurricular activities were in agreement, alignment, with what was being taught in the home. But the culture of school has shifted. Something is wrong, very palpably wrong, with the modern system of education. How do we teach our youngest citizens to hope, to dream, and to fully engage with the world around them? How do we turn the tide so we can once again raise compassionate, intelligent children who love God, their parents, and one another?

Social scientists say that our worldview is formed by age 13, and our sense of attachment is formed by age six. Thus, the formative years are vital seasons to invest into the next generation, to help them find their identity, to discover their purpose, to experience the joy of walking in wisdom. The early years are a prime opportunity to teach our children God's ways, how to lean in and hear his voice from a young age. Sadly, Barna has shown that only 2% of the current living Millennial population has a biblical worldview. I have tested this stat personally by assessing Millennial and GenZ leaders through PEERs analyses (see the Nehemiah Institute for details on how you can apply these assessments in your organizations). The results were not pretty. If we don't turn the ship around, GenZ and Alphas are likely to perform even lower on the worldview scale. And since half of 2% is 1%, that doesn't leave us much margin for error.

Again, we must ask, what led us to this place in history? In my 2009 book *The Science of Social Influence* (then titled *Emerge*), I wrote about a tragic timeline that has paved the pathway, brick by brick, for the drama we see unfolding around us. We are caught in a serpentine root system that has subtly wound its way into the hearts and homes of the vast majority of America families. Let's unpack this timeline, the decisions and steps that led us here over the last few decades. Why does a timeline matter? It's like a pathway through the wilderness. If you get lost, you can retrace your steps to find your way home. And that's exactly what we need to do today with regard to American education.

In talking with many wayward GenZs who have been raised in church but not discipled at home, their worldview is clearly evidenced by what they care most about. They are more connected to and concerned about friends, money, and popularity than family, futures, and eternity. They are more committed to values and interpersonal connections outside of the home than within it. "Even a child is known by his actions," Proverbs 20:11 says. Our treasures expose our hearts, so it's important to look at the patterns of cultural decisions that underscore our values. Perhaps you recall the lyrics to the 1989 song "Living Years" from Mike and the Mechanics: "Every generation blames the one before, and all of those frustrations come beating on your door. I know that I'm a prisoner to all my Father held so dear. I know that I'm a hostage to all his hopes and fears. I just with I could have told him in the living years."

Though the song centers on generational discord and finding peace with one another before we die, the first few lines underscore the point that each generation has a way of projecting blame onto past generations, of failing to take responsibility for our own role in the matter. Though all of humanity is certainly knit together, and our parents' and grandparents' failure to disciple their children led to the spiritual vacuum we see today, we must each come to the place in our own lives where we become the agents of change, the generational curse breakers, the pioneers of hope and faith in our family line.

When we are unwilling to forgive and release, to break off generational blameshifting and take responsibility, we allow ourselves to be held hostage, as the song posits, by our forefathers' hopes and fears. The youngest generations' brokenness is the result of a systemic model, Barna notes, namely the lack of parental discipleship compounded by the parasitic nature of the public school system. Stepping into the vacuum left behind by family leadership, schools have exacerbated the thirst for vengeance, flooding young minds with concepts like white guilt and holding innocent students hostage for actions perpetrated by ancestors they never met. Unforgiveness and exploitation have become a rhetorical pathway to this kind of pseudo-peace that continues the cycle of victim and oppressor. However, as leaders, as living change agents, we are tasked with retracing our steps in order to find our way out of this urban jungle.

Generational change can be tracked in cyclical patterns, and when we step back to the wide angle of the century perspective, we see an aggressive downward lunge on the graph in the scholastic arena. My grandmother, Clara Mae Biby, taught in the public elementary school system for most of her life, 40 years, and then volunteered another 15 years in public school reading programs. Her early classrooms were filled with school-district-issued hymn books and prayer books. Students in her class learned to read from the McGuffey Primer, which underscored biblical concepts like "in Adam's fall, we sinned all."

She often talked about the differences she saw across five decades. Certainly, in terms of student behavior, the 1950's "crimes" of chewing gum and cutting in line would be welcomed today in exchange for the horrors faced in the modern public school, from gang warfare to sexual assault to school shootings. The lack of parental connectivity puts children in a dangerous quagmire here. As a culture, we have sown the seeds of family disengagement. We have looked the other way when the Great Commission was outlawed on our watch. We have applauded politically-correct, woke doctrines of demons, and tragically, we are now reaping the harvest for this egregious cultural error.

Without a parent to moderate the madness of the schools, the hype of social media, and the general insanity of the culture, our students remain trapped in a downward spiral of dysphoria. They are more vulnerable today, more easily persuaded than ever before because of that unholy juxtaposition of parental neglect and the government school's extreme possessiveness. The battle for control over the child's heart and mind is all too real.

Again, most of this is not new. We can track increasing government control of children through the school system for over 30 years. In fact, most of the changes in the school system, both ideologically and methodologically speaking, center on one distinct moment in the timeline.

Schools had one identity pre-1964 and have touted a completely different identity since 1964. Several of my favorite public-school-exposé quotes in *Outsourced* were actually written 30 and even 40 years ago, and yet they sound exactly like the public school classrooms of today! Why? Because they are the same. Very little has actually changed since one singular scholastic earthquake forged a crack across the classroom culture.

Why are the schools of today so similar in content and methodology to the schools of the 1970s and 1980s and 1990s and 2000s and 2010s? Because the gaping dividing line has very little to do with increasing (or decreasing) intelligence. It has nothing to do with the job market. It has nothing to do with the addition of the internet or even technology in the classroom. The equator line dividing the educational hemispheres, the corpus callosum of the academic brain structure, is the marker of one singular moment in scholastic history: BC and AD. Schools were different before the Bible was removed. What? Can the answer really be that simple? Well, it's culturally complex, as there are a number of highways and byways surrounding that neural matter, but the removal of the Bible from the public school classroom has created a forceful undertow whose power is only now being unleashed. The tectonic plates have been shifting slowly for years. The water has been rising, the dams have been crumbling, and now the full tsunami is in view.

In the 50s, there was a consensus among leaders. Pastors, parents, and the general culture largely walked in stride. Values education was an extension of the home. Students were educated through inculcation and modeling, and parents and teachers were almost invariably speaking the same language. The schools and the social culture underscored traditional family values. Parents did not have to counter the culture or the school boards. These macro institutions worked in tandem with the micro institution of the family. But in 1964, when the Bible was forcibly removed from the public school system, a swift transference of power took place. Suddenly, we saw a questioning of traditional roles, a disdain for traditional relationships and religion. Overnight, the entire culture started acting like a rebellious teenager.

In the 1960s, moms were told emphatically that the grass was greener on the corporate side of the fence. They left junior with the babysitter and checked out of the home in order to clock in at the office. As a mass Mom-exodus hit the homefront, the newly-remodeled school value systems were right there to fill in the gap. As I explained in *Emerge,* while TV dispensed its "age-appropriate" diet of clever consumerism to the kiddos at home, public education was undergoing the most significant facelift in the history of the United States school system: The Values Clarification Movement.

We often blame the culture for the change in the school system, but what if it's actually the other way around? What if the school system is actually the cause of the shift in the culture? Think about it. The vast majority of students in America were "educated' under this system, and these students go went on to lead companies with the ideas they learned in school. The seed is planted in the young heart and then bears its fruit in the culture when the student is fully growth. The student becomes like the teacher, and then the student's ideologies, passed on from the teacher, continue to spread. The whole cyclical model continues to sow and grow and train up one generation after another. Kirchenbaum called this shift in values a "critical moment" in the history of education, because there was a tangible shift in the teacher's role. In an instant, the chasm between right and wrong was sealed shut. There was now only "your" truth and "my" truth, "your" wrong and "my" wrong, no absolutes. This moral relativity is now intrinsically woven into the scholastic system. Once the rope to the anchor of truth was severed, morality took on an entirely new definition. Instead of the "well-formed conscience" through which previous generations had contemplated their social, intellectual, and spiritual pursuits, students were now being trained up in a system devoid of moral absolutes.

How do these ideologies affect a home, a city, a nation? Remember the words of John Adams: "Our Constitution was made only for a moral and religious people. It is wholly inadequate to the government of any other." The surest way, then, to conquer a nation like America would be to undermine its moral and religious values. And that is precisely what the VCM movement, coupled with the removal of the Bible from the public sphere, set out to accomplish. Even today, almost 60 years later, the Values Clarification Movement remains the most influential methodology ever to strike the scholastic market. John Heenan, one of several national leaders in the movement, says that VCM gathered such widespread attention that in one decade, there were 40 books published on the "values clarification" approach, one of which, *Values Clarification: A Handbook of Practical Strategies for Teachers and Students*, sold more than 600,000 copies—almost unheard of in the field of education at that time.

In fact, so sweeping was the movement that it became a foundation for every possible scholastic subject: religious education, health education, sex education, and drug education—and its pervasiveness was not limited to school alone; in addition to public school classrooms, VCM found its way into families, sports teams, churches, workplace communication, and volunteer organizations. Even today,

VCM it is still being used widely because its methodology and philosophy has been readily and subversively incorporated into curricula and training in diverse fields. It has become such an accepted foundation of teaching that few recognize its presence enough to question it.

Across this span of time, then, students have been indoctrinated with the idea that how they *felt* about a matter largely governed the rightness or wrongness of the occurrence. Morality has been subordinated to personal experience and interpretation. Truth is now moldable, pliable, situational—dependent on the needs of whatever circumstance we find ourselves in. Values clarification itself actually owes at least part of its history to the 1890s philosopher Frederich Nietzsche, who was set on "proving" that Judeo-Christian values were "imprisoning," and that values should be defined individually, not corporately. Almost 60 years later, C.S. Lewis saw the seeds of Nietzsche's philosophy beginning to take root in American soil, and he countered with a global research study in search of common values that would disprove Nietzsche's focus. Lewis discovered eight such "objective values" such as honesty, generosity, mercy, and duty, and he said that without these, the body corporate will cease to function. As Lewis put it, "In a sort of ghastly simplicity we remove the organ and demand the function...We laugh at honour and are shocked to find traitors in our midst. We castrate and bid the gelding be fruitful."

Studied at face value, the idea of fluid morality is utterly nonsensical. Like many of the foibles evidenced in modern schools, it's difficult to comprehend how any rationally-thinking generation could have been so swept up by the concept. The entire United States legal system, for example, is based on a set of universal values: Stealing is wrong, lying is wrong, murder is wrong. These morals-turned-laws are proverbial stop signs that remind us of the ultimate authority and the sheltering protection of absolute laws. Without an acceptance of universal values, our society would collapse in a downward spiral of selfishness and stupidity. The VCM regime celebrated personal choice and rejected ultimate authority, starting with God and ending with the parent. Even in the 1970s, parents already noted that their children were coming home from school with an air of distrust for parental authority. As we will discuss in a later chapter, this division of family has been one of the tragic markers of the reign of traditional education. It is grossly magnified in today's public school classroom.

Even in many "Christian" educational institutions, professors who were themselves trained by atheists are now trying to muddle through the integration of their faith with their academic discipline. They lack the biblical and historical context to do what their academic deans insist: integrate faith and academia. Again, Plato's two questions must be reflected on here, as the lack of biblical literacy points to an extraordinary, transgenerational influence. Who taught these children, who are now teaching our children? What were they being taught, and what are they now teaching? May we take heed to ensure that we are both ingesting and passing along doctrines of truth and not, as Paul so piercingly described them, "doctrines of demons."

In his book *The End of Education*, Neil Postman writes of another subversive train of thought moving swiftly through the public school systems, this apparatus-driven, bureaucratic monster that, he says, inhibits the natural flow of teaching and learning. "Free human dialogue, wandering wherever the agility of the mind allows, lies at the heart of education. If teachers do not have the time, the incentive, or the wit to provide that; or if students are too demoralized, bored, or distracted to muster the attention their teachers need of them, then that is the educational problem that has to be solved." The breakdown in education is a metaphysical problem, he says, not a technical one.

Postman made that statement in 1995. Looking back in the rearview mirror of America's belief-to-behavior harvest, the seeds of division that we see sprouting up in America's public school classrooms today were sown thirty, forty, even 50 years ago in those same classrooms. So when we say that education has radically changed, that's only partly true. The level of distinction from then to now has only slight variations. The fragmentation was already present in the foundation, and the key element influencing change was the removal of the Bible from the public sector.

As Postman says, the idea of public education depends "absolutely on the existence of shared narratives as well as the exclusion of narratives that lead to alienation and divisiveness." Without agreement, without a shared vision and goal, education can't, by definition, be public. This is the irony of the public system today—parents have finally become aware that the "public" schools are not serving the public agenda after all; they are simply serving their own institutional agenda. "What makes public schools public is not so much that the schools have common goals but that the students have common gods," Postman reminds us. Public education does not serve a public; they create a public." Since 90% of America's children are educated in the public school system, it is without a doubt the most significant impetus for faulty, Brave-New-World-esque socialization. Our worldview is formed by 13, and even a child is known by her actions. Thus, these early foundations are a trajectory predictor for the fragile future of our great nation.

Dallas Willard writes in *The Great Omission* that many Christians defy God not only because of their sins of commission, but also because of their sins of omission, things they didn't do or didn't say. Jeremiah 44 provides an interesting parallel. The men of the city are keenly aware that their wives have violated God's law by making offerings to other gods. The husbands apparently take no action. In fact, the women tell Jeremiah publicly that they won't listen to him. They complain that when they tried to stop giving offerings to their false gods, they "lacked everything... and were consumed by sword and famine." They then caustically remind Jeremiah that they had their husbands' "approval" to violate God's law. Ouch. Jeremiah tells them again (and again) that their land will become a desolation, a waste, and a curse if they continue their ungodly practices.

Like Jeremiah, we live in a nation where evil is celebrated, encouraged, practiced and paraded on the screen. But parents, it doesn't matter who signs off on the misguided behaviors. It doesn't matter what publicly acclaimed source promotes these errant beliefs. It doesn't matter if the upside-down world defines good as evil and evil as good. We have to know the word of truth that will protect our minds and hearts from both the sins of commission and the sins of omission. The world needs a people of courageous conviction who will go against the flow of the culture. The world needs truth tellers and culture shapers. "Broad is the road that leads to destruction, and many will enter in," Matthew 7:13 tells us. "But narrow is the way of life, and few will enter in." That mission starts at home, which is where the wives of Jeremiah 44 missed the boat.

Alice Walker, upon returning from a life-changing journey to impoverished Jamaica, penned a revelation about the difference between offering her resources to strangers across the globe and investing in her own family. "We find our deepest rest and most meaningful service," she said famously, "at home." When the world shut down in 2020, families whose hearts were oriented outside the home suffered extreme disorientation, distress, and dysphoria. But there was a significant difference for homeschool families. Homeschoolers typically like being, well, at home. They typically enjoy one another's company. They might even be referred to as "homebodies" at times, preferring home and family to external sources and places. When the world shut down and restaurants were closed, they were still rooted and oriented, anchored, because their place of comfort was the home. They knew how to care for themselves, how to feed themselves, and how to relate to one another. Their attachments were whole. If we can reorient ourselves and redefine our priorities, there will no doubt be an outpouring of peace, joy, and purpose in this generation. May our own hearts be rooted in family first so that they may overflow to the world from a place of peace and not fear, hope and not regret, purpose and not pain.

Though there have been many bifurcation points in the tragic timeline of the public education system, the most compelling ones are those of lasting impact: the home and the church. These two powerful entities of influence have willingly and naively handed the steering wheel of life over to the public school system. Thus, the confluence of parental separation, church impotence, and public school authoritarianism have created the monster that prowls subversively in our midst. To redeem the next generation, we must reignite the engines of church and family, pulling the plug on our Frankensteinic creation, that behemoth usurper known as a "public" school.

CHAPTER FOUR

Generational Jurisdiction: Whose Kids are They?

Looking in the rearview mirror of life helps us process the decisions we've faced, the actions we've taken, and the impact of those actions, whether positive or negative. This is one of the reasons I love social science. Just as we can look back in the field of personal or cultural history and see what decisions led to where we are today, we can actually look forward in an almost prophetic sense with the social sciences and see what decisions will come out of what is happening in the culture today. In this lens, we can effectively answer a vital question that has been spiraling upward through the legal and scholastic circulating in America right now: "To whom do America's children belong, to the parents or to the state?" Now, as parents, we would probably answer immediately with a hearty "back off, government; these are my kids." But when we look at the number of laws and practices in the scholastic culture that have migrated toward government control over children and the decisions our children make, the rearview mirror's account is actually quite chilling.

Several years ago, the Maryland Board of Education hit front page news with its overtly anti-family proclamation: "While we recognize the right of parents to direct the education of their children, we must *bend their will* to the state's obligation to educate its citizens" (italics mine). In 2007, 11-year-old students in Portland, Maine were granted legal rights to obtain a birth control patch without their parents' knowledge or consent (which brings greater tragic clarity to the stats on teen pregnancy and STDs). In 2011, California passed a law allowing children as young as 12 to obtain the Gardasil vaccine without parental knowledge or consent. This vaccine was developed to allow even a prepubescent girl to engage in sexual intimacy with as many boys as she wishes without the consequence of disease that naturally occurs in those with multiple partners. The human body was created for monogamous relationships. The vaccine does nothing to prevent the mental, emotional, or psychological damage caused by the hookup culture, of course; instead, it promotes promiscuity in the same manner that the public school system does.

And, of course, the same is true now of many public school districts regarding abortion, including LA county. In 2019, the *Washington Post* announced Planned Parenthood's "reproductive health initiative," opening 50 clinics at LA County high schools. The *LA Times* listed the "benefits" to include "more extensive birth control options" stating that the clinics will be a great option for a student "who wants to become sexually active but is not yet comfortable talking to her mom about birth control." There's that battle for control again—the parent versus the state. The Planned Parenthood clinics offer doctors appointments right on campus, outside the realm of parent knowledge. And of course, no surprise: California law supports minors age 12 and over in receiving counseling, birth control, and even having abortions without parental consent. Again, these centers are right there on the school grounds, away from the proverbial prying eyes of parents.

The same thread of perversion resonated through the system when a "public" university in southern California defended an art professor who required that his students fully disrobe for their final exam. Parents complained, and *Christianity Today* wrote an article denouncing the professor's behavior, but the college administration defended the professor's actions, saying, in essence, that students shouldn't take the class if they don't want to follow the professor's rules. Parents complained that they didn't know about the class until their children had already been emotionally scarred by the experience, but administration just shrugged their institutional shoulders and looked the other way. The number of unsuspecting parents and students who have been negatively impacted by the perversion of government school agendas such as these is difficult to comprehend, but the battle for control rages on.

As HSLDA President Mike Smith notes, prior to the Troxel v. Granville Supreme Court case in 2000, government systems consistently supported parents as the decision makers in a child's life. But since that landmark case, we have seen a gradual attempt at eroding the rights of parents and buttressing the rights of the state. Some of the laws have become increasing bold and overt in their anti-family stance: The U.S. Ninth Circuit wrote in 2005, "Parents…have no constitutional right…to prevent a public school from providing its students with whatever information it wishes to provide, sexual or otherwise, when and as the school determines that it is appropriate to do so." The Ninth Circuit went on to say that "the parent's rights end at the school door." In 2010, SB 543 gave schools the "right" to remove kids ages 12 and up from the school campus and transport them to off-campus counseling without parental knowledge. The author of the Senate Bill, Mark Leno, wrote that parents are "a barrier…especially harmful to…lesbian, gay, bisexual, and transgender youth." More recently, in 2021, Gavin Newsom signed AB 2016, which introduces into the classroom a mandatory study encompassing both the tenants of Critical Race Theory and the gender "spectrum" in relation to oppression. The vast majority of parents surveyed in public response say that do not want their children taught these principles, and yet the school system continues to press forward with its own agenda. Learn more about some of these rulings from our friends online at Rescue Your Child.

When I was in graduate school, we spent a lot of our study time looking at how many of the issues we were facing in our culture were the result of parenting choices we had made as a society. For example, Mel Levine, who was an expert on the Millennial generation, would predict behavioral patterns for that generation based on how they were being parented. Cultural sweeps like the decline in discipline, the lack of maternal care, and the rise of social media have all had significant implications for the home and, as a result, the future of our nation. Looking in the rearview mirror from a cultural perspective helps us to connect outcomes to actions. It helps us see the power of responsibility. It helps us become personally aware of the fact that ideas have consequences. Our actions influence the future.

One of Mel Levine's famous points of research was that the parents of the last generation spent a lot of their parenting time in highly structured group activities, rather than simply giving their children the individual freedom to "go outside and play." It's been a few decades since we actually heard that advice, to go outside and play. Instead, there was this very structured experience of play, and Levine projected, he culturally prophesied in a sense, that the next generation would have difficulty thinking outside of the box, that they would be captive to groupthink, that they would not know what to do if they weren't given very clear and specific instructions. And we've absolutely seen this play out in the workplace.

When I was writing the book *Multigenerational Marketplace*, I talked to many CEOs who were frustrated with younger workers because they didn't know how to lead with initiative, how to "find" work, how to think outside the box. It's fascinating and sobering to see these cultural predictions come to life. Likewise, researchers for the generation following Millennials, GenZs, said that due to the constant onslaught of selfie pressure, the constant posting of their own faces, the rise of violent video gaming, and the lack of parental connection, GenZs would exhibit a spirit of narcissism that was not balanced by empathy. And, indeed, this is what we've seen. The youngest generation, Alphas (born after 2010) are projected to be the most educated generation, partly due to growing up with knowledge at their fingertips. Projections for their generation include a redefining of what true education looks like. They are predicted to be the largest generation ever, so whoever educates them will literally rule the culture through the norms, values, preferences, and convictions that are implanted in them.

Researchers Mark McCrindle and Ashley Fell have noted that Alpha's adolescence is beginning earlier, what's called "upageing," earlier rates of maturity (both from synthetic foods and from a socialized environment of hypersexuality). At the same time, markers of adulthood like marriage are being delayed, which is similar the studies we discussed earlier from George Barna for the current generation, GenZs. McCrindle predicts that Alphas will be physically, socially, psychologically, educationally, and commercially sophisticated well beyond their years. However, as other researchers have noted, there is a caution, as they won't necessarily have the emotional maturity to balance out that "sophisticated" palate. Alphas have access to more technology and more external influences outside the home than any other generation in history. Parents, be aware. This generation is poised for being influenced and for influencing the larger culture in a way that no previous generation could have imagined.

There has also been a gradual transference of power, a shifting of the locus of control in the lives of the next generation. As a result of the shift of power from parent to screen, we have seen a shorter attention span, the development of a "mean and scary" worldview (parents, remember, the collective body of research suggests no screens for ages 0 to 2, and no more than 2 hours of screen time for ages two to adult). When we look around at the current generation, a massive glut of 51 million students being swept away by the indoctrination of the public school systems, and when we see how they have fallen captive to anxiety and fear, we have to question the influence this upswing will have on the cultural psyche of the next generation, especially in the light of the loss of parental power.

Both the social sciences and traditional "hard" science underscore the plans and processes of process of development within human relationships. When we see, for example, the rise in cortisol, a physiological demonstration of stress on a preschool child's body when he or she is in nonmaterial care, that tells us that a child needs his mom. Not too complicated, right? Science literally answers these questions for us. What is God's design for marriage? It's answered in biology: the definition of the species is the ability to procreate. It's important to consider the newness of the virtual world and its impact on social depth and narcissism. In many ways, the internet has created a world where many people, especially the youngest generations, appear to have lost their grip on social skills and appropriate levels of disclosure. Many are simply spinning out filament into the air (to cite Wordsworth's poetic reference) hoping that some ethereal concept, some gossamer thread, will cling somehow to someone, and a "connection" will be forged. We are beginning to see many young people growing less capable at the subtle arts of listening, turn-taking, both verbal and nonverbal communication in general. The rapidity with which some seem to develop "true friends" online fosters a surge of concerning behaviors, such as disclosing personal information far more readily than is deemed healthy for the relationship—far more readily in fact, than would ever occur in a face-to-face relationship. If as one of my favorite developmentalists puts it, "speech is an expression of that process of becoming aware" (Vygotsky, p. 30), then learning how, why, and when to speak is a vital component of the process of development—and a vital component to our own health both as individuals and as a culture.

In Romans 12, Paul writes of the Christian's transformation which begins with the renewal of our mind, allowing us to "discern what is the will of God, what is good and acceptable and perfect." He goes on to describe the marks of the true Christian: showing genuine love, holding fast to good, being fervent in spirit (in great contrast to the emo culture driving a spirit of depression through music and dress) outdoing one another in honor, rejoicing in hope, and being patient in tribulation. These are part of what Paul calls the believers' "reasonable" service, *logikos,* where we get the word *logic.* This list of our logical service is a great litmus test for our children's heart condition. Do they serve, love, honor (evidenced in the treatment of others) and can they be patient and hopeful (evidenced in the measure of self-control and self-discipline) in all circumstances? Is there at least some processing in that direction? Think how many significant crises could be readily avoided today if people simply learned to speak with honor and to utilize self control!

Again, this is further evidence for the vital role that parents play in the development and discipleship of the next generation. Children do not learn these traits from their peers. They do not learn them in secular indoctrination centers. The beginning of wisdom, its very starting point, Proverbs tells us, is the fear of the Lord. Children will learn mockery of the laws of the Lord in California's public schools; they will learn oppression of its truths, but they will not learn the fear of the Lord in centers that are linked with an aggressive, secular agenda. I know there is a push in some circles to try to mend public education, but I believe it is too far gone. I believe it's time for a new breed of education, one that is tried and true, proven in its efficacy and return on investment for generations. Christian parents are called to rise up and carry the mantle. Our time and energy would be better spent not mending schools, but ending them.

As Nabor and Mate write in one of my all-time favorite parenting books, *Hold on to Your Kids: Why Parents Need to Matter More than Peers,* the parental dynamic, correctly applied, answers life's most profound questions about childrearing. Remember our Romans 1:20 model? God's character, his nature, is evidenced in the creation he designed. As international experts on child development, Nabor and Mate show in their well-researched work that peer orientation undermines, literally sabotages, parenting. They call it parental impotence, and we see it all around us today. Children are being driven by their scholastic peer groups like little mini gangs bent on selfishness and destruction. Peer orientation must be dethroned for the natural process of parenting to be effective.

And yet, the government keeps pushing for control. O u r friends at Parental Rights have done tremendous work this arena to expose the erosion of parental rights in medicine, in government, and in education, but the battle continues. Maybe you've heard the echo of that rhetorical question that often surfaces in America today, "Whose children are they?" In other words, what agencies have the right to make decisions for the next generation? Do America's children belong to their parents or to the state?

When we look at the predictive power of the next generation, he who holds the gold makes the rules. Hitler intentionally designed programs like Hitler Youth and the League of German Girls to train up a generation, indoctrinating them in the Nazi regime. Just read the history of how Hitler banned the Boy Scouts and forced scouts to join Hitler Youth so he could control what they learned. In early 1930, the Nazi state abolished all youth groups in Germany, closing off all the competition for worldview development. By 1937, they had 5.4 million youth members (65% of the 10-18 population) and by 1940, 7.2 million —a full 82% of the 10-18 population belonged to Hitler Youth. One of the most chilling historical citations was the stated goal of these Nazi organizations: to "dismantle existing social structures and traditions and to impose conformity." Sound familiar?

Parents, in 2019, over 90% of students in America attended secular public schools. Are you hearing what I'm saying? The power is in the hand of the educator. Let's go back to Plato's question for every civilization throughout all time and space, for this is truly the determining factor in America's future: Who is teaching the children, and what are they being taught? Christian parents must be mindful of the fact that schools, especially in overtly liberal states like California, are literally inculcating the values that will drive the future of our nation. And lest we think that private schools are faring much better, let's go back to the research by Ken Ham and Brit Beemer on how few Christian schools are actually making Christian disciples.

My friends at The Nehemiah Institute have devised a test called PEERS that is designed to assess one's biblical worldview in the areas of politics, education, economics, religion, and society. The founder of the Institute, Dan Smithwick, tells me that less than 20% of Christian teachers he tests in the United States pass. The vast majority, 80%, do not have a biblical worldview. Thankfully, his test also provides opportunity for training, so we can shore up the worldviews of teachers who have been trained up in the public system and have not yet dealt with their own indoctrination prior to entering a teaching contract at a Christian school. In our work at both Awaken Academy and Chula Vista Christian University, we are partnering with the Nehemiah Institute for Biblical worldview training, and I highly recommend the PEERS assessment to anyone considering starting your own private Christian school or homeschool program.

One of the most significant missing elements in modern schooling is the apprenticeship or mentorship model. I am not at all surprised that we lack an apprenticeship model because the social science statistics tell us plainly that parents have failed to replicate themselves and their faith in the Christian process we call "discipleship," which is ultimately the reason the next generation is where it is and maintains the level of atheism that it does. But it is not too late to turn this ship around and create a mentorship or "scaffolding" model.

Lev Vygotsky was a Russian author and theorist (1896 – 1934) who contributed a great deal to human development. His writings were suppressed by the Russian government during his lifetime, but many of his ideas have begun to make a resurgence in recent years. Vygotsky believed that the most effective learning environment for children was one built on scaffolding, where a parent or an older sibling provides an apprenticeship model that challenges the child while still providing "scaffolding" for support, creating an environment for growth that offers attainable challenges for the child in training. Vygotsky called this process the "zone of proximal development." The word "proximal" means in close proximity, so we could see this process as one of mentorship, discipleship. Family is our closest proximal zone. Again, back to social science and the Romans 1:20 model—this is a logical delineation in the training up of a child.

Another one of my favorite researchers, Uri Bronebrenner, is famous for a theory he called ecological systems theory, which underscores the need for intergenerational mentoring as a primary influence in healthy human development. In the book *Two Worlds of Childhood: US and USSR* (1973), Bronfenbrenner said, "Children need people in order to become human.... It is primarily through observing, playing, and working with others older and younger than himself that a child discovers both what he can do and who he can become--that he develops both his ability and his identity.... Hence to relegate children to a world of their own is to deprive them of their humanity, and ourselves as well." How much simpler could it be, friends?

Children need people in order to become human! They don't need screens or toys or even books: they need human interaction with someone they naturally love and respect.

Children (and arguably, all of us) need mentorship. This is one of the reasons we use the one-room schoolhouse model in much of our homeschool academy work, because children need older models with likeminded values who will show them what the next phase of life will look like. We all need that. We all need to be reaching up to someone 10 years older and reaching out to mentor someone 10 years younger. In this way, we can effectively pass the baton, leave a legacy, and train up the generation coming up behind us.

As Bronfenbrenner notes, "Development, it turns out, occurs through this process of progressively more complex exchange between a child and somebody else—especially somebody who's crazy about that child." Bronfenbrenner's ideologies remind us that children don't develop into healthy young adults by being trained by television or parented by peers. They need the love and nurture of a parent who loves them in order to reach their true potential. Later, Bronfenbrenner added, "In today's world parents find themselves at the mercy of a society which imposes pressures and priorities that allow neither time nor place for meaningful activities and relations between children and adults, which downgrade the role of parents and the functions of parenthood, and which prevent the parent from doing things he wants to do as a guide, friend, and companion to his children." This was in the 70s! How much more so now!!

Bronfenbrenner believed that the age-segregation in our society was a great detriment to children, which has created a sense of isolation from the world of work. In the past, children were much more integrated into the world of work, even sharing in the task of the family business and the agricultural needs. Today, children have a very muddled sense of what the adult world of work consists of, and Bronfenbrenner believed this created an unhealthy disconnect from the reality of the child's future world of work. In the same way, children are also disconnected from the adult responsibilities of caring for children. As Bronfenbrenner notes in *The Ecology of Human Development* (1979), "In the United States, it is now possible for a person eighteen years of age, female as well as male, to graduate from high school, college, or university without ever having cared for, or even held, a baby; without ever having comforted or assisted another human being who really needed help...No society can long sustain itself unless its members have learned the sensitivities, motivations, and skills involved in assisting and caring for other human beings."

And yet, everywhere we look, there is a force attempting to undermine this core system of the family, a battle for control. In our current state of educational affairs, parents' rights end at the public school door. This is why parents walked into their kids' bedrooms in 2021 and heard teachers on Zoom saying, "Parents are not welcome here." This is why, in public schools across the country, there is a resurgence and redefinition of racism, Marxist philosophies that are determined to divide, to create a victim and oppressor mindset from which no one can escape. Be sure to check out my podcast interview with Keven McGary to hear about the dramatic indoctrination of Critical Race Theory sweeping the schools, the rewriting of history, the pulling up of traditions, the toppling of statues. And of course, this doesn't even begin to address the hypersexualized, overtly anti-Christian culture that has sprouted up in the government school system. There are over a dozen new sexual agendas targeting children in the public school just in the last decade. And tragically, many of the parents I talk to who are breaking free of the public school system say that one of the most significant pressures their children were facing in the school system was actually not the teachers—students and parents alike say they expected indoctrination and pressure from their teachers (which is tragic in

70

its own right). What they weren't prepared for was the level of negative peer pressure their children would face from other students. The pressure is embedded in the system.

There's a term in social sciences called third-person syndrome. It's a self-protective mechanism that convinces us that other people are vulnerable to something, but we ourselves are somehow above being influenced by it. Third-person syndrome plays a significant role in the worldview of parents who keep their children in government indoctrination centers despite hearing about the horrific performance of the public school system. Third-person syndrome creates a sense that we are somehow above the level of being influenced by those around us. This is naivety at best and arrogance at worst. Even in studies of parents' opinions on school districts, third person syndrome reigns. Most parents believe the problems described in American public schools are referencing schools "somewhere out there," not the public schools in their own districts. It's similar to the idea that 75% of Americans believe they're above average. The math doesn't add up. It may be more comforting to point the finger at another district, another state, another scapegoat. But the reality is that these issues are happening across the nation. These pressures are not just local, they're national, generational. The roots run deep and wide.

The Bible tells us that we are absolutely, without a doubt, undeniably influenced by the company we keep. Whatever the age, we must be aware of the power of influence. Paul said that if someone is living a life contrary to the word, we are to have nothing to do with him, and yet parents are sending their kids to these cultural indoctrination centers where the very proximity of relationship means that they will be peer-driven instead of parent-directed! In the current system, the battle for control is clear. Parents' rights end at the public school door. Parents were told they couldn't listen in on classroom instruction, and they couldn't "opt out" of the anti-Christian teachings of the public school.

Thankfully, parents across the nation have begun awakening to the ludicrous nature of the rhetorical question, "Whose children are they?" Our children do not belong to the state. They belong to the parent. And as a parent, you have the God-given right and responsibility to raise, educate, and train up your children, to transmit the truth of God's word to the next generation. As parents, we can no longer afford to delegate away our rights and responsibilities to strangers who don't love our children like we do, people who don't carry the same mantle of authority and responsibility we do. We must stop outsourcing our children.

In his powerhouse book *Abolition: Overcoming the Christian Establishment on Education,* lawyer Kevin Novak explains the basis of law and jurisdiction in a manner that perfectly exemplifies the reasoning of a legal mind. After a lengthy and convincing argument on the grounds for educational control, he cuts to the chase: "The civil government has no right to operate a school system, because the civil government has no jurisdiction over the heart and mind." The word jurisdiction, he explains, is comprised of the prefix *juris*, Latin for the word "law," and the suffix *diction*, which is Latin for "to speak." So, jurisdiction means "to speak law." That's exactly what's happening today: The public schools are trying to speak law, to claim their own brand of jurisdiction over the minds and hearts of America's children.

And, Novak says, a failure to teach this principle of governance will prove to be "catastrophic to the gospel." Every decade, he says, "in each successive generation, more and more of the power is shifted to government and away from family." This has been a decades-long battle with government education, vying for cradle-to-grave control of the American people. Novak says these two constructs are mutually exclusive: The "growth of civil government lessens the growth of family government, which impacts the transmission of the gospel." In other words, as a direct result of the empowering of government school systems, the transmission of the gospel is weakened. Isn't this ironic, considering how many parents send their children into the atheist dens of the public school system thinking they will serve as mini evangelists and win over the hardened atheists who are making a living leading astray impressionable youth? In essence, the opposite is happening: "The gospel suffers because humanists are then in the position to utilize their physical sword to advance their ideologies through civil government," Novak says, "and naturally, those humanistic government actors are not facilitating the gospel, but hindering it." Parents, when we put our money on the table in the form of attendance at a local public school, we are empowering the secular vision, furthering the humanistic mission. If we want to topple the structure, we have to cut off the financial stream.

If you listen to my radio show or podcast, you've probably heard me say all-too often that here in America, we have allowed the Great Commission to be outlawed on our watch. I think we would be kidding ourselves if we thought this travesty could be turned around without some heavy lifting on our end. We must make an honest assessment of where we are as a country, as a church, as a family in order to establish a new course of direction and action. Years ago, I heard visionary education pioneer Dr. Michael Farris predict three waves that would come against the parent-directed movement. The first two were unfounded and have been disproved (naysayers said homeschoolers would be ignorant and unsocialized, but of course the stats now show they are the most emotionally mature, identity secure, academically equipped, civically engaged group of all students). But the third wave, that parent-directed education was a threat to the secular state because it is the most effective process for transmitting the gospel and making disciples—that part is true. When we make the sacrifice to invest into our children academically, socially, emotionally, mentally, and spiritually, we will reap a harvest. God's word will not come back void. It will accomplish his desire. He is right now, even now, watching over his word to perform it both in our generation and in the one to come. What seeds are we planting today toward that future harvest?

Our best offense for the next generation is not increasing government regulation; it's empowering parents. As a lifelong educator, I wholeheartedly believe that parents can successfully educate their own children. I believe this responsibility falls on the shoulders of the parent, not the government. Our end goal is different from theirs: We don't want to produce dispassionate intellectual children—we want a passionate, educated, wise, culturally savvy generation to be the head and not the tail, to have the courage and the tenacity to go into all the world and make disciples. The oppression in the current system is teaching children to compartmentalize their faith, not to speak up boldly for what is right and true. How can we make disciples if we can't make conversation?

The two youngest generations have incredible cultural power at their fingertips, and Alphas will be one of the largest generations in the history of the world from a numerical perspective, so whoever educates them will literally rule the culture through the norms, values, preferences, and convictions that are implanted in them. The next generation is poised for being influenced and for influencing the larger culture in a way that no previous generation could have imagined. As believers, we must heed the times, the signs, and the seasons and take an active role in discipling the next generation. Let's take a deeper look now at the twelve toxic traits that are currently fueling America's public education system.

CHAPTER FIVE

Toxic Trait #1: The Making of a Snowflake

In the book *The Coddling of the American Mind*, lawyer Greg Lukianoff and professor Jonathan Haidt write about their observations of the Great Untruths being taught across college campuses, untruths that are harming students and setting them up for failure by teaching them to trust their feelings, to avoid discomfort, and to encase themselves in proverbial bubble wrap to avoid the wounds of the world. The authors saw an alarming trend happening in classrooms across America: students were claiming their mental health would be jeopardized if they were "triggered" or "feel unsafe." Discomfort, as Lukianoff and Haidt put it, was being classified as a medical response. Students whined that they would be unable to function if they had to listen to certain topics, especially topics they personally disagreed with. Now, if that cultural crisis in itself didn't clue us all in that something was terribly wrong with American education, the next wave of idiocy should have flipped on the light for all of us: Suddenly, college campuses were awash with safe spaces equipped with the weapons of modern warfare: playdough and puppies, coloring tables and bubble rooms designed to help fragile 19-year-old students process the horrific trauma of hearing a different opinion.

Though I spent most of my 20 years of education in the private school environment, the markers were still there: parents calling to tell me their child wouldn't be able to give a speech in front of the class because she might pass out from nervousness, or being asked not to post articles from the Institute for Creation Research because it might "trigger" someone if I dared to suggest in a Christian institution that the Genesis account is historical fact. Or the notes excusing Susie from PE because she "couldn't run fast" and the emails excusing Jonnie from completing his homework because he was "overwhelmed with his current workload." Twenty years of classroom teaching and conversations with both parents and students led me to this chapter's topic, "How to Make a Snowflake." But first, a little background on the historicity of the key word here, snowflake.

Years before *The Coddling of the American Mind* hit the streets, former college president Dr. Everett Piper saw the blizzard coming, and he wrote the iconic letter that sent the word "snowflake" soaring to its now-viral status. Piper's 2015 letter, "This is Not a Daycare; It's a University" tells the story of a student who felt victimized by a sermon at the university chapel because the speaker used the word "divorce," and that word made the student feel terribly unsafe and uncomfortable. When the student complained to a dean, Piper called out the student, as well as any other fragile students who might be tempted to bemoan the message, calling these snowflake students to account for their childishness, their selfishness, their narcissism, and their unwillingness to engage in authentic discourse.

"We're not comfortable with the discomfort," Piper later told *Today* reporter Megan Molohan. "As a culture, we raised a generation that cherishes comfort more than freedom. It is not a surprise to see such immaturity and selfishness in our students when we have been perpetuating immaturity and selfishness for decades." A generation that values comfort over freedom will never truly be free. This pattern of rebellion bound up in the heart

76

of mankind is evidenced when we crave smooth talk instead of the truth, flattery instead of facts, the easy road instead of the rewarding journey. Isaiah faced the same issue. "Now go, write it before them on a tablet and inscribe it in a book, that it may be for a time to come as a witness forever," Isaiah 38:8-11 says. "For they are a rebellious people, lying children, children unwilling to hear the instruction of the Lord, who say to the seers, do not see, into the profits, do not prophesy to us what is right; speak to us smooth things; prophesy illusions." Isaiah's cultural distress, much like ours today, was fueled by a community of adults who didn't want to hear or speak what was right, who didn't want to face what was true, people who preferred to live in a grand illusion.

Parents, training up our children and making disciples means that we must have difficult conversations. Children (and adults) need to hear information they don't necessarily like, corrections that aren't comfortable, pleasant, or flattering. There must be discipline (root word = disciple). There must be truth that refuses to coddle sin. Little offenses may seem benign in the moment, but in just a few years, those seemingly benign character flaws will yield a harvest that can twist a city, state, or nation. I often encourage parents to add ten years to that seemingly small disobedience. What does that seed of rebellion look like when it's full grown? The end result is often sobering. May we not be a generation that closes our eyes to the visions of the seer, a generation that drowns out the voice of the prophets, craving in its place the artificial sweetness of candy-coated compliments. Instead, let's be a generation that embraces the truth, the life, the way, and the hope of the world. As leaders, as parents, as industry disruptors, we have to work diligently to create resilient, growth-oriented mindsets in the next generation.

Postman saw this love of comfort spiraling down the track like a bullet train. Postman wanted to persuade his readers that the content our modern public discourse has become what he called "dangerous nonsense," demonstrating the downward spiral of behavioral expectations where we grow "getting sillier by the minute."As we listen to the conversations of the culture, whether in written word, in speech, in songs, or in other media speak, the gravity of Postman's (and Morse's and Thoreau's) observations become painfully clear: The art of authentic conversation, of civil discourse, has been traded in for a shallow din of surface conversations that flit from subject to subject like a butterfly on a limb. There is no depth, no challenge, no exposition. Alternative viewpoints are banned, canceled. This is such a striking contrast to the necessary developmental foundations of critical thinking!

Our students won't learn resilience in echo chambers and safe spaces. They will never reach the peak wisdom without exposure to the truth of God's word and even the historical documents of real struggled endured by real people. What is the collective effect of this dangerous nonsense? Certainly, people have lost the ability to engage in meaningful conversation. They've lost the ability to be sharpened or challenged by a thought that differs from their own, even to agree to disagree. Civil discourse has died. Lukianoff and Haidt link this steady decline has its roots in the American college system, where students have been provided with "safe spaces" to protect them from any thought that might "trigger" them. In other words, we have baby-proofed the college, and, as a result, children have failed to develop the self-discipline and maturity that would have come from exposure to from those trigger words, phrases, ideals, and dangers. Without these anchors, students will become snowflakes, not champions.

It's highly ironic that secular college and secondary programs accuse Christian education as being myopic. One of the core courses in any solid Christian education program is apologetics, a course that exposes students to the many various worldviews that exist on the planet and teaches them how each of these worldview lenses encourages people to think, see, and process information. In other words, students are taught not just what to think but how to think. They begin to reason and wrestle with questions in their belief systems, and they learn not only what they believe but why they believe it. This is one of our foundational methodologies at Chula Vista Christian University. Our students are taught how to think, how to reason, how to distinguish between lies and truth.

As Lukianoff and Haidt note, the coddling of the American mind has resulted in absolute mayhem in colleges around the nation. When Dr. Piper first heard that his students claimed to be "triggered" by hearing words like divorce in chapel, he knew the writing was on the wall. His not-a-daycare essay eventually grew into a book with the telling subtitle: "The dangerous consequences of abandoning truth." He and many other presidents have noted the rise of Postman's dangerous "din of nonsense" as they watch the spiraling of the modern student. These mentalities should concern us not only for today's colleges and college students; they should warn us of the trajectory for the future of our nation. Colleges are not just teaching today's students; they are training tomorrow's workforce, leaders, culture shapers, and pace-setters. We do not develop resilience by avoiding uncomfortable or painful topics. We do not become mature, civically-engaged citizens by lying in a fetal position with our fingers in our ears to keep us from being exposed to "trigger" words, blocking our auditory receptors from perceiving anything unpleasant or contrary to our existing paradigms.

As the tragic timeline showed, there has been a natural progression to this point in history. The enemy of our souls was perfectly poised to hijack the emotions and the reasoning skills of the American people. Each year, 51 million K to 12 students absorb the doctrines of the godless, soulless public education system. Decade after decade, we churn out millions of drones whose educational indoctrination has taught them what to think, but not how to think. As a result, the world system is spiraling out of control with a counter logic that is increasingly difficult to comprehend. But don't be fooled: the issue is not a physiological one. The issue is a spiritual one. We are, as Dallas Willard once put it, living in an upside down world. Let's further unpack the thorny, thistly path that led us to these specific GPS coordinates.

When I was in graduate school at Regent University, my professors did a phenomenal job of exposing us to the deep thinkers and social prophets of the day. One such author at the time was Mel Levine, who was a foremost expert in what was the then-youngest generation, Millennials. He predicated behaviors coming down the pike because he could tell what patterns of belief and behavior were being engrained in these children and how, if they didn't turn in a new direction and embrace neural plasticity, their own parenting would be negatively affected by these decisions. Levine saw that Mommy and Me cultures, constant social engagement, and the lack of creative outdoor time alone would foster a groupthink that would make kids want to conform to social norms rather than think for themselves. Sound familiar?

In his book *Ready or Not, Here Life Comes,* Levine details the struggles of the youngest generations and their lack of accurate knowledge about themselves. He says that cognizance about one's background, strengths, weaknesses, tastes, and inclinations help chart a course for what he calls the "startup years." Children amass this self-knowledge through daily osmosis through direct or indirect teachings of parents and by comparing and contrasting themselves with others. However, if the child has been what Levine calls the "victim of brain neglect," where specific needs of the mind were never met, that child will have significant difficulty moving from adolescence to adulthood (a common challenge we see today in what Postman called perpetual adolescence, or the childified adult). This "brain neglect" comes when a child grows up misunderstood or emotionally disabled "because crucial capabilities...were never cultivated during childhood or adolescence."

The parent-directed movement of education, on the other hand, provides an opportunity for mentorship, apprenticeship, scaffolding, discipleship. We can call our children up to greatness because we have dedicated time with them, intentional training opportunities. In the traditional classroom, a child spends 7 hours a day trapped in someone else's paradigm, driven by someone else's governance, never allowed to think or act freely outside the walls of the box in which he is imprisoned. And we wonder why, by age 7, most boys in America say that they hate school.

In working with the current demographic of American parents, we see two realties emerging today. One extreme is that of highly enabling parents, whose behavior has created in their children a sense of total and utter dependence. Instead of empowering their children to think and act independently, these parents create a parasitic parenting model, often living vicariously through their children's successes. On the flip side of that model, we also have a polar opposite, increasingly prevalent, and painful reality of detached parenting—mistuned and unattached parents whose love for some other entity rivals their love of being a parent. Placed side by side, these two parenting extremes are a strange outworking of modern day authoritarian versus laissez-faire parenting, distal versus proximal styles of relating.

Let's look at the first one, enablers. We saw this format evidenced in the college payoff schemes, the pseudo sports, the fake testing, parents who would do absolutely anything to get their kids into that "great" college (you know, the college with such questionable ethics that they would actually let a kid bribe his way in). In the payoff education scandal, parents shelled out roughly $25 million to a group of universities from 2011 to 2019 to bribe coaches and university administrators into providing their children unwarranted admission to the university. Some parents were charged. Some colleges shed crocodile tears, telling the press they were "shocked" that their own trusted sports programs could display such uncharacteristically corrupt behavior. With these shallow admissions of repentance, the world suddenly felt better about the colleges again—at least until the next round of payoffs. But this was certainly not the first time we've seen such corruption in the academic sector. Remember when 176 Georgia teachers were indicted for changing the answers on their students' tests in order to inflate their grades so that the school would get more money?

Now, the stories are not always so overt or dramatic. Sometimes it's as simple as a parent's unwillingness to face a child's character flaws. A parent in a local private school recently rose up in arms over a teacher calling her 6-year-old princess to account for her behavior in class. "Are you insinuating that my child would lie?" The mom asked with great incredulity. How dare the teacher challenge a parent's perfect princess on her behavior! The art of protecting, turning a blind eye, defending crooked character—these measures will play out in unattractive ways in 5 years, 10 years, 20 years. College coaches tell me that many of today's athletes have been trained to think of themselves as above average. They complain when they aren't listed on the starting lineup because they have never been confronted with the reality of their weaknesses. These snowflakes have been propped up on a parental pedestal of pseudo perfection. It's time to help them melt down their icy protrusions so they can discover the truth. We can't remove the anchor of morality from the public sphere and then expect integrity to reign. We can't keep castrating the gelding and bidding it to be fruitful. There is one sure path to avoiding the systemic corruption we find ourselves immersed in today: The fear of the Lord is the beginning of wisdom.

One of the most sobering realities of working with the next generation is seeing the damage done by passive, permissive leadership. The trait of parent protectiveness and an inability to see wrongdoing in their children nurtures a spirit of narcissism and egocentrism, not to mention an unwillingness to face and correct weaknesses. Jeane Twenge points out that the youngest generations have burgeoning level of narcissism, but they lack the appropriate level of empathy to balance that out. They are devoid of the appropriate level of self-awareness that would help them develop a realistic assessment of their strengths and weaknesses. We all have both. Blind spots can be extraordinarily debilitating if we don't have someone in our lives to sharpen us, to shape us. As parents, we have the unique opportunity unlike any other influencer in a child's life. Through our actions or inactions, our discipline or our laziness, we will raise up and send out into the world either brats or bullies. A future spouse, employer, or civic leader will be the recipient of either the blessing or our curse of our posterity.

As a culture, we spend an extraordinary amount of time running in circles like a hyperactive three year old. We go round and round with no destination in sight, using our energy for meaningless activities, trivial pursuits, cruises to nowhere. In the 1960s parents stomped their feet at the teaching of evolution in the public schools. Has it changed? No, for the last fifty years, it has been taught as fact every day across the United States. In the 1980s parents stomped their feet about the pervasive teaching of sexual education that contradicted with the values of the home and the Bible. Has it gotten better? No, it's gotten worse, far worse. The agenda is now far more aggressive, far more perverse. Read the grotesque standards and lesson plans in San Diego County schools on the SHEP site. It's shocking.

Parents are up in arms about medical mandates in California right now, and rightly so. But really, where did we draw the line of what's acceptable, and when did we just give up? Do we care about the content taught in sex ed? Evolution? Perversion? The rewriting of history? Critical race theory? As Postman describes CRT in 1991, it's already been embedded in the government school structure for 30 years! The definition of insanity is doing the same thing over and over and getting a different result. I know we all want to believe that the system can change, but hear me: the system we are working against is not human. It's not people; it's principalities. Why are we constantly trying to yoke ourselves with evil and think that no one will get burned? As Gatto said, the public school system is totally unreformable. It has to be reconstructed, rebuilt from the ground up. Instead of wasting our energy stomping our feet at an unreformable, irreversibly crooked entity like the government school system, why not use our time and resources to innovate, to dream, to create a brand new, highly effective, and life-altering educational methodology for the next generation?

Dr. Simone Gold, founder of America's Frontline Doctors, recently spoke at our church. She was the third national speaker in a row to step on the stage, and without provocation, turn the topic to education. She called on parents to pull their students from traditional education and homeschool them. In fact, she said that when parents ask her broad questions about medical procedures, her first question is, "What are you doing right now to make it possible to homeschool your kids?" If they are doing nothing, she said, then she won't answer their question. Why the hard line? Because at the national level, all of these cultural leaders, from Candace Owens to Charlie Kirk to Dr. Gold, see the insidious push of indoctrination in traditional education. They see it dumbing us down, creating a planet of sheep who have no ability to think critically, to reason, to speak up, or to properly direct the future trajectory of our great nation.

Let's consider again Plato's two most important questions: who is teaching the children, and what are they being taught? How would you answer these questions for your own family? The reflective response should include not only what we are allowing them to be taught in oppressive government schools but also what we are echoing in our own homes. Having a safe haven, what Bowlby (1944) called a "secure base," gives people a sense of confidence, and many of our younger generations have not grown up with that sense of safety or connection. "Over the (last) five decades," van der Kolk (2014) writes, "research has firmly established the idea that having a safe haven promotes self-reliance and instills a sense of sympathy and helpfulness to others in distress." In fact, these skills are paramount in helping younger students (future employees!) get "in synch" with the needs of others. They learn the "self-awareness, empathy, impulse control, and self-motivation that make it possible to become contributing members of the larger social culture," van der Kolk notes. Parents, you play a key role in the creation of resilience simply by being present in a child's life. Deadbeat dads, that one is for you. It's time to get off the sidelines and onto the field. The dramatic decline of resilience in the youngest generations tell us that something is missing.

Twenty years ago, former Washington Post author Pete Hamill wondered aloud in an essay entitled "Crack in the Box" whether television addiction in the young mirrored drug addiction in adulthood. As neuroscience later proved, it did, and it does. Following in the footsteps of educational prophets like Postman, Huxley, and Levine, I too have wondered, in the same way, whether the dopamine-driven behaviors of social media's incessant vying for vain approval have left a generation of narcissists unable to attach. I wonder whether, as Drs. Bush and McIlhaney have written in the book *Hooked,* the casual sex culture has unleashed a mass of sticky-less tape, leaving behind an unanchored, unmoored generation that fails to commit to healthy adult attachments.

This lack of attachment, this drift from the moorings of committed relationships, has a significant impact on every aspect of adult life, including emotional health. The National Alliance on Mental Illness observed a "crisis of mental health" on college campuses in the United States in 2015, with over 5 million students dealing with anxiety, depression, and related issues. Suicide, is, tragically, the second leading killer for college students, says the American College Health Association. An article in *The Chronicle of Higher Education* called "Prozac Campuses" notes that today's students have an "overwhelming need to seem flawless." They are uncomfortable with anyone, even their closest friends, knowing that they have defects or frailties. The airbrushed perfectionism of social media has transplanted itself into our collective cultural consciousness, and the result has been a paralyzing perfectionism that keeps our young snowflakes frozen in their tracks.

It's not that college students are experiencing new pressures, of course; the college experience has always been known for its high-pressure environment. What's different today, researchers say, is the level of efficacy: Today's young adults simply do not have the same markers of resilience as that of previous generations. They don't know how to push through the struggles of life. They don't know how to climb back up when they're thrown off the horse. Researchers attribute this deficiency and concurrent lack of problem-solving skills to childhood environments where they were not allowed to fail, where everyone received a trophy, regardless of the level of excellence or incompetency. If they just *tried*, they were rewarded. Mediocrity became the celebrated norm. Largely because of this mindset, today's youngest generations have not yet developed the stick-to-itiveness needed to persevere through life's challenges. This is yet another crisis caused by the snowflake culture.

Stanford University professors have coined the term "duck syndrome" for this Gen Z phenomenon. What we see on the outside when we watch a duck gliding across a lake is an effortless, graceful display of beauty. However, underneath the surface, the creature's legs may be paddling frantically to keep its body moving forward. When I share this Duck Syndrome visual with GenZ, they nod enthusiastically in agreement. They relate to the image. They have been culturally conditioned to defending an image, to pretending they have it all together—so much so that it can be difficult for them to ascertain what they are really feeling. Younger generations are terrified of failure, and since failure is a very real part of life, we need to help desensitize them against that irrational fear. And like all hopeful and permanent change, we need to begin the process of training at home. These strains of parental dysfunction must be addressed if we are to heal as a nation.

And, parents, we might do well to exhibit some resilience ourselves. If we have a habit of dissolving friendships or business partnerships or church memberships over every tiny offense, then we are not modeling relational resilience to the next generation. Mom, Dad, if you're fleeing your fractured state in the hopes of finding greener pastures elsewhere, that may not be the best role model of resilience to the GenZ and Alphas who are watching your example. When the going gets tough, the resilient get robust. There is an end-of-the-ages parallel here, parents. If we are constantly trying to avoid pain and find greener pastures, we will miss opportunities for growth. As the saying goes, we can't outrun the rapture. Certainly, no man knows the hour, but we know the hour is coming. In the event that we may be living out the book of Revelations right now, we might want to man up a little bit. Read some missionary biographies. Read Rod Dreher's book *Live Not By Lies*. Find some sure footing for your faith because even though we don't know for sure *when* the day is coming, we know for sure that the day *is* coming.

If we raise a generation of snowflakes, they will melt when trouble comes. If we raise a generation of champions, they will stand strong and hold back the wave of darkness rushing over our nation. And isn't that our goal, when we've done all we can do, we will stand and stand strong? It's our responsibility to speak life and purpose, to inject courage and hope into the next generation. If we want to raise resilient kids instead of snowflakes, we need to turn the ship around.

In their book *The Power of Resilience*, Drs. Brooks and Goldstein explain that a resilient mindset is characterized by several features: Resilient people feel a relative sense of control over life; they are empathetic and know how to fortify "stress hardiness." Resilient people demonstrate effective interpersonal communication skills, problem-solving skills, and decision-making skills. They know how to establish realistic goals and expectations and how to learn from success as well as failure. Resilient people are compassionate, contributing members of society who live responsible live based on a set of thoughtful values. Which of these characteristics did students learn in traditional education? In school, student's days are spent doing the work someone else determines as important, 65% of their social time is on a screen, and they are segregated from anyone outside of their exact peer group. Their work is limited to ethereal constructs that have no connection to the real world. There are no truths in the public system, only "my truth" and "your truth." Students have no control over their days, their actions, even their thoughts. Everything is governed by someone else. In short, through their actions and interactions, America's public schools are teaching an anti-resilient mindset; day by day, class by class, lecture by lecture, government schools are sculpting a generation of snowflakes.

When we look at the implications of stress and efficacy under the microscope, we see some biological markers that can help us understand why the traditional school system is not built for developing emotional health and resilience. In a study on stress, Michael Marmot of University College in London reported in the *Lancet* journal that clerks and secretaries were more likely to die of a heart attack than senior executives were. Taking into account all variables, researchers found that "the lower the job category and the less control, the more likely people were to suffer from heart disease." Why? Because they had a perceived lack of control over their circumstances. This idea of circumstantial control or agency is also linked to a desirable educational outcome known as intrinsic motivation. The bulk of neuroscience research shows that the two key ingredients necessary for moving a student from external motivation to internal motivation are efficacy and curiosity. How many traditional schools completely undermine these two essential mindsets by crushing curiosity and labeling students by their inabilities instead of their strengths?

A mom was talking with me recently about how thankful she is to have rescued her child from public school. At age 10, her son was already saying he "hated" school and didn't want to go back. Uncertain of her options, she called the administration to find out what was happening. They called a meeting with her, and she described the experience to me. She sat down, encircled by an entire team of teachers and psychologists like a sheep surrounded by wolves. She quickly realized that they were repeating the same "remedies" they had been peddling to her family for the last five years. This mom saw with a moment of clarity that the school administration did not have her child's best interest at heart, and his entire vantage point was being driven by scholastic labels. Her son had become a hollow shell of his former self, begging her every day not to send him back to the school that was crushing his spirit. In that moment, the light went on. She pulled him out of public school and began homeschooling. Within just two weeks of taking back her son's education, she told me that she hardly recognizes her son. He's now excited about life and learning, talking nonstop and reading books on his own. And when he recently had the opportunity to take a day off from their homeschool coop and go to Disney, he didn't want to miss the class about the biology of an octopus! The student who was labeled slow, lazy, and "messy" by his teachers now has a new love of learning and a new lease on life.

Brooks and Goldstein note that "a life that is not balanced

or authentic is one ripe for discontent, shallow relationships, and stress, all characteristics that are not in accord with a resilient mindset." In the social media culture that has literally groomed the next generation on what is perfect and lovable, children are constantly exposed to this inauthenticity. Resilience is developed through self-discipline and self-control. In fact, psychologist Daniel Goleman called self-control one of the top five elements of emotional intelligence, and King Solomon ranked it higher than warfare: "Better a man who controls his temper than one who takes a city."

Now let me ask you this. Do you think the peer-driven culture of traditional education is a model of self-control, self-governance? Do children learn maturity and wisdom in the presence of their peers? No, definitely not. More often, in the company of their peers, they learn folly, immaturity, and reactivity. They are trained up by peers who lack self-governance, so they exhibit a lack of self-governance. Bullies beget bullies. Snowflakes beget snowflakes. The cycle continues ad nauseam. As Drs. Nabor and Mate have shown, it is not in the company of peers that our youngest citizens will grow up to be responsible, mature citizens. They must be molded by adults—adults who will refuse to coddle them, to make excuses for them, adults who will apply godly discipline to their lives (in pre-snowflake days, we used to say that parents "apply the rod of learning to the seat of correction").

The point of discipline is to teach self-government. Hebrews 12 reminds us that God disciplines those he loves as a father the son he delights in. This is an opposite point of view to the world system, because hedonism has infiltrated our parenting. But discipline (again, root word = disciple) is a vital component of later self-government. If we don't learn to discipline ourselves, someone else will have to discipline us later on. Those who don't learn self-government will be subjected to the government of others. Think how many crimes are committed for the simple lack of self-discipline!

Hezekiah was one of the "good kings of Judah." However, like many leaders before and after him, he failed to equip his descendants, to disciple his family line. Scholars even go so far as to call him "disappointing as a man and a father, but even more so as the steward of David's dynasty." When Hezekiah learned that the pride that led him to show off his wealth to the Babylonians would lead to his descendants being enslaved as eunuchs (thus threatening the family line) Hezekiah said, "At least there will be peace and security in my days." This undercurrent of selfish preservation spoke volumes about his lack of concern for his future posterity. What about us? Are we willing to make the necessary sacrifices to prepare our children and our children's children for the future? Are we prepared to fight for a nation that needs us to engage in the battle? If you're a parent, be a disciple maker, a mentor, an apprentice. Help your kids follow you as you follow Jesus. Our families need us, our state needs us, our country needs us. The future is birthed in the present, and it's up to us to steer the ship in the direction of hope, purpose, and destiny.

This is one of the key reasons I encourage homeschooling families to belong to a cooperative or homeschool academy. There is a benchmarking process, a sharpening process when you permit just enough peer exposure to allow your child to see that a) there will always be someone better, stronger, smarter, cuter, faster, and more able that your child. And that's okay. Find your lane, kid, and stay in it; b) being around people who are better than you will always expose your character. This is good. When character issues rise to the surface, we can deal with them. Yes, Thoreau thought he could go into the wood to "live deliberately" and alone, but without the interaction of other human beings, we don't reach our full measure of potential. Remember, the human brain is a social organ, as Dr. Dan Siegel puts it. We are molded in the context of our relationships, for better or for worse.

In his book *The Developing Mind: How Relationships and the Brain Interact to Shape Who We Are,* Siegel demonstrates definitively that our relationships throughout life provide a basis for neural growth and transformation. Both the potential and the need for these connective patterns exist lifelong. As Ainsworth's (1978) groundbreaking studies on attachments in early life demonstrated, in order for a healthy, secure attachment to develop, the parent must have "the capacity to perceive and respond to the child's mental state." This is physically impossible if the parent sees the child for the typical 15 minutes a day, the average amount of one-to-one time invested by dad in modern American families.

Neuroscientists have observed clear causation between socio-emotional deficiencies in the early years and specific affective responses later in life. For example, if there is a lack of worth, connection, or assurance in early life, a pattern of anger will be developed. Without connection, affection, and approval, a pattern of sadness and shame emerges. If there is a lack of assurance, certainty, security, a pattern of anxiety or fear shapes the neural world, and eventually, the individual's outer world. In order to heal, says Siegel, there must be a move toward coherence, an attempt to integrate all of these fragmented parts into a whole and become less rigid, more adaptable. "As integration is achieved across the numerous dimensions of living," Siegel says, "a sense of the unity of being is revealed." As Bowlby (1973) states, because attachment relationships are "a principal key to the mental health of the next generation, we need to know all we can about (their) nature and about the manifold social and psychological conditions that influence development for better or for worse."

From a developmental perspective, some stressors are necessary to sustain life and to extend the growth experience. Muscular tissue, for example, is strengthened through periods of stress and rest, as any weightlifting participant knows. From a metaphorical perspective, beneficial stress is akin to the experience of a butterfly breaking free from its cocoon, pressing its wings against the outer walls of its shell in order to enhance blood flow, to strengthen cellular structures, and to ready the creature for its flight to freedom. In the same way, humans need the impact of stress to create the physical and emotional fortitude needed for success in life. As any professor can attest to, these mini-stressors often function as the building blocks of socio-academic success in the college environment.

We do need some stresses; however, there is a limit to stress's effectiveness. Too little stress leads to apathy, but too much stress leads to emotional overload. In the earliest phase of human life within the intrauterine environment, the effects of stress are already visible. As developmental psychologist Kathleen Stassen Berger notes, too much maternal stress can create a child that is either emotionally "flat" or, an opposite response, a child who is prone to overreaction. We also see these stress responses Stanford preschool studies, where cortisol rises and negatively impacts behavior when children are removed from non-maternal care. Even the stressors of being in an environment that is not their home elevates their cortisol. Why? Because it's not natural. They were designed to need their mommy, not a rotating daycare provider. The biological responses tell the story. As Romans 1:20 reminds us, God's nature is evidenced in the created realm.

Stoltz (1997) writes in the book *Adversity Quotient* that repeated actions stemming from an internalized system of belief can lead to the creation of neural superhighways, what he calls a "habits only" lane in our neural network. This development is highly effective and beneficial for the task of learning a new skill, but unfortunately, it is also equally effective and non-beneficial for learning a destructive habit. What would happen if we took the ten steps to resilience Stoltz outlines, stir them in a pot with John Taylor Gatto's *Dumbing Us Down* observations, and reverse engineer the list? We would see, up close and personal, the steps schools use to create a generation of snowflakes, a veritable *Screwtape Letters* directory of anti-resilience. Stay with me here for a satirical moment:

1. To make a snowflake, we must limit children's sense of autonomy and control. This is perfectly achieved through the public school's goal of controlling every minute with a bell or buzzer, requiring a raised hand for teacher permission for anything from getting a drink to going to the bathroom, and, like a prison, regulating every second of their day.

2. To make a snowflake, we must continue to reduce students' sense of empathy by replacing it with cynicism or disconnect them from humanity with facial barriers and plastic cubicle cages so they feel alone and isolated.

3. To make a snowflake, we must keep the language oriented toward victimhood so there is no opportunity to develop "stress hardiness." Critical Race Theory, which has been in play in public schools under different monikers for 5 decades, does an excellent job of creating victims by pitting people against each other in a bourgeoisie-versus-proletariat, victim-versus-oppressor mindset. This also goes a long way in reducing empathy, step number 2.

4. To make a snowflake, we must keep students focused on petty disagreements and interpersonal conflicts, never allowing the Matthew 18 principle to be part of their daily dialogue. That way, they won't develop relational resilience. Social media is highly effective at this one, pitting people against each other and hiding behind the walls of anonymity to utter cruel and degrading comments like weapons hurled from a walled fortress.

5. To make a snowflake, we must keep their school work from connecting to anything meaningful in the real world so that they won't possess any actual problem-solving skills. This will also limit their sense of autonomy and efficacy, step number 1.

6. To make a snowflake, we must keep students segregated from what Bronfenbrenner called "the adult world of work" so that they have no idea how to make important decisions. Instead, they will become what Postman called the childified adult. Keep children in age-segregated peer groups for as many hours as possible each day, from school to sports to church services. Keep them away from older students and parents who might call them out on their immaturity, which would cause them to raise the mental ceiling of possibility over their lives.

7. To make a snowflake, we must restrict students from establishing realistic goals and expectations, setting their ideals too high to be attainable, and surrounding them with materialistic celebrities who will misrepresent realistic levels of material success. We must follow in the footsteps of the university-payoff-parents by doing all the work for student. Never let them fail. Never allow their ideas to have consequences.

8. To make a snowflake, we must prevent students from learning from successes as well as failures. This can be done one of two ways: We can keep them from failing by cleaning up every mistake they make, or we can keep them from learning from their successes. They must be trained to see success as accidental, not the result of hard work; otherwise, they will develop a sense of autonomy that will save them from the snowflake syndrome.

9. To make a snowflake, we must twist the 9th rule of resilience: that resilience comes from being a compassionate, contributing member of society. If we want to create a snowflake, we have to keep children segregated from meaningful work and

civic engagement. They must be made to feel that there is no rhyme or reason to the political process and that their voice doesn't matter. This one is clearly working even now; Project Votesmart says the number one reason the youngest generations don't vote in elections is because they feel their vote won't make a difference. To make a snowflake, we must also shield children from correction. If their coaches won't let them play, make your demands known as a parent. If their Sunday school teacher says they wouldn't obey, defend the child, stomp your feet, and vow never to return to that mean-spirited church that would dare to question the character of your little prince charming.

10. And finally, to make a snowflake, we must never let the next generation know that resilient people live "responsible lives based on a set of thoughtful values." The public school system has worked overtime on this one since the introduction of the Values Clarification Movement in 1964. Remove values from the schools, pull up the moral anchors, and watch students become increasingly disenfranchised, depressed, purposeless drifters. We didn't reach the treacherous heights of statistical norms by accident; there is a reason GenZs are the most anxious, depressed, atheist generation in the history of our nation.

This *Screwtape Letter* satire is hopefully an eye-opening appeal to the works of darkness being played out in the public sector today. Parents have often unknowingly played into the hands of Wormwood. When we look at the characteristics needed to develop resilience in children, it's a sobering analysis: Every single characteristic required for developing resilience is undermined by the public school system! So parents, if you want to raise a snowflake, just keep sending them off on the big yellow prison bus to the local government indoctrination center. Press, shake, freeze, and voila, there you'll have your very own snowflake.

And what will the outcome be? What socio-emotional challenges will that icy, fragile little snowflake face in 10 years?

20 years? Suzie snowflake won't last in college because she may run into the last remaining teacher who actually cares about truth and who will thus offend our little princess, who will then drop out of college. Suzie snowflake won't be able to maintain a healthy adult relationship because she will learn to curl up in a fetal position every time her spouse points out a flaw. She will storm out of the relationship over irreconcilable differences and then take that baggage to the next relationship. Suzie snowflake won't be able to hold down a job because it will be an average of 50 days between every commendation, and Suzie snowflake will feel overlooked, devalued, and mistreated because she doesn't get constant recognition for her below-average work.

But if we want to raise a generation of champions, then we need to take an opposite approach to our modern anti-resilience methodology. We need to stop filling students' days with busy work when authentic education only takes 2-3 hours a day. We need to stop overcomplicating education when skills like reading and arithmetic only take 100 hours to master. We need to give students a sense of control over their lives instead of ruling them with an electronic buzzer and a raised hand. We need to give them the opportunity to interact with people of all ages, not just age-segregated microcosms that keep them from learning mentorship and intergenerational communication.

We need to make their school work relate to the real world so they can learn problem-solving skills and decision-making skills that will help them navigate the issues of adult life. Perhaps then they will stop posting #adulting announcements that celebrate mediocre milestones like cooking dinner. We need to help them develop realistic goals and expectations, to connect the dots between their failure and their success. We need to teach them civic engagement, how to become a compassionate, contributing member of society. Children don't become responsible members of society by hanging out all day every day with other children. They learn these values by being parented—

by having regular, authentic, intentional interaction with adults. Resilient children know how to think, respond, and live devoted to a set of values, walking in congruence with the morals they have been trained up in. Parents, this training, this discipleship, rests squarely on our shoulders.

When Dr. Piper's students refused to listen to conversations that brought up unpleasant memories or feelings of discomfort, they launched a process of pseudo self-preservation, a form of emotional bubble wrap that would eventually cause their downfall. The human brain is wired to process traumatic events bi-hemispherically. We actually heal in the context of authentic conversation and supportive relationships. In graduate school, I studied the effects of trauma on the brain and saw the incredible potential for processing past and present traumas of all shapes and sizes within our conversations and communities. The most important step we can take to prepare the next generation for adulthood is not to shield them from painful memories; it's to help them process these experiences so that what was once painful or uncomfortable can become a testimony of triumph.

If we raise a generation of snowflakes, they will melt when trouble comes. If we raise a generation of champions, they will stand strong and hold back the wave of darkness rushing over our nation. And isn't that our goal, when we've done all we can do, that we will stand and stand strong? Parents, it's our responsibility to speak life and purpose, to inject courage and hope into the next generation. So let's say no to snowflakes and yes to resilient visionaries who will help turn this nation around.

CHAPTER SIX

Toxic Trait #2: Exponential Emotionality: The Age of Anxiety

Almost three decades ago, I was part of a discipleship-based church in northern Florida where the pastors started to notice a trend in their children. Their boys were coming home from the local public school—in the Bible belt—with increasing levels of fear over what seemed to be the most minute of actions. They would panic when anyone ran the shower too long. They would stress out if mom or dad let the water run unabated while brushing their teeth. One day, the mom asked her youngest son why he was so worried. "Mom," he said, his little eyes welling up with tears, "we're going to run out of water! There isn't enough water for everyone!" Mom assured her son that there was plenty of water and that God had built into the earth a natural recycling process that literally reclaims water from the ground to the sky. She reminded him that no new water has been created nor has needed to be created since the dawn of the universe because God's provision is perfect. But her son remained unconvinced. Like many parents, the pastors initially thought that a simple conversation with their children would open their eyes to the truth. "But mom, the teacher said so," the children echoed again and again. The root of fear and the teachers' authority in all matters had already been well-established in their hearts, even in the early childhood years.

These sweet, innocent children were coming home from school literally terrified of turning on the tap water. Their mother suddenly saw quite clearly the root of the fruit: the public school system was indoctrinating her children with a spirit of fear. Their teachers were warning them over and over that the earth was going to run out of resources, and a classroom of children came home paralyzed with anxiety about the future of their world. The children couldn't think logically through the lens of faith to see God's provision and protection; instead, their impressionable little minds and hearts were gripped with terror. Looking into the eyes of their worried children, the pastors recognized this deception and decided to do something about it. They stood up and took action by starting a Christian school at their church, just as we have done today at Awaken Academy, and just as you can do at your church. Their Christian school, birthed as a mission of freeing their own children from public school indoctrination, has now been impacting their city for over 25 years.

Now, you and I know that the God who created the heavens and the earth also created the resources to sustain them. In fact, as the creation scientists at Fourth Day Alliance have shown, we could fit the entirety of the earth's living population in one single state: All 7 billion of the world's men, women, children, and babies could fit in their own 1,000 square foot homes across the 267,339 square-foot-state of Texas, leaving the rest of the country—and the planet—completely void. Did you catch that? The entire living population of the world can be housed in one single state. The world is not overpopulated. We are not running out of resources. Some cities are overpopulated; however, the world itself is not overpopulated. But this is one of the fear-driven models of teaching in the public system, and it's even more pressing and overtly influential today than it was 30 years ago.

Fear has been the controlling force in school systems for generations, of course, and, more recently, it's also been the driving force for parents to keep their kids in schools that they know are broken and harmful. Fear is a terrible master. Most of the parents who come to us wanting help with breaking their children free of the public school's indoctrination centers are gripped by one singular emotion: fear. They don't feel capable, qualified, equipped. They fear that they won't have the resources, the intelligence, the patience, the organization, the know-how. They have been trained in the expert culture, conditioned to believe that they are, at the core, simply not good enough. This is a root of fear, insecurity.

It's important that we understand fear in both its physiological and spiritual implications. Fear is a manipulative emotion that keeps people shackled, living under what God has called them to live over. And this is where we now find ourselves, in the age of anxiety. I recognizer it well, as I spent the first two decades of my life struggling with anxiety, depression, and PTSD. I was still afraid of the dark when I was a freshman in college. Fear was an intrinsic part of my worldview from childhood to young adulthood. When I was a little girl, I was convinced that someone was hiding under my bed with a long sword just waiting until I fell asleep to thrust the sword up through the mattress. I would practice my track and field long-jump skills by leaping onto the bed from two feet away so that the imaginary intruder couldn't grab me by the ankles. Once I made it safely to the surface, I would cover my head with a blanket—because apparently the blanket made me impervious to sword-induced injury. But one night as I lay there trying to fall asleep, I suddenly had the realization that for a sword to pierce through both my mattress and my box springs and still do damage to my body, it would have to be so long that it wouldn't actually be able to fit under the bed! Aha! It was an epiphanic moment in my prepubescent brain, and armed with a tiny grain of logical evidence, I was able to talk myself out of that irrational fear and start climbing up onto the bed like a normal human being.

If you've ever dealt with fear, you know that it causes a variety of human responses, many of them irrational. A mindset of fear can cause people to lash out unreasonably. It can cause people to withdraw completely from human contact. It can cause people to become hypervigilant or suspicious of everyone or just plain mean-spirited. Many of the fear-based arguments blazing across social media today quickly disintegrate into the childhood version of name calling with ad hominem fallacies that attempt to defame the person. These conversations are often devoid of logic but fueled by fear.

Since fear and anxiety are some of the key emotional responses tumbling out of the youngest generations today, let's take a moment to unpack their causes, effects, and impact on the body and brain. From a physiological perspective, fear has a number of deleterious effects on both our biology and our neurology. Fear hijacks our emotional response system, which is what causes people to become irrational. It damages the hippocampus, it impairs long-term memory formation, and it impacts our ability to regulate emotion in general. A study by the Pacific Lutheran University School of Nursing showed that chronic fear can cause immune system and hormone system disruption, nervous system changes, sleep changes, eating disorders, headaches, chronic pain, and difficulty breathing.

Fear can also be extraordinarily debilitating from an emotional perspective as well. Dr. Mary Moller, director of Psychiatric Services at Northwest Center for Integrated Health, says that emotional impairments from fear can include learned helplessness, phobic anxiety, mood swings, obsessive-compulsive thoughts, and an inability to experience feelings of love. That last offshoot, an inability to experience love, is of signifiant concern in a generation where paralyzing idealism and the fear of commitment often keep young people from marrying until later and later. According to the US Census Report on marriage medians from 1890 to present, the average age of marriage for women has gone from 20 in the 1950s, 60s, and 70s to age 25 in 2000, age 27 in 2010, and age 29 in 2021. While there are many reasons for the delay, fear of commitment is a known causative factor. The delay affects birthrate, as fertility decreases with age, and it affects what I call "bachelor habit formation," which may make longterm relationships more difficult to sustain. Young adults need to be trained in a family, not by living with a group of other bachelors as they await the culturally delayed onset of marriage. Biblically, a child goes from the covering of his or her parents to the covering of the spouse. There is no in between stage.

In the social sciences, there's a term called the mean and scary worldview. It's a phenomenon that happens in the brain of someone who has a high viewing rate of screen time, with "high" being defined as over two hours of screen time per day. This viewing habit causes people to see the world as a more dangerous place than it really is, which means they become more fearful, more suspicious, and less trusting of others in general. When we hyperinflate the danger of something in our mind, we don't respond logically. Jumping across the room to avoid a sword-bearing, under-the-bed-dwelling boogeyman is a case in point.

Fear actually drives our response to the world by creating a view of reality. A study at the University of Minnesota found that fear can interrupt the neural process that helps us regulate emotions and read nonverbal cues. So instead of having a normal emotion or reading someone's nonverbal response correctly, our brains respond through the lens of fear, which means we are more likely to be impulsive and hyperreactive to situations. Fear also affects our digestion and other autonomic bodily responses. The body devotes all of its energy to fighting off that perceived threat —real or imagined. And chronic fear, like that which often drives panicked parents in their search for educational options, even impact our memories of experiences. Our brain is dependent on certain chemical states to retrieve certain memories, and fear can impact both our recall of and our storage of memories. The chemical changes caused by these chemical changes can actually distort our memory and our perception of reality! Fear impacts our behavioral, autonomic, endocrine, cognitive, and even our interpersonal responses. As author Gary Chapman once said about emotions like fear, they are designed to be visitors, not permanent residents, in the human heart.

What we feed on grows. If 90% of the conversations in our head focus on fear, and if we fail to balance that with conversations founded in rationalism, that's a breeding ground for a fearful worldview. And this worldview affects more than just us as individuals. Like a virus, these beliefs and behaviors can be transmitted from one individual to another. If we don't begin to assess and address some of these problematic paradigms in our own minds, we will persist in passing these mindsets on to our children, our families, our friends, those within our realms of influence. Fear can drive us to be hypervigilant, constantly worried, or obsessed. As Harvard Professor Steve Pinker says, this exposure to fear can lead to us becoming "miscalibrated."

A relentless consumption of negativity makes us fatalistic, gloomy, desensitized, anxious, and even hostile. Why? Because it creates a mindset. And let's remember how mindsets form: When a working model or paradigm goes unnoticed and unquestioned in our lives, it creates a pervasive worldview, a lens, a mindset of fear, what Besser van der Kolk described as a "misinterpretation of innocuous stimuli as potential threats." In other words, it creates a worldview of fear and defensiveness where we would be better served by healthier responses like trust and hope and openness. What a great reminder to discipline ourselves not to dwell on the negative, but to think, as Philippians 4 reminds us, on what is true, honest, just, pure, lovely, virtuous, praiseworthy, of good report. The lack of fully present, mature adult role models has dramatically limited the next generation's ability to stay calm and respond well. Their irrational responses have been culturally conditioned by the ongoing presence of their emotionally immature peers. We have actually become a nation of overreactors who literally thrive on conflict, who thrive on being stressed out.

If we remind ourselves what that fear-induced stress does to our brain and body, we can see the danger—and the preventative ability we have to protect ourselves from that danger. Other than a temporary state that protects us in a moment of potential harm, fear should not be residing in our hearts, reigning in our homes, or ruling our country. Fear is a terrible master. So what can we do to start walking in a new normal, a faith normal? It starts with parents leading the way, recognizing our own habitual patterns and then teaching the next generation the art of freedom. It starts with parents stepping up like our Floridian friends did, becoming agents of change, and rescuing their children from the fear-based education systems that are training up a generation of fear-driven protégées. Because of its refusal to acknowledge biblical truth, the secular humanist education system can't accurately assess or address the spirit of fear. The best the world can offer is a non-Christian, clinical approach that assigns problems without cures and offers only Band-aid approaches. But I've got good news: There are many, many scientifically and scripturally proven ways we can deal with these issues effectively. What that means is that we must fit our lives and our expectations into the word of God and not the other way around. His word is a lens through which we view both our definitions and our solutions.

We all see through a glass dimly. We have to know the word of God and define our terms through the lens of truth, or we will absolutely be led astray. In terms of emotional health, that means we begin by defining, naming, identifying what's really happening in the space between our ears. Clarifying the emotion you're experiencing can help you (and your children) learn the skills of naming and emotion regulation. Maybe you've heard the saying from Abraham Maslow, "If the only tool you have is a hammer, you tend to see every problem as a nail." Naming is a tool in your tool belt. It switches the power dynamic. Perhaps that's why God gave Adam the important role of naming the animals he was given dominion over.

People who haven't learned to differentiate between what emotions they're feeling often have a general sense of being overwhelmed or helpless. And those feelings can lead us astray. If we are feeling fearful about stepping into the leadership role of our children's education, that emotion can drive our vision of the potential experience and keep us from taking action. Emotions are certainly not negative in themselves. Emotions are designed by God to protect us or to bring us closer in relationship to him and to others. However, emotions are our servants, not our masters. "Why so downcast, oh my soul?" King David said to himself, to his emotions. The problem: he was downcast. The solution? He said, "Put your hope in God."

When my husband and I had been married about 10 years, I had an experience with fear that illustrated its power in shaping belief and behavior. It was late at night, the kids were asleep, and I was doing laundry, when suddenly, I heard our garage door open. I got up and looked in the garage to make sure it wasn't imagining things, and sure enough, the door was standing wide open in the middle of the night. My brain immediately spiraled to a probable rash of serial killers in the neighborhood. I hit the switch to close the door, locked the door leading from the garage to the house, and asked my husband what would make the garage open on its own. "It's probably connecting to a neighbor's circuit or something," he said casually.

I was not happy with his response or his calmness, but I went back to folding my laundry. It happened again. And again.

By the fourth time, I was ready to attack the perceived intruder. My heart was racing, and I told my husband I was calling 911. I was very worked up, both due to the overwhelming sense of fear and my husband's British stiff-upper-lip response to what I had firmly and completely convinced myself was a life-or-death situation. "There's no one outside," he said again in his calm European manner. "I looked." Unconvinced and absolutely livid, I stomped upstairs and angrily flipped open the dryer door, only to discover the culprit. The remote control to the garage door was flipping around wildly in the dryer, opening the door at random.

Fear keeps us from responding rationally. Just as it can create wild scenarios of impossibility in our minds, it can also keep us stuck in unhealthy cycles. Fear can push paralyzed parents down into a rat-race cycle, rushing through the morning routine, hustling everyone into the car, slamming back some nonnutritive breakfast substitute, and dropping their kids off at the front door of a local public school that they know is pulling them further away from truth, further away from family relationships, and further away from God. Fear keeps families from fully stepping out into what they often sense God is calling them to do. It holds us back, pins us down.

Besser van Der Kolk is a Dutch psychiatrist who worked extensively with Vietnam vets in the early days of PTSD (his book *The Body Keeps Score* is one of the most insightful psychology books I've ever read). In his research, van Der Kolk was surprised to see that the main issue war veterans struggled with wasn't the presence of memories. It was actually their inability to get along with other people; they couldn't engage well with others, they blew up and overreacted at small things, they felt no emotions toward those they knew they loved. They didn't feel alive in the present. They were disconnected from emotion. To help them heal and reconnect to humanity, van Der Kolk would coach them to physically recall moments of joy in their past, playing a sport they loved, or an experience with a loved one. And then he said this: "When those feelings of joy have stopped, it means something is frozen within you; it's time to deal with it and unplug the river of life."

What are the implications for a generation trapped in fear? Personal and professional paralysis, certainly. Hopelessness. Stagnation. And excessive fear can lead to an extreme desire for control, circumstantial manipulation. I'm sure if we looked back in the history of Jezebel's life, we would see some origin stories that made her want to threaten prophets and murder anyone who got in her way, even over the sale of a vineyard (overreact much?). She was bitter and vengeful toward anyone who opposed her plans, and the Bible says in 1 Kings 21:25 that she stirred up wickedness in her husband Ahab, inciting him to do evil. Control and fear can lead to some significantly irrational responses.

This ongoing exposure to fearful situations creates an anxious worldview. Just as an unstable relationship with a parent creates an abnormal attachment between the parent and the child, so too, this lack of security in the emotional realm creates a lack of healthy responses and reactions to life's circumstances. And it can keep us bound and fearful about stepping out make a change for our family. If you see the downfall of our nation's government school system, but you feel unable to make a step forward, that may be a sign that fear is holding you back. This measure of personal control, this intentionality to balance and regulate ourselves and our emotions, is a vital component of growth: Self-regulation is a key to mental health. It's not the existence of trauma but the response to it that makes all the difference.

The level of bullying in the public school system is a tremendous inducer of fear in the hearts of young students. Students tell us stories of being stalked in the hallways, in the classrooms, in the bathrooms. There is no safe place to escape from the schoolyard bully. Thus, the roots of trauma are planted early and run deep by high school. When there is trauma in the early years, as neuroscientist Dr. Schore has shown, the brain organizes its development around that experience. "Overwhelmingly stressful experiences may have their greatest impact on the growth of the mind at the times when specific areas of the brain are in rapid periods of development and reorganization," he notes. "For this reason, the early years of life may be a time of enhanced opportunity as well as of vulnerability." In other words, our children are more vulnerable to the long-term neural impacts of stress when they are young. For parents who have been conditioned to believe that their little children are called to be salt and light in the wolves' den of the public school classroom, it's important to note these age-specific vulnerabilities. Because of these early traumatic experiences, students can be left with lasting effects on the deep brain structures that help us process our responses to stress and encode memories.

These influences color every aspect of identity, belief, and behavior in the mind of a young person. The mind, as Dr. Dan Siegel notes, is literally formed through "the interaction between neurophysiological processes and interpersonal relationships." Though these alterations certainly continue throughout our lifespans, neuroscience shows that a foundation is laid in early life in this regard: Our worldview is formed by 13. Parents, when we train up a child from youth within the context of a certain mindset, a belief system, that belief system will persist. If a student is trained up in mistrust or general fearfulness, those patterns have to be unraveled, unlearned, through the process of connecting in healthy relationships. It is this continual shaping, this pliability, that creates new growth, new hope, new possibilities. Conversely, if a student is trained up in Marxism, CRT, evolution, racism, or hopelessness, those patterns persist. When students are forced to remain in environments that thrive on fear and control, they learn unhealthy defense mechanisms that will carry into adult life.

When we look at the construct of fear under the

microscope, it's sobering to see its potential power for sweeping cultural influence. As believers, though, we know there is only room in the human heart for one focus of our fear, one worthy object of that emotion. There is only one entity in the universe deserving of our fear, and that is the creator of the universe. We don't talk about the healthy function of fear much today, but Jesus actually said in Matthew 10:28, "Don't fear the one who can harm the body; fear the one who can throw both body and soul into hell." That's a mindset shift, mom and dad. There is only room in the human heart for one fear, the fear of God. We have to pass along these truths, these weapons of warfare to the next generation. Our youngest citizens don't yet have the needed access to the weaponry that is so mighty for the pulling down of strongholds because they have been taught in classrooms where "character education" has replaced the wisdom of the word.

The *Harvard Business Review* recently published findings from a study of the two youngest working generations, Millennials and GenZs, and said they are the most anxious generations of all time (which is not new; a host of other researchers have already been saying this for years). But what is new is the evidence of the fruit: the study showed that 50% percent of Mills and 75% of GenZs said they had left a job for mental health reasons, and 65% had experienced "overwhelming anxiety" in the previous year.

The Bible says in 1 Peter 5:8 that the enemy prowls about like a roaring lion seeking whom he might devour. That's not just a catchy tagline; that's reality. We face an enemy. And right now, that enemy has unleashed his full-fledged power on the two youngest generations. We've seen the tragic stats on anxiety, depression, abortion, STDs, suicide ideation, and atheism. We've seen the vacant expressions of the youngest members of our culture: stuck, jaded, cynical, disinterested, passive, spectators who don't care about their parents, their siblings, or the loving God who created them in his image.

Fear has been perpetuated and politicized in the public school system, from the school board Jezebels to the false prophets with their proverbial red pens and their cancel culture coercion. Fear has been the puppeteer of parent and student alike. When Candace Owens spoke at our church recently, she outlined this same movement of fear throughout history in the public sector, where fear has been manipulated to force a mental or physical dependence on the government. As parents, we have the opportunity to set the record straight on fear. We have the opportunity to teach our children freedom from worldly anxieties. We have the opportunity to provide a biblical education that teaches the next generation to steward the earth without worshiping the creation. We have the opportunity to reset the focus from "what if" and "why me" to "He can" and "He will."

In a generation sporting the highest recorded rates of anxiety on record in the history of our nation, imagine being able to share those revelations and those myth-busters with your children before they become embedded in their behavior as habits of the heart! Imagine what it would be like to reset our kids' mindsets from fear to peace even as toddlers. There is so much more to life than dedicating 7 hours of energy to a screen or a bowing to systems that have hijacked human emotion and held the next generation hostage to fear. We were made for more, and our kids were made for more. The possibilities of renewed hope and purpose and vision are endless when children have a lifetime of faith-filled responses, a fountain of hope, from which they can draw living water.

As we've been launching this education revolution across San Diego County, I've been talking with an overwhelming number of parents who have realized that they have allowed some other lesser god to be wrongly placed in the driver's seat of their affections. They are awakening to the fact they had given their hearts over to the wrong focus. It's an easy trap to fall into, this incremental refocusing of our time and attention that gradually veers off course over a span of time. But the reality is that, just like our earlier analogy of fear, the human heart can sustain worship of only one entity at a time. Consider the dichotomy of serving: We will serve either God or money as our master, Matthew 6:24 says. We will hate the one and love the other. The same is true for fear. We will fear either God or man, one or the other. King David prayed in Psalm 86, "Teach me your way O Lord, that I may walk in your truth; unite my heart to fear your name." Unite, *yahad,* means to unify, to concentrate our affections. Our hearts must be united, not fragmented. They must be focused completely on loving, serving, and fearing God. And this service, this fruit, is to be productive; as Philippians 2 says, we must be mindful to work out our salvation with fear and trembling. The offshoots of a unified heart should be great productivity for the kingdom of God.

This is a litmus test for our homes and our children. The larger culture outside our windows swells with celebrity worship, with fragmentation of identity, of idolatry. We have the unique ability as involved parents to help steward our children's hearts so they will not be vulnerable to these permeations. In fact, one of the cultural norms I've noticed in working with both public schooled and homeschooled students over the last 20 years is that by and large, my homeschool students have a far greater sense of identity by the time they reach their teens than their traditionally-schooled counterparts do. In public schools across the nation, identity is one of the key foundations being attacked in the lives of students right now. We have to help our children develop a stable sense of self, an understanding of who they are and the intrinsic value they carry as a son or daughter of God. This includes their resolution to follow faith over fear.
It's time to gear up for battle.

Dads, this is a war cry especially for you. In a study on faith practices in the family, Promise Keepers found that if a child is the first in a household to become a Christian, there is a 3.5%

likelihood that the rest of the family will follow. When the mom is first, that likelihood increases to 17%. But when the father is the first person in the family to become a Christian, there is a 93% likelihood that the rest of the household will follow. Dads determine destiny. Pastors, this is a great lesson for church growth too. We can go after the kids in the school system, bussing them into church sans family on a Sunday morning, but if we can pluck up that anchor of the family, the father, from his easy chair and get him planted in the house of God, our effectiveness, our impact in growing the kingdom, will be exponentially multiplied.

Of course, this is not a politically correct call and response. The biblical worldview, more often than not, stands in direct contrast to the cultural worldview. Zephaniah 2:3 says, "Seek the Lord, you humble of the land, who do his just commandments, seek righteousness, seek humility." The three main constructs of this verse are rather unpopular ideologies in the common culture. Obedience is taught in the limited conversations of military life and childrearing, but even less common than these two concepts is the idea of seeking humility. The Hebrew word here, *anava*, means meekness, modesty. That's certainly not a concept we hear promoted in the secular system. In fact, the self- esteem movement taught in the public school system is not at all modeled in the balance of humility. Instead, it places full confidence in the flesh, something the Bible clearly warns us not do. Unsurprisingly, it has not ended well for the self-esteem movement. Social science research shows that the self-esteem movement has actually bred little more than narcissism and promiscuity.

Proverbs 27:21 says that a man is actually tested by the praise he receives. Does praise puff us up or does it foster a spirit of gratitude for all that God has done? I love what Dr. Henry Morris says about meekness: "A meek spirit enables a a Christian to maintain composure in the face of opposition, to accept adversity without complaint, promotion without arrogance, demotion without resentment." The more we know the Bible, the more we can recognize the counterfeited rules, norms, and mindsets of the culture.

I vividly recall the moment I was delivered from a mindset of fear. I was 18 years old, a freshman in college, living 1217 miles from my hometown, and still sleeping with a light on. I'll say that last phrase again in case you missed it: I was 18 years old and still sleeping with a nightlight. But this particular night, I went to turn on my nightlight, and it popped audibly and blacked out. That was odd. Okay, I thought. I'll just use the hallway light instead. So, I got up to turn that one on, and POP! It went out too. Oddly enough, that was a holy moment. I knew God was speaking to me, sharpening me, healing me, and I resolved in my heart in that very moment that I was going cold turkey on my fear of the dark. And I did. Today, I am not afraid of the dark, or drains, or attics, or mannequins, and I can kill spiders all by myself if they dare to cross the threshold into my house.

Parents, we must watch for the warning signs of fear in our lives and in our children's lives: If you have symptoms of excessive control, feeling detached from others, being angry for no reason, if your relationships keep failing apart, if you blow up about small things, or feel emotionally distant from those you love, if you have low levels of compassion toward self or others; these, van Der Kolk says, these may be symptoms. You've got to shift into the mode of intentionality to break free of those destructive mindsets.

Today, we find ourselves in an all-hands-on-deck moment in our nation. National crises are opportunities for the church to rise up, not to shrink back. Hebrews 3:13 says that we are to encourage one another daily so that we won't be hardened by sin's deceitfulness. If our social media posts are way more fear-inducing than encouraging, we must question the root, the mindset. As leaders, mentors, parents, we have to be intentional about the way we choose our words, especially in a time of national upheaval. Our words can further the emotion dysregulation around us, or they can help bring peace.

Philippians 4:6 tells us not be anxious about anything but "in every situation, with prayer and petition, with thanksgiving, to present our requests to God. And the peace of God, which transcends all understanding, will guard your hearts and your minds in Christ Jesus." This is a decision, an act of the will. We will not be anxious, because we know that anxiety does not serve our brain, body, or behavior well. It doesn't change anything. It only hurts; it never heals. If there was ever a time we needed to have peace set as a guard over our hearts and our minds, this is that time. Isaiah 28:3 says that God keeps in perfect peace the one whose mind is stayed on him because he trusts in God. We have to determine that we will place our eyes and our minds on the one who is able to do immeasurably more than all we can ask or imagine. One really important marker between fear and hope is that fear leaves you feeling helpless, and hope leaves you feeling empowered.

"May the God of hope fill you with all joy and peace as you trust in him," Romans 15:13 says, "so that you may overflow with hope by the power of the Holy Spirit." A national crisis is a great time to check our personal fruit. Are you overflowing with joy, peace, trust, and hope? If not, consider what type of messages you are allowing to crowd your neural space. It might be time to practice a little emotional distancing from the information sources that are causing panic. Instead, fill up your tank on the word of God. Because if there's one thing we know about fear, it's contagious. But so is faith.

When we place our eyes on the storm instead of the one who calms the storm, we will find ourselves drowning in the crashing cultural waves of fear and terror. But when we place our eyes on the author of our faith, and we live proactive but not panicked lives, we will find rest, even as Jesus did, right here in the midst of the storm. Let's communicate hope to those in our realm of influence by modeling appropriate emotion regulation and serving as beacons of hope in a unique season of history. Let's be people of faith, not fear. Parents, it's time to rescue a fearful generation from the grips of a government school system that is profiting from the downfall of our youngest citizens. It's time to turn the age anxiety into an era of peace, purpose, and promise.

CHAPTER SEVEN

Toxic Trait #3: Overexposed and Underdeveloped

As a professor in California for many years, I saw in my classrooms daily the devastating effects of the aggressive, liberal, sex education propaganda in the public sector. Even though I taught mainly in private universities, the vast majority of all college students—public and private—are products of California's K to 12 public school environment.

As a result, caring professors must be prepared to pick up the shards of students' shattered lives after they have been misinformed, misguided, and maltreated by a lifetime of "education" in the public system. Remember, a child's worldview is largely formed by 13. This is why evangelizing to anyone under 18 is illegal in China. It's also why Hitler targeted 10-18 year olds for his socio-cultural indoctrination programs.

By the time they enter college, students have usually decided what they believe and are firmly rooted in the behaviors that underscore those beliefs. Sadly, for the majority, this means sexual activity before marriage and the resulting emotional distress that comes from living outside the boundaries of healthy behavior. Looking from the outside, I realize that it's difficult to imagine just how embedded the perversion truly is in the foundations of the school system. By way of example, a parent told me recently that her public school district has canceled literature class in 9th and 10th grade. Why? To replace it with a new and better class called "Identity and Relationships." After all, who needs the time-tested anchor of classical literature's morality and character training, when we can instead immerse students in the perversion of what government schools term "identity exploration" and relational diversity?

According to the San Diego Unified website, the Identity and Relationships course being taught across the county "allows students to explore their own identity as well as the different identities of those around them in their diverse communities." (Oh, and the course conveniently counts toward the "ethnic studies graduation requirement," in case you were wondering).

Parents, read between the lines here. We've all seen how schools are dumbing down students with common core, which we will talk more about in a later chapter. But one of the most aggressive of the ten toxic traits is the attack on purity. America's students are overexposed and underdeveloped.

And it's not just the teachers, of course, it's also the peers. A parent told me recently that her son was being mocked in public school constantly because he wouldn't "experiment" with same-sex relationships. His pushy peers call him "double-straight," which is apparently a severe cutdown in the mind of a secular humanist. Not only is he standing firm as a straight man, he won't cross over to their pressures of perverse practices under the weight of a bully's oppression.

The stats tell the story: the next generation is hurting, anxious, lonely, and desperate for the good news that they have value, that they are worth more than the objectification of their bodies. However, instead of offering hope, the current system preys on generational insecurities, dragging behavioral expectations to the lowest level.

This debauchery is not limited to the state of California. I hear it from parents all over the nation. In fact, a parent from Mormon-centric Utah told me recently that she was leaving her 15-year post as a kindergarten teacher because she was chastised for not accepting and promoting transgenderism—in five year olds.

In San Diego, parents can easily look up what's being taught in the public school classroom: the Sexual Health Education Program (SHEP), details are available at 3rs.org and at sandiegounified.org/SHEP. Find the teachings of your district, and trace the beliefs to public behavior, which is sadly very easy to spot. If you are a parent who has placed your precious children in the public school's care, whether traditional or charter classrooms, note especially the specific lesson plans for each grade: The elementary curriculum introduces 10 – 12 year olds to the idea of bathing together as a measure for avoiding sexually transmitted diseases, and the 9th grade study of biology, which should begin with zygotic life and the analysis and classification of bacterial kingdoms, is instead riddled with aggressive lobbyist views on sexual identity. The very first lesson in the public school's 9th grade biology book preaches gender fluidity. Ironically, it's difficult to find a hint of actual science in the public school's science textbook.

The teachers' guide for SHEP notes on page 8 that "rather than attempting to be 'values-free,' (the curriculum) conscientiously embraces a set of values that are *widely accepted* in our society (italics mine)." However, it remains to be seen exactly whose values are represented therein. As the California Family Council (2018) notes, if a school were truly representative of the public, as the name implies, the public school board and the curricula would represent a "spirit of inclusivity, (inviting) people of faith and cultures different from their own to participate in selecting an acceptable curriculum that respects all beliefs and is scientifically accurate." But this has not been the case. Not even close.

Parents persist in crashing school board meetings and doing their best to speak up, but their speaking times consistently are pushed out to the last minute of the meeting, cut short, ignored, overlooked, even stopped mid-sentence by the school board. Time and again, year after year, the same issues are pushed through, and parents try in vain to voice their opinions. But the system continues to repeat its folly, to bully parents, to silence them.

And then the cycle repeats again the following year. It's almost like a domestic abuse victim who so desperately wants to believe the best of her boyfriend that she keeps getting back in the ring. The boyfriend doesn't change. The school board doesn't change. It is linked to a higher agenda, its own subversive higher purpose, one that is being unpacked chapter by chapter, line by line, in this book.

As Mary Rice Hasson writes in the *The Family in America* (2014), there has been a radical increase of sexual perversion on American college campuses. As Hasson notes, the main goal of these institutions is to reframe sexuality outside the boundaries of Christian thought, normalizing perversion and "abhor(ing) the constraints of traditional sexual morality," driving home what Hasson considers to be the most damaging of phrases: "no judgments allowed." Hasson explains that many public institutions now teach that the hookup culture is a "healthy" outlet that helps students moderate stress without commitment. Colleges promise that the public school system will be certain "not to pass judgment" on students' perverse decisions.

Parents, there will be a judgment, a final judgment, for both our behavior and our children' behavior. And our job now is to teach our children, in the words of the Great Commission, to obey everything that Jesus taught. We can't justify sending our children off to institutions where they are taught that the hookup culture is a beneficial exchange that allows them to "focus on studies" and have their life of perversion without the "drag" of a relationship.

The agenda is pervasive, and parents are clearly not the voices the university system or the local school board wants to hear or obey. In fact, the board's unwillingness to listen to the arguments of the parents is a symptom of a bigger challenge, one that is currently wreaking havoc on the next generation. This hypersexual culture promoted and promulgated in the American classroom has several foundational components that are currently cultivating mayhem in the minds and hearts of our youngest citizens. Instead of hearing the concerns of parents, school boards shoo parents away, kick them out of Zoom classrooms, and bolt the proverbial door behind them. My top ten concerns with the moral miseducation of this agenda are as follows:

First, the current sex ed curriculum promotes promiscuity, not purity. The prevailing belief in most modern sex ed programs is that abstinence is not only unlikely, but that teens and young adults are virtually incapable of sexual purity. In other words, they are no better than animals driven by instinctive behavior. With this viewpoint, we are setting them up for mental failure before they even begin the relational race. As any good educator knows, low expectations lead to underperformance. If we tell kids they are "not capable" of sexual purity as children, how can they be we expect them to be faithful to their long-term relationships in adulthood?

Second, though sex education curricula was purported to have a positive impact on the rate of sexually transmitted diseases, the opposite has been true. Since 1964, when the Values Clarification Movement first hijacked the minds and morals of educators and planted its permissive seeds in the fertile soil of America's classroom, STD rates have gone up, not down.

VCM prohibited any education from a "sectarian" viewpoint, promoting instead the religion of secular humanism and hedonism. What happened as a result? Let's look at the data: According to the Center for Disease Control, 50% of all new

STDs in our country today are contracted by the 15 to 25-year-old population. Every day in the United States, 8,000 teens and young adults are diagnosed with an STD—that's 3 million new cases per year! Liberal sex ed programs, which abound all over the country, have not reduced the STD rates in the students they serve. Instead, the rates continue to climb.

Third, the current sex ed agenda is driven by a liberal powerhouse that promotes promiscuity, giving children as young as elementary school sexual ideas that they were most likely not even thinking of before they had these classes. This agenda promotes promiscuity, pornography, and hypersexual lifestyles as normal choices open to all people, ideas that are at odds with the Christian worldview: Believers are expected to treat one another as brothers and sisters, in all purity (1 Timothy 5), to flee sexual immorality (1 Corinthians 6:18), and even to avoid *looking* at someone we aren't married to in a lustful way (Matthew 5:28). Clearly, the current sexual education agenda has fallen far outside of these boundaries.

Fourth, the current sex ed culture omits the truth about the mental and physical damage that stems from multiple sexual encounters. First, humans do not contract an STD from a mutually monogamous lifelong relationship. We contract an STD from using the body in a way it was not designed to be used, with multiple sexual partners. Furthermore, the curriculum overlooks the damage done to oxytocin, the bonding hormone, as teens move from one partner to another ad infinitum.

As board-certified obstetricians Drs. Bush and McIlhaney have noted in their book *Hooked: The Brain Science on How Casual Sex Affects Human Development* (2019), overuse of this bonding hormone leads to an inability to bond over time. If we are not more proactive in protecting our children, the ongoing cultural atrophy of this neuropeptide may have tremendously negative impacts on future marriages and future families.

Fifth, public schools should, by their very name, represent

the public view. According to a 2018 study by Christianity Today, 80% of Americans believe in God, and though their beliefs differ denominationally, most agree that God has provided us with rules and guidelines for sexual behavior for our protection. Instead, in America, Christians are marginalized for their belief system, and Christian schools are denied financial support from our collective tax dollars—discriminated against for their beliefs—even though the students within those schools are just as much citizens of our state as those students attending public schools.

Sixth, the sex ed culture, as with the public school culture in general, promotes an excessively peer-driven environment where the voice of reason is decidedly and deliberately absent. The lack of parental governance in these systems, where students spend 8 hours a day with peers and then another 2 to 3 hours in sports or alone with homework, creates a peer-driven environment that limits maturation.

Kids do not grow up to be responsible, respecting, mature citizens in the tutelage of peers. They need adult intervention in order to grow and develop in a healthy, responsible manner. A voice of reason must preside over the hallways, the classrooms, and the playgrounds of the public school, especially in the arena of sexual behavior.

Seventh, the casual sex culture has had dramatic lifestyle effects on the youngest generations, resulting in skyrocketing rates of cohabitation amongst Millennials and GenZs: 51% of Mills are currently cohabiting, living together in a sexual relationship. Marriage, if pursued at all, is being delayed longer and longer, decreasing the range of fertility for childbearing. Cohabitation is linked to a higher rate of domestic abuse, drug use, and a lower likelihood of long-term relational success.

Are these the stats we desire for the next generation? Early life practices, such as those learned in elementary school, carry through to adulthood. What we tolerate today, we will embrace tomorrow. Because we have tolerated excessive sexual impropriety at the elementary and secondary levels, it now runs to the extreme in local colleges and universities.

One of the largest universities in San Diego County has for many years unabashedly showcased annual "condom fashion show," shamelessly normalizing and promoting the culture of promiscuity to 18 to 22-year-old students. The sexual focus at this institution has not been cathartic in any sense of the imagination; in fact, *Business Insider* recently ranked this particular university as one of the top 25 most dangerous college campuses in the US.

And don't believe for a moment that the hypersexual culture on college campuses is any more appropriate simply because the kids are over 18. Experientially and statistically, we see that college students need ongoing adult intervention, coaching, guidance, and positive role models in order to succeed in life.

Eighth, the current sex ed culture is promoting an environment of hypocrisy. On one side of the fence, we rake public officials through the coals for promiscuous behavior three decades earlier (in their teen years), and, at the same time, promote these same behaviors in school and mass media!

The current curriculum is teaching the youngest age groups to draw from an arsenal of sexual fantasies provided by their educators. Like Hollywood, the public system has no anchor, no moral mooring on which to build an argument, which is why it is so incredibly ineffective at moral boundary setting. Parents must be part of this process. In fact, an ongoing study at Harvard University called FINE (Family Involved Network of Educators) has shown that the singular most important factor of a student's success from kindergarten to college is an involved parent! If the public education system truly desired to positively impact those soaring rates of STDs in our youngest populations, they would partner with parents, not cast them aside. This brings me to my final point.

Finally, parents have been disempowered in the realm of influence in government schools, which is a key reason for the growth of home education. Even before Covid graciously blew the cover off the public school's indoctrination agenda, homeschooling was already recognized as one of the fastest growing segments of American academia. Modern public schools have not listened to the needs, desires, and goals of parents. Instead, they have thrust Huxley's *Brave New World* upon us without our consent.

Parents need to be aware and involved, making wise educational decisions for the sake of the next generation. Let me put it this way: moms and dads, if teachers are not listening to you, and if the public sector is not representing the public it was commissioned to serve, don't just sit back and let your kids be indoctrinated on your watch. You are the gatekeeper of your child's heart. You have the legal right to choose a better system for your child. You can join the ranks of the now millions of children being educated at home across the US. Yes, it's a sacrifice. Find a way. We pay a price to live set apart.

Of course, the public school system is just one aspect of the social culture where reason and morality have pledged divorce from one another. But with over 50 million K to 12 students and another 14 million college students enrolled in government schools across America, it's a vital starting point for discussion. We are already sitting at a higher rate of enrollment than Hitler's Youth programs experienced, and the propensity for influence is tragically exponential.

As a result of the hypersexual culture, today's students are overexposed and underdeveloped. Our nation's youth are sick, hurting, angry, confused. We have higher rates of anxiety, depression, and suicide ideation than we have ever seen before in the history of our nation. As parents and educators, we can't look at the rates on self-injurious behavior and convince ourselves that kids are okay. They are not okay. The rampant STD rates are symptoms of a much deeper problem—one that can never be solved by a hypocrisy-laden, secular system that has absolved itself of any connection to moral absolutes. The launching point of wisdom is the fear of the Lord. Without a deference to a moral authority, our wisdom will be nothing more than a wilting, worldly shadow of the true original.

One of the most beautiful aspects of the parent-directed education movement, and something we are seeing coming alive across the county of San Diego today, is this Luke 1:17 model of the restoration: the hearts of parents and children are being healed, relational attachments are being restored. As new homeschooler Corie Di Matteo shared on our Communication Architect podcast interview, many parents are beginning to feel a relational shift and a thawing of their hearts (which they didn't even know were frozen).

God is turning hearts of stone into hearts of clay. As a result of these shifts, dads are getting more time with their kids now that the average 15 minutes a day we saw in previous years. A family revival is happening in our midst! And that's a vital addition because this is a generation that desperately needs fathering.

"When a man's folly brings his way to ruin," Proverbs 19 says, "his heart rages against the Lord." This is a vital verse for today. Did you know that the most common reason GenZs don't believe in God is because they don't understand God's judgment? They falter because they believe a good God would never allow such consequences as sin brings. However, Proverbs tells us that folly is what actually brings these consequences. The fool, Proverbs says, projects blame on to someone else (here, he rages against the Lord) instead of taking responsibility for his own folly and its repercussions.

The same patterns are evidenced in children who have not experienced godly discipline in the home. Parents, our children need to understand that their ideas have consequences. They can learn even from childhood to take responsibility for their actions. Teach them to ask forgiveness when they've done wrong and to give generously out of their own well of forgiveness to those who have wronged them. The small step in discipleship will help turn a generation away from narcissism, blame, and projection, and back to personal responsibility.

Parents can no longer afford to look the other way. It's time to speak up, to stand up, for the sake of our children. The mental, physical, relational, and spiritual health of the next generation is at stake. This gradual decline of values and truth and integrity have brought us to where we stand today: at a national crossroads. As Neil Postman always said, it's up to those of who see the older, clearer waters to speak up.

In San Diego County, parents have seen with their own eyes the horrific agenda being played out in the schools, a grotesque reenactment of Aldous Huxley's *Brave New World*. And these parents have said, "Not on our watch!" They've decided they want no part in this degradation of the minds, hearts, and souls of the next generation. They are pulling out of the public schools in droves. Parents have waved goodbye to the big yellow prison bus and rescued their children from eight hours of indoctrination and incarceration in the government system.

In my book *The Science of Social Influence*, I wrote about a parent who was so disconnected from her child's needs that she was literally playing a game on her phone while her son committed suicide in the next room. This is a dramatic example, of course, but it does parallel what has been happening all around us in the culture. Parents have been apathetic and oblivious to the tragic disappearance of attachment, the bruised souls of the next generation. The public school crisis didn't just take over American minds and souls overnight. It's been a gradual turning up of the heat, a gradual decline of values and truth and integrity until we reached the point where we are today: the most anxious, depressed, atheist generation in the history of our nation.

Thankfully, parents are now waking up to both the cause and to the call.

Hypersexuality is just one of the twelve toxic traits being spewed out of the sewers of government indoctrination centers. Stay with me as we unpack the next trait, generational segregation, along with its horrific offspring, peer orientation.

CHAPTER EIGHT

Toxic Trait #4: Generational Segregation

It is no secret that the family is in great duress in our culture today. It has been divided, confused, misnamed, misguided, and, often, robbed of its true purpose. Whether you are someone's child, someone's parent, or someone's grandparent, we all have a role in the family, and we have all been impacted by the experience of the family environment. In 1973, Uri Bronfenbrenner summarized the overarching concern of family disintegration in his book *Two Worlds of Childhood:* "A society which neglects its children, however well it may function in other respects, risks eventual disorganization and demise." When we neglect the family, we stunt the development of the culture.

Sociologist Anthony Giddens defines family as an entity whose purpose is to "contribute to society's basic needs and...perpetuate social order." Family was God's idea. He sets the solitary in families, and healthy homes model the beautiful hierarchy of Christ and the church, his bride. Since it was "not good" for Adam to be alone, God made a helper for Adam and told the very first couple in the history of the world to multiply and become a family. Healthy families make healthy cultures. The reverse is also true, and we see it exemplified even in the structural makeup of a city. When cities multiply apartment buildings, crime increases. Why? Crime increases not because of poverty but because of brokenness. Multi-unit housing draws hurting people who are "solitary," living apart from connection. Social science documents this phenomena. The family is the foundational community of society. If we can alter the course of the family, we can alter the course of the culture.

One of the many significant reasons that public schools have had unparalleled access into the hearts and minds of children is because the school system has spent decades creating mental and physical barriers that isolate students from their families. The sheer volume of time away from the family unit has been increasingly detrimental, creating a steady decline in connectivity and weakening the family structure as a whole. As Gatto notes, "Schools are already a major cause of weak families," as they draw family members apart into separate life tracks that often lead in opposite directions. Traditional school systems have also pulled away from the one-room schoolhouse model, which is now the brunt of jokes despite its rate of socio-academic success in comparison to today's segregated scholastic models. This overall lack of connectivity has created a generational gap, a distancing from the natural role model orientation that exists organically in the family hierarchy.

As I look out at the landscape of the American teenager, having spent two decades teaching the next generation, I see a pattern that links together these influences across the timeline, a transference of belief and behavior that begins in the family system. If the average kid has 15 minutes alone with dad each day, if 90% of Christian parents don't read the Bible together outside of church, and if traditional education pushes parents out, creating an expert culture where parents are replaced by peers, we see the makings of a perfect storm.

Many of us spend our lifetimes rebuilding what has been broken—both in others' lives and in our own. In fact, the statistics are sobering. A number of researchers (such as Felitti et al. 1998) have found that severely mistreated children have a greater risk of developing alcoholism, depression, and drug abuse, of attempting suicide, of smoking, of having multiple partners (upwards of 50 by some studies), acquiring a sexually transmitted disease, and becoming obese as adults. They also have a higher risk of heart disease, cancer, lung disease, skeletal fractures, hepatitis, stroke, diabetes, and liver disease (van der Kolk 2003, p. 168). Clearly, the systemic challenges of abuse can run deep—from mind to body to culture. And again, maltreatment is not simply a physiological trauma. We have an entire generation of students who feel abandoned, and this crisis is playing out in their interpersonal and interpersonal behavior. Parent education is a vital link between the hurting world of the present and the healing world of the future.

But the traditional education system undermines the role of the parent, constantly isolating and segregating family members from one another. Modern education, whether public or private, separates us all from the inborn needs of familial community, severing the ties between each age group and dislodging the connective experiences that unite generations. Now, sending your children to a private school is, in most cases, a better option than public school if you absolutely had to make that choice, but it's very important to look at the model and honestly assess the strengths and weaknesses of each particular school prior to making that decision. If we plan to send our kids out the door every day to be discipled by someone else, we must readily admit that we are outsourcing them. And if we want a good harvest, we had best make sure that the people doing the discipling share our values, our vision, and our educational and spiritual outcomes. There are a small handful of private schools in America that are rising above the norm, incorporating parents in the mix, and seeing some hopeful outcomes. Though some private schools are a better option than being yoked with the secular indoctrination centers of the government school system, there are also many testimonies of people becoming promiscuous, addicted, and even atheistic in private schools. So what's the differential between the systems?

Most Christian private schools have not fared much better in their Christian retention rate than public schools. Shockingly, as Ken Ham and Brit Beamer have demonstrated in their research, students are almost as likely to walk away from the faith upon graduation from a "Christian school" as they are from a public one. However, the commonality in private and public schools' high rate of failure here is not the academic content— don't miss this—it's the lack of parental involvement. From a biblical perspective, parents have been given the mantle of spiritual authority for their children's wellbeing, and when this mantle is outsourced over and over again, whether to teachers or coaches or even pastors, students grow up with a discipleship deficit. This is where we find ourselves today.

The parent-directed model of education endeavors to turn that stat around by keeping parents in the seat of spiritual and intellectual authority. The addition of a homeschool support network can also give them the ability to delegate some of the practical applications of that coursework to trusted adults in a likeminded Christian environment that partners with parents instead of attempting to replace them. In short, this means providing a Bible-based educational support system that centers on both spiritual and academic formation. Without parental involvement, the risk of both academic and spiritual failure is great. Let me say it this way: Parents who do not engage with their children in a discipleship modality and who do not take upon themselves the spiritual mantle of parenthood will, at least from a statistical standpoint, fail to reproduce strong followers of Jesus.

As we look around the campus of almost any church in America today, we see the missing generation, GenZ, as evidence of this tragic statistic. The most depressed, anxious, atheist generation in the history of our nation was "trained up" not only by aggressive Marxist indoctrination in the public school, but also by confused, dispassionate parents and teachers in the private sector who failed to equip students with a biblical worldview. In 20 years as an educator, one of the things I found to be most maddening was the deliberate and overt attempts by school administrators to keep parents out of the lives of students. Even if a parent was paying $130,000 for a child's college education, that parent did not have the "right" to know what was happening to the child. We will talk in a moment about where that led, but realistically, even the best teacher in the world can't replace a parent. A teacher has an opportunity to invest into the child for a year, maybe two at most. Is the teacher going to stay in the game the next 10 years, the next 15 years? Of course not. And yes, I know there are bad parents. I grew up with one. But that doesn't mean we have to sever the rights of good parents. It's a bit like sequestering the healthy instead of healing the sick.

The Bible calls leaders to account for how we manage our children and our households, and that fruit is actually measured in a child's willing obedience to parents. "Here is a trustworthy saying," 1 Timothy 3 says. "If anyone sets his heart on being an overseer, he desires a noble task...He must manage his own family well and see that his children obey him with proper respect." In fact, even the readiness for leadership in ministry is measured by our success in the home! As the Apostle Paul noted, "If anyone does not know how to manage his own family, how can he take care of God's church?" The family is our living resumé, a daily document that visibly demonstrates to the world how the humans we were given to steward turned out. The proof is in the pudding. Having spent thousands of hours in our presence, what is the fruit of our children's lives? Parents, we replicate who we are; thus, our children are a magnifying lens for both our strengths and our flaws.

Parents, you are the key to success in your child's life! The Harvard Family Research Project found that the positive impact parental involvement bears on academic success doesn't stop after potty-training. It doesn't stop after kindergarten. It doesn't even stop in adolescence. In fact, parent participation is equally relevant in post-secondary academic achievement! As former University of Illinois professor Evanthia N. Patrikakou has shown, parent involvement tends to decline as children reach the upper grades. Some reasons for this, she says, are the complex structure of school systems, fewer schools requesting help from parents, and curricula that can leave parents feeling intimidated. It's almost as if parents were being squeezed out. According to a 1992 report by the National Association of Secondary School Principals, the majority of parents express an interest in being involved in their children's education. "Family requests for involvement are constant," noted one researcher; however, many parents feel unable or uninvited when it comes to their children's education. Movements like the UN Rights of the Child, which seeks to overthrow parental rights in favor of child rights (i.e., a child has the right to decide what is best for herself without parental "intervention") make these messages even more confusing for parents. Many parents, out of a supportive but decidedly uneducated desire to help their children, hand over the reins to someone else.

In an extensive longitudinal study, Harvard University researchers followed a cohort of students from the eighth grade through high school, college, and into the workforce. The study found that parents' expectations and, essentially, their belief in the students' academic capabilities, were predictors of the students' success: "The further in school parents believed their adolescents would go, the clearer the adolescents' perception of such expectations, the higher their own academic expectations, the higher their academic achievement." What they believed, they achieved. What we think about, we bring about. What we

134

speak, we reap. That's not some new age rhetoric. The tongue has the power of life and death, and those who love it will eat its fruit. And the marker for the Harvard study did not diminish as students aged. "The long-lasting effects that parent involvement variables have on the academic achievement of adolescents and young adults," the researchers noted, "indicate that parent involvement during high school and beyond still remains an important source of guidance and support for the developing individual."

Psychologist and author Dr. David Walsh explains the need for parental guidance well into young adulthood. The brain, he says, develops in spurts until the age of 25. Until this quarter-of-a-century mark, the prefrontal cortex is still "under construction," and since this neural region regulates impulse control, aggression management, emotional control, and self-regulation, it is important that adolescents have a good grounding in parental oversight. Dr. Ruth Kraus, assistant professor of clinical psychology at the University of Chicago, agrees. "Adolescence is a time when everything is out of kilter, and nothing is stable in the body or mind." Parents, she adds, must step in as the "designated prefrontal cortex," offering common sense, guidance, and advice. Many of my post-25 students tell me they can clearly recall the moment when they started thinking differently, where their whole brain was engaged in the problem-solving process. Until that point, they really do need to have conversations with adults, especially parents, to help guide and direct their decision-making process.

Instead of incorporating family and school, though, the modern K to college educational environment attempts to decentralize the family unit, drawing the core of power out of the family and into an external system—a system that lacks the power to properly regulate these vital components of judgment and self-regulation. Thus, the unformed and inconsistent patterns in the adolescent's mind remain undeveloped. If we desire for young adults to progress socially, scholastically, and emotionally, we have to put a permanent end to the processes that attempt to sever relational ties between parents and children.

The friction on the topic of parental rights and control has been ramping up over the last three decades. This year, there was an attempt to pass a bill that would allow an 11-year-old child to circumvent his or her parents' desires and get a vaccine if the child believed it was the right choice. This example follows many others before it, from schools that allow a variety of adult decisions, from birth control to abortion, to be made by a child without parental consent. This is an age-old battle over control. If the left can't kill us off through abortion, it seems like their next best hope is to indoctrinate a generation of children and turn them against their parents. One such example that I wrote about in a previous book is a model of academia positioning itself against the structure of family accountability, the Family Educational Rights to Privacy Act (FERPA). The U.S. Department of Education defines FERPA as a federal law "designed to protect the privacy of student education records."

In effect since 1974, this archaic, misguided law applies to all schools receiving funds through the U.S. Department of Education. At its core, FERPA severs all parental access to records pertaining to the student's education, including grades and academic standing, attendance records, financial standing with the college, results of any disciplinary proceedings involving the student, hospitalization, treatment for any emergency or life-threatening medical or psychological conditions, missed classes, and disruptive or erratic behavior. Only through a written release from the student can a parent gain access to her child's file—even if that parent is completely funding the student's education and the student is living at home with the parent. Is the lunacy coming through loud and clear here? Neither the professor nor the administrator has the "right" under FERPA's regulations to speak to a parent about the student's records. In a number of recent cases, this has been problematic, even life-threatening.

Thomas Baker, associate dean of students at the University of Iowa, notes the increasingly dramatic number of college students engaged in self-destructive behaviors and the challenges FERPA regulations have presented in some of these cases. In light of an increase of tragic suicide attempts on college campuses, Baker has written about the challenges of parental disconnect, including administrative decisions not to notify parents of prior suicide attempts. Baker argues that violating a student's privacy rights may be a necessary step in protecting the student's well-being. In a court case, a college dean had learned of a student's suicide intentions. The dean then met with the student and required him to sign a "statement pledging not to hurt himself." The student committed suicide two days after signing the pledge (Baker, 2005).

Obviously, most parents would recognize the futility of asking a suicidal patient to sign a note promising he wouldn't hurt himself. This is a naïve oath at best. Yet, as schools are increasingly called upon to take the parental mantle upon themselves, such faulty decision making is likely to be more the norm than the exception. To this end, Baker says he desires to see parental notification as part of the overall strategy in suicide prevention and mental health. "Protection from harm includes the ability to influence the student's behavior, and…parental notice influences the behavior of a troubled student" by reinforcing positive feelings that exist between the student and his or her family members. Inherent in this system of disclosure is a belief in the value of accountability: "Sending a copy of the parental notice letter to the student encourages the student to refrain from self-destructive behavior in the future."

Having navigated these tragedies, can you guess what Baker's recommendations are? "A more open relationship with the student's family," he says, "will prevent further self-destructive behavior as well as address and heal any existing dysfunction within the family." In other words, we need to involve parents more, not less. Pulling power from parents and assigning it to any other entity runs contrary to the biblical worldview. Children do not belong to the state. We do not co-parent with the government. Children belong to the family. The state has absolutely no spiritual jurisdiction over the raising of children, including their education.

As they begin to imagine a more effective model of education for their children, parents often share their legitimate concerns with me about the education process. What if I work? What if I'm the breadwinner? What if I don't feel capable or qualified or even excited about being more involved in my children's education? Parents, all you need is conviction and community. These will drive your vision and help you feel less alone in the process. At the end of this book, I give some practical solutions for taking this next step. But for now, let me give you a couple of concepts to think about. First, being a parent educator takes less than three hours a day. And depending on the level of support, the student's age, and the existing drive and motivation, it can even be as little as 2 hours a day. When parents assess their schedule through the lens of possibility, most find that they can unearth 2 hours a day to spend with their child.

The amount of time spent with our children is most definitely a behavioral influencer. Social scientists have analyzed the research on family dinner down to the minute, and what did they find? Spending even just a few nights a week having dinner together in the context of conversation and a lack of distractions (like phones and television) bears a significant impact on students' performance, mood, health, grades, and even improvement of delinquent behavior.

Anne Fishel, executive director of the Family Dinner Project, has calculated that it takes five meals a week to solidify the benefits, whether that's breakfast, lunch, or dinner. But in her interview with Harvard Graduate School of Education (2020), she revealed some compelling data about why family's often don't eat together and what age group actually rates family dinners as more important that might be expected.

Fishel found that families across all socioeconomic backgrounds had the same excuses: they are too busy, it's too much work to cook for everyone, there's too much conflict at the table, and their teens won't want to be with the family. However, the data challenged these mindsets, especially the last one, with a full 80% of teenagers reporting that family dinner is something they like and that it's the most likely time of the day they talk to their parents. Parents of teens, listen: the research tells us that teens want to have family dinner. In fact, Fisher, a family therapist, says that if families actually ate dinner together regularly, it would put therapists out of business. "Many of the things I try to do in family therapy actually get accomplished by regular dinners," she notes.

In fact, a study at Columbia University found that teens who eat dinner with their family twice or less per week were 1.5 times more likely to smoke, drink, or use illegal substances than teens who had dinner with their families 5 to 7 times a week. Joseph Califano, President of Columbia University's National Center on Addiction and Substance Abuse, said that increased dinner time frequency equated with a lower likelihood of sexually active friends. Clearly, the pseudo stability sought in illicit relationships is moderated by the authentic stability of a loving family.

When our kids were little, time in the kitchen was a favorite. The kids learned to bake and cook at a young age, and it's still fun for them to impress their non-culinary peers with their homemade bread or gourmet desserts. Those recipes we developed together are representative of hours spent laughing, talking, and learning in the kitchen, inventing and experiencing moments of trial and error (we keep a catalogue of the recipes in our *Very Veggie Cookbook* on my website as a free download for families who want to try out new menu ideas).

Similarly, when we look at studies of time spent in nature, the two-hour-a-week mark is the minimum requirement for improvement in mood, physical health, and mental health. A formula exists! There are actual numerical factors that influence these quantitative results. I encourage parents to make an honest assessment of how time is being spent investing into the home compared to the work environment to see what windows may exist for developing a system that increases family togetherness. From this connectivity will come a wellspring of hope, efficacy, and purpose.

As Barna says in *Revolutionary Parenting*, if we want to succeed as parents, we must have a "radically realigned pool of personal and family relationships." Most Americans, he reminds us, will not relate to the prioritization of family. They will find it threatening, archaic, or otherwise out of touch. But, Barna notes, "parenting cannot be revolutionary if it adopts the core assumptions and practices of the prevailing culture." We have to rise above the norm. Parents are more likely to raise spiritual champions, Barna notes, if parents accept the fact that from day one, their parenting efforts will stray from the norm and will put them at odds with the vast majority of American parents, the ones who are going with the flow. Broad is the way that leads to destruction.

Barna lists a number of behavioral markers that successful parents (what he called Revolutionary Parents) shared in common: They were most often from single-income households (meaning that one parent worked and the other cared for the children), they were from intact families with two parents, these parents spent more time with their children than those who did not raise spiritual champions, they came from all economic walks of life (money or the lack thereof did not determine the making of spiritual champions), and these parents identified parenting as their most important focus in life during their parenting years.

In talking with parents who are considering exiting the public school system, some tell me with great regret in their voice that they can't find a single hour to spend with their children in a given day. As the words leave their lips, they often realize that something is out of balance, out of whack, in their familial system. I promise to pray with them for God to provide a way where there seems to be no way, to open up doors for flexible scheduling, entrepreneurship, or even a new career field all together. Peter writes in his second letter, Peter 1:3, that through his divine power, God has given us everything we need for life and godliness. Everything! Mom and Dad, God has called you, equipped you, and given you the resources and brain power you need for this task! We'll talk more about your ability and your call in the last two chapters of this book.

As parents, it's time to take back what is rightfully ours. Our children thrive when they are raised by involved parents who are willing to invest in them, disciple them, search out their gifts and talents, and provide them with the freedom of an individualized learning model that doesn't aggressively undermine the family's values. And if it hasn't already been stated clearly enough here, family matters. At the start of the 20th century, it was not well-known how early family experiences affected one's longterm behaviors in adulthood. In 1929, John Bowlby, world famous psychiatrist and the founder of attachment theory, was working in a school for behaviorally challenged children when he began to wonder how early family experiences affected the behavior of the developing child. He became passionate about what he titled "the making and breaking of affectional bonds" because he saw the direct mental health implications when those family bonds were broken. John's son, Robert, recounted his father's frustration and disappointment at the reluctance with which his work was received. The scholarly community, much like the traditional scholastic community today, rejected his findings, as they no doubt found them offensive, personally attacking, guilt invoking.

Attachment theory, Bowlby notes, can press buttons and bring to mind sensitive memories. Sadly, he noted, most people prefer to preserve an idealized version of their attachments rather than explore the idea that their attachments may have been more insecure than secure, more neglectful than loving. The sudden awareness of brokenness can rock one's sense of security and stability. But in truth, it is the only place we can start. Parents must assess their own influence on their children while there is still time for that influence to be positively affecting.

Just as Cicero said that gratitude is the parent of all other virtues, my research and observations of families coming out of the traditional education system has caused me to consider another cause-and-effect relationship: the root of peer-orientation, which stems from parental neglect, is the foundation of much of our modern developmental evil. And peer-orientation only flows in when there is a vacuum in parent-orientation. Parents, peer-orientation will not be broken off without your intervention! No scholastic support program, no Sunday school teacher, no basketball coach can successfully replace you! Your child was born with a unique biological attachment and need for you that cannot be outsourced to someone else. We must step up and take the reins. We must apply the spirit of wisdom and discernment; we must follow the biblical mandate for training up our own children in the way they should go. This is our responsibility as parents.

Many parents, though, feel they are battling against the clock. Time is their greatest nemesis. In her book *The Overworked American* (1991), Juliet Schor says the typical American is working the equivalent of 13 months a year. Americans in general have more leisure toys but less time to enjoy them. Comparatively, Americans vacation about 7 days a year, whereas European nations vacation 5-6 weeks a year. And listen to this: despite our overwork, Americans are still underperforming: We produce the same amount that our European counterparts do—even though they take an extra five weeks off work! "All work and no play" is a mindset that has infiltrated every aspect of work and home life in America. Over the last thirty years, the percentage of time working outside the home has increased significantly for both men and women. And the amount of hours both parents work outside the home affects the amount of time we can spend investing inside of the home. It's a fairly simple equation.

The family-centric model of education, embraced for thousands of years before the current era of media-centralization, remains the primary system of educational health. According to Dr. John Wherry of the Parent Institute, children with involved parents are more likely to earn higher grades and test scores, attend school regularly, have better social skills, demonstrate positive behaviors, and adapt well to their environment. "The research evidence is now beyond dispute," Wherry noted. "The most accurate predictor of a student's achievement in school is not income or social status, but the extent to which that student's family is involved in the child's education."

In fact, in the more than 30 years of research on parent involvement, researchers have consistently found that parent involvement produces positive results for children. The Manitoba Department of Education and Training (1994) notes that, "Parents are more significant than either teachers or peers in influencing educational aspirations for the majority of children," including improved academic performance, improved school behavior, greater academic motivation, and lower dropout rates. When we look behind the scenes at schools were new programs are hailed for increasing student performance, we almost always see a common fact (hough not one commonly pointed out: Parents have been invited into the mix. In other words, it's not the social system that is improving grades: it is the inclusion of family in the process.

Sadly, many parents today seem unaware of the powerful role they play in the lives of their children. Some of these beliefs stem from the continued mockery of authority and parenthood in general, as well as the chasm of disconnect between this generation of parents and the former generation. Today's parents have been conditioned to believe that someone else can do a better job of inculcating values, but this is simply untrue from a statistical standpoint.

When we look at the comparative retention rates for Christianity across all scholastic backgrounds, the data is compelling: 85% of students who grow up in Christian homes but attend public school will walk away from the faith by the time they graduate. Only 15% survive. Why? Students are indoctrinated daily, constantly, oppressed not only by teachers but by peers. And this is happening daily in our K to college environments across America. A student recently told he was trying to start a conservative club at his secular university, and the very small number of professors that were rumored to be conservative told him quite plainly that they would never put their name publicly to those clubs because their offices would be burned down. What? Turning Point USA faces these same attacks when they try to create conservative space on secular campuses. Let's think about that for a moment. Parents, these are the schools American Christians are sending their children to in droves. Over 14 million students attend state universities in America. K to college, the American public education system has become an indoctrination station, and the next generation is paying the price. If we stop feeding the monster, we can starve it out.

Next on the Christian retention rate is private schools, which are still abysmally low—if parents are not involved in the discipleship process. Sadly, too many private schools cater to a drop-off mentality where parents hope someone else will train up and discipled by someone else. In his study of 200 Christian colleges and universities, Ken Hamm wrote in *Already Compromised* that the vast majority of Christian institutions of higher education have defaulted to a godless education system that has watered down the word, forsaken their mission, and essentially looked the other way when it comes to authentic discipleship. The one bright spot for Christian Education is the parent-directed model of homeschooling. As Dr. Brian Ray has shown, less than 5% of homeschoolers walk away from the faith when they graduate. Why? They have been discipled by a parent. The home is in order. There is no escaping the fact that parents are the first line of defense for discipleship, and our children are the first line of our living resume. The fruit of their lives is the tangible evidence of where we've invested our time, talent, and treasure.

Remember, Luke 6:40 tells us that the student will become like the teacher. We will become like the company we keep. There is no more capable person for training up your own child than you, the one to whom God gave that incredible child. The foundations our children form in childhood and their teenage years will guide them in the way they think, the way that act and interact, in the way they work, in the way they vote, in their selection of spouse and all other major lifestyle decisions. Many parents tell me that they feel a sense of apprehension about their ability to care for their child, and this sense of inadequacy persists across the variants of age and socioeconomic status. One parent told me she felt unprepared because she had her first child at 19. Another mom, who had had her first child at age 28, said she felt just as unprepared. Much of this tendency toward fear and outsourcing comes from the lack of hands-on experience in an actual family! Prior to the last century, learning to be a parent was a natural part of being a member of a family that worked together daily toward common goals. Today, however, this is often not the case. A teen can grow up and go to college having never held or cared for a baby. For this reason, many young adults feel (and truly are) underprepared for parenthood.

When I walk parents through filing their very first private school affidavit, which in California is their one and only annual conversation with the state, their sense of relief is palpable. "That's it?" They ask with great incredulity. The moment they click the submit button, many parents weep. The vast majority of the parents I work with in our academies have come straight from the public system, and they feel the weight lift as soon as they click the submit button. Many message me to tell me of the incredible sense of freedom and excitement they feel surging through them. It's tangible, palpable. There is a reset coming, a great reset that teeters on the edge of revival. It starts in the home and floods into the church, the marketplace, the neighborhood. It is, as Maya Angelou once described the impact of an artist, a "great and gorgeous light" that is illuminating minds and defrosting hearts. The Great Resignation may just be one of the linchpins in the next Great Awakening.

As a leader of your family, you're called to be a watchman, a keen observer who eyes the streets from the tower wall, scanning the horizon for intruders, whether natural or spiritual. We all have to keep an ear to the ground, a finger on the pulse of our cities, our homes, watching and warning those who depend on our courageous vision for their safety. We need a sweeping cultural awakening sooner rather than later, because as a result of the segregation of family, we see a new cult arising, one that is described in the next chapter. The cult of peer orientation has replaced parental attachment, and the results are sobering, truly devastating, for an entire generation.

CHAPTER NINE

Toxic Trait #5: The Cult of Peer Orientation

When I started researching for this book, I was prepared mentally (for the most part) for the cultural carnage in the youngest generation. I've followed George Barna for years. I've read all of Ken Ham's books. I've been steeped in research on media socialization and GenZ identity formation since I started graduate school years ago. And, of course, I've seen it experientially, as I've been immersed in the classroom for two decades. It might sound a bit cynical, but I completely expected the fallout we are seeing in the youngest generations. What really gripped my heart, though, was the fallout in the lives of parents, Millennials.

Traditional education has created a multigenerational emotional deluge, and the floodwaters are just now beginning to recede, leaving in plain view the dramatic destruction: a generation attempting to cope under an inability to think, to reason, to attach, to function as God designed their minds, hearts, and families to operate. It is from this place of malformation, this place of cracked foundations, that we have to begin our rescue mission.

One of the more significant offshoots of the system's influence is the mindset of inability: the culture of the expert has replaced the wisdom of the parent. Two generations have been swayed to believe that parents are somehow less capable, less informed, even less passionate about their children's successes than a stranger would be. It's so counterintuitive on paper that it's a difficult train of logic to follow. I think an example from almost 100 years ago, an early push of the expert culture, helps make the parallel clear. From the 1940s to the 1960s, an ongoing advertising campaign tried to convince mothers that nursing a baby was a lower class undertaking, and that smart upper class mothers gave their babies formula. The belief among childcare "experts" at the time was that breastfeeding was an old-fashioned and archaic technique and that "modern" science could surely outperform nature. Sound familiar? It's a refrain that has been echoed throughout generations, attached to a plethora of parenting topics.

Misleading ads like these formula-is-best campaigns have been banned today, and baby formula companies are now required to post a disclaimer stating that mother's milk is best for a baby. In fact, mother's milk is an incredibly complex nutritional formula designed by God to be perfect for the baby's needs— both physical and emotional. The act of nursing brings the baby close to the mother, where eye contact is fostered. The mother's body releases endorphins that enhance the emotional connection between mother and baby. In nursing, as in with other activities requiring closeness in physical proximity, a chemical dance between mother and child ensues: This "dance" is known as a parasympathetic expression; that is, the biochemical response of one individual influences the biochemical response of the other. In the case of mother and child, there is a slight acceleration of the heart and a rush of hormones that further foster the mother-child bond.

In addition to meeting emotional needs, nursing provides the perfect sustenance for a growing baby. The composition of the breast milk changes with the needs of the baby, beginning with colostrum (a thin, high calorie fluid), and then *changes in*

composition with the physical needs of the growing baby's body.
In other words, the mother is already intrinsically equipped with
everything her baby needs! Human milk, as opposed to cow milk,
is higher in fat and lower in protein, ideal for the period of rapid
brain development a baby is experiencing. The iron in mother's
milk is easily absorbed by the baby's system, so there is no need
for supplementation. Breast milk offers a degree of immunity
from respiratory illnesses, allergies, ear infections, diarrhea, adult
obesity, and, according to the American Academy of Pediatrics, it
may also enhance cognitive growth, leading to higher intelligence
in adulthood. What synthetic substitute can promise a genetically
designed formula perfectly suited to the changing needs baby's
body? The natural design supersedes any chemical composition
fashioned in a human laboratory.

The same is true for the family. Family is God's design.
The institution of marriage was his invention. And just as he
designed a mother's body to care for the needs of the baby, he
also designed the family to care for its children through the
provision of unique differentials both mother and father bring to
the mix. Just like the commercialized socialization of formula
that kept mother's from following biological logic, it's important
to keep our finger on the pulse of covert social pressures that
attempt to replace the genuine with a saccharine substitute. At the
macro level, parent orientation has been replaced by a twisted
offshoot, peer orientation.

This subversive intruder of peer-orientation has been
looming on the horizon for decades, slowly inching its way
toward the doors of our homes, toward the hearts of our children.
Watchmen have called out here and there throughout the years,
but for the most part, parents have done one of two things. They
have either looked the other way, hoping that ignoring the
problem would make it go away. Or, they've stomped their feet at
the enemy, trying to use carnal tactics to overcome a spiritual
battle. This force of darkness has been seeping in for decades like

a dark flood spreading across the classroom floor, gradually gaining depth and mass and literally suffocating the light and life out of the next generation.

One such watchman on the wall was a research prophet named James Cooley. In 1966, he told his contemporaries that he saw the underpinnings of a concerning behavioral trend looming on the horizon. He said that his research and experience was showing a shift: that the hearts of teenagers were starting to orient more toward their peers than toward their parents. His colleagues laughed at him and said that this research trend was a figment of his imagination. But of course now we look back over the last 50 years and see that the trend was real, and there has beee a switch of attachment. The young are now attached to the young instead of to their parents, and their parents are now attached to their own peers instead of their children. The need for healing of attachments now spans two generations.

This segregation is easily traced back to the literal training ground of community—the traditional education system. Long gone are the multi-age schoolhouses like the one where my grandmother taught in Dupo, Illinois, riding her horse to class and spending the day teaching twelve grades in one room where the older students served as role models and mentors for the younger students. In her model, all ages learned to work together, to play together. Schedules were built around agrarian cultures where each member of the family had a chore that contributed to the betterment of the field, the home, the family. But the closer we inched to institutionalized, grade-segregated learning, the more we lost those community and familial ties that bind, and the further children slipped away from connections to the adult world of work, of responsibility, of caring for other human beings.

Developmentalist Uri Bronfenbrenner once marveled that in the modern era, unlike any time in human history, a student could graduate from college having never held a baby or cared for another human being. The roots of narcissism, isolation, and certainly, the peer-driven modality, are formed and fashioned in this peer-centric environment.

A peer is a person in one's social circle who typically informs and enforces societal norms. The terms "peer influence" and "peer pressure" are both centered on this definition. Maybe you've also heard the term "superpeer." Just a decade ago, we referred to the superpeer as the one most influential person in the group, the ringleader. Now, if you look up the term, it has shaken off its previously negative connotation and has become a pathway for global influence.

If you've ever been the unwitting victim of peer pressure, you understand the power of the peer group, especially for young students who also lack the mooring of a family structure. Maybe it was something as simple as finding yourself dressing exactly like someone you looked up to, or maybe it was pressure to attend an event you didn't want to attend. When I was in high school, the girls on my volleyball team said it was "cool" to shoplift. I told myself constantly that I would never follow in their footsteps, but one day, I gave in to the pressure to fit in. Of course, I was caught, and to make sure we got the point, the store called the police and then called our parents to come pick us up. In my case, that meant my dad—who also happened to be an undercover police officer—had to come pick me up from my waiting "cell" inside the squad car outside the local Kroger grocery store. I'm sure that probably ranked right up there as the most embarrassing moment of his life. But the more time I spent around my peers, the more I became like them. We become like the company we keep, said King Solomon, considered to be the wisest man who ever lived. Precisely what values are being inculcated through the ubiquitous presence of public school indoctrination, and what can we do to combat this inculcation?

The modern American family has been a picture of fragmentation, segmentation—at least until 2020, when American families began to wake up and then to rise up. Parents heard their children's public school teachers spewing out anti-Christian philosophy. They saw their children depressed and sullen, hollow shells of their previously joyous childhood selves, and they wondered what had happened to bring them to this place. A lack of family connectivity is one of the markers gang recruiters look for in 4th graders: a fatherless child will be more likely to bond with a peer group because he lacks a sense of belonging in his family group. This makes him an easy target. The generational disconnect strips power from the parent and ascribes it instead to that underperforming scholastic counterpart, the peer.

The culture of the expert, so celebrated by the public school system, has silenced two generations of what Maya Angelou called the "mother wit," that powerful source of inspiration that helps mothers know instinctively what their children need. We have allowed that internal compass to be thwarted, tipped on its side, until we feel like we don't know which way is north. Modern parents are convinced they need an expert to explain everything to them, to do everything for them. They experience a profound sense of discomfort and frustration when we tell them to figure something out or to function "off book" in their educational processes. Why? Because they too have been victims of the same traditional education system that taught us what to think but not how to think. They are paralyzed by the same sense of perceived lack, inadequacy, and doubt that their children are! It's time to break these generational cycles, friends.

Thankfully, God has equipped us with biological, sociological, and spiritual support that gives us exactly what we need to accomplish the task at hand. As 2 Peter 1:3 notes, God's divine power has given us "everything we need for life and godliness." He provides not just some things but *everything* we need! Moreover, neural plasticity studies show that we can change and grow throughout the entire lifespan! When Paul told the church in Rome not to conform to the pattern of the world but to be transformed by the renewing of their minds, he was speaking to adult men, not children. He had faith that the men in his audience could change. He didn't give qualifiers by age. The word he used for transform, *metamorphoo*, is the same concept we use for changing one entity into another, like a caterpillar becoming a butterfly.

The term for conform, *syschematizo*, means to be molded according to a pattern. Though the biological concept of neural plasticity didn't yet exist, Paul was saying that we can grow, change, and develop throughout our lifespans, breaking free of the worldly pattern around us, if only we will renew our minds in the word of God! So don't be discouraged if you hear your own thoughts of failure, hopelessness, and inadequacy echoed in these pages. All is not lost. There is hope. God can supersede the brokenness of our generation when we look to him, trust him, and live in wholehearted devotion to him.

I received a beautiful testimony from one of our new homeschool academy parents that illustrates the power of transformation well. Their 13-year-old son went to a friend's birthday party, and there were many younger students present. The parent immediately recalled the pressure to conform in public school. "In traditional school," she said, "it's socially unacceptable and frowned upon to associate with other age groups and grades. You are made to feel like an outsider and weirdo if you are seen talking to younger students." However, because her teen had been learning in multi-age classrooms and spending more time with his parents and siblings, his mom noted that he completely resisted the social pressure to shun the younger kids. Instead, he was bold and unafraid to relate to everyone, to be inclusive in the best and truest sense of the word. What a culture of value older students create when they encourage, inspire, and set the pace for younger students!

"As adults, we know that when you grow older your circle may consist of folks of all ages and demographics," the mom told me. "Sadly this isn't nurtured at the younger ages. Division is praised and welcomed." In the homeschool academy format, students gain this valuable experience of relating to (and caring about) other age groups. As the parent put it, "The academy is strengthening our future leaders' character, and that is far more important to us as a family than anything else."

But does one child matter? Does one town, one county, one state make a difference? There's a poem often circulated by teachers, where a child is standing at the ocean's edge saving every beached starfish he can find by throwing it back into the ocean. The sandy shore is literally covered with the starfish, suffocating on the beach, a few feet from the life-giving source of water. A passerby asks the little boy why he persists in trying to save some starfish when he can't save them all. "Why waste your time? In the grand scheme, your effort is meaningless," the passerby says, chastising the boy. "Well," the boy says, tossing another starfish into the sea, "It matters to that one."

As a parent, each one of us has a little starfish that may be shriveling on the sand, gasping for breath in the anemic ecosystem of the public school classroom. Your rescue matters to that one. Pastor, your rescue matters to that child, to that family. Friend, God equips the called. If he called you to be a parent, he has equipped you to be a parent. And these early years, the years where children are often shipped off to school for a stranger to cheer them on as they reach all of their milestones, these are prime years of emotional real estate where we can grow deep roots for a future harvest.

At each stage of prenatal and postnatal development, specific social and internal characteristics are developed. Toward the end of a child's first year of life, cognitive processing ability is forming through the organization of the orbitofrontal region. As UCLA psychiatry professor Dr. Allan Schore notes in "Back to Basics: Attachment, Affect Regulation, and the Developing Right Brain Linking Developmental Neuroscience to Pediatrics," poor attachment or relational trauma in this stage results in a lack of attachment, a lack of empathy, a reduced capacity for play, and a lack of emotion regulation, especially with regard to aggression. Parents, these are all characteristics we are seeing in the youngest generations. Later, for a healthy developmental system to form within the infant, there must be reciprocal connectivity will develop to regulate emotion, to respond to stress, and even to evaluate facial expressions (the inability of which is actually a common theme among violent criminals). This latter characteristic is especially concerning for "pandemic babies," many of whom are growing up without the warmth of human expression as their guide to the adult world. As Dr. Schore says, these components of development "are all directly influenced by the attachment relationship."

The most vital of parent-child connections, research shows, are intuitive, beyond conscious control, which is why dysfunction can so easily be transmitted transgenerationally. These connective opportunities, often numbering upwards of 20 per minute, give the child a sense of connection to the parent. This requires an investment of both time and intentional focus. At the cellular level, there is a connective, intuitive, synchronized interplay, almost like a "dance" between the parent-child dyad. When the mother exhibits an expression, the baby "learns the rhythmic structure of the other and modifies his or her behavior to fit that structure, thereby cocreating a specifically fitted interaction," where, as Dr. Schore puts it, the "mother's psychobiologically attuned external sensory stimulation frequency coincides with the infant's genetically encoded endogenous rhythms." In other words, mother and child can "read" each other, and their responses to those needs and continuing responses create a sense of safety and connectivity.

Through this process, we are creating and strengthening the sense of self within each person, developing what Dr. Dan Siegel has called the "relational mind." As sociologists such as

Pearce (2007) have said, we are capable of co-creating a world through our communication. Through our vocalizations, our eye contact, our responses, and our reading of the needs of the other person, we shape the inner world of the "other" in our parent-child dyad.

One of the most sobering aspects of working with a new generation of parents is observing the impact of decades of government schooling, which has created gaps in their personal awareness of parenting needs. In a strange and illogical mental cutoff, parents seem to have been convinced that they are "needed" only through potty training, at which point they should give their children to the "experts." Like the mothers of the 1940s who were told that their own bodies were incapable of sustaining life and should be given over to the "expert" formula makers, today's moms have been victims of the same repackaged lie. They've felt like their job was over once the first two or three years were checked off, and they feel they must invariably hand them over to the "expert" government ruler who will shape and fashion them into the desired image. Let's return to Plato's question: Who is teaching the children and what are they being taught?

Two emerging findings that are coming out of our early studies on students (and parents!) who are migrating from years of public schooling are these elements of peer-orientation and its offshoot, atrophied self-government. Now, this can be painful to address, but as William James once observed: "Not everything that is faced can be changed, but nothing can be changed until it is faced." So, first, the bad news. Students coming out of the traditional system, whether public or private, have two distinct expressions: They lack of self-government, and they are highly peer-oriented. Of course, these two challenges are closely intertwined. Perhaps the best book I've ever read on the dangers and downfalls of peer-orientation is the gem by Drs. Neufeld and Mate, *Hold on to Your Kids: Why Parents Need to Matter More than Peers.* This construct of peer verses parent orientation is the root of relational evil and the foundation of immaturity in self-control, self-government. Children and teens have developed strong orientations toward and attachments with their peers, and parents have outsourced their children to the larger culture. This combination of the drive for man's approval and the parental neglect has created this rift.

This is the reality, the tragic trend that we are seeing across the landscape of the rescue mission. As students are stepping out of the government school system, we expected to see low levels of engagement, low academic performance, and high rates of disinterest and disrespect. But what we didn't expect to see was the depth and breadth of the root in the parents as well. Two generations have been dramatically impacted by the lie of the expert culture. Just like the parents of the 40s and 50s who were tricked into trusting "the expert formula" over God's design, many parents today are beholden to the same lie that is producing the same sobering outcome.

How do we break off the peer-orientation in today's generation? Institute for Excellence in Writing (IEW) founder Andrew Pudewa was recently teaching a parent educator session for our academy families, and he talked about how many parents coming from public schools are literally afraid to help their children succeed. This is rooted in that same "culture of the expert" that makes parents feel incapable of teaching their own children anything. He gave simple techniques to help students succeed, giving them small tasks that would help them feel a sense of agency, ability, efficaciousness. These are simple tools that yield significant results, like a tiny acorn budding into a mighty oak. These simple measures unlock the doors of intrinsic motivation. Do you remember the two essential elements we talked about? They were efficacy and curiosity. If we make the work too hard and we don't ever give our children, especially our young children, the ability to succeed, they won't develop intrinsic motivation.

We also talked in an earlier chapter about the importance of time, most specifically in that segment, family dinners. There was a marker, a minimum, of a number of meals that helped families hit the threshold of positive social shaping. In the same way, an investment of time, energy, and focus is needed to shift the hearts of children back to their parents and the hearts of parents back to their children. Luke 1:17 echoes the cry of Malachi 4:6, that God would turn the hearts of parents and children back together, "or he would strike the land with a curse." Peer orientation could readily be seen as a cursed offshoot, a harvest for the trading of our time, our treasure, for something of far lesser value. From ages 1-13 especially, our children have a season of significant influence from their parents. We must not squander it.

I'm sensing the winds of change upon us. A parent messaged me recently to say she would be missing an annual event that she normally really enjoyed attending. Her young son was sick, and normally, she would have called a babysitter, left the child at home, and attended the event. But after being part of the homeschool community for a year, something was different this time. She said, "I'm thankful to you for teaching me where I need to be." It wasn't the party friends that needed her in that moment. It was her child, who had the great satisfaction that night of knowing that he was the priority in his parents' lives.

I teared up at her words, experiencing the overwhelming evidence of a shift taking place in our midst, on our watch. Right here. Right now. The poet Christina Rossetti asked, "Who has seen the wind? Neither you nor I, but when the trees bow down their heads, the wind is passing by." I can feel that wind stirring up around us right now. Change is coming. A cultural shift is on the horizon.

Isaiah 56:9 speaks of leaders who became so distracted by gluttony and selfishness that they lost both their vision and their bark. "His watchmen are blind; they are all without knowledge; they are all silent dogs; they cannot bark, dreaming, lying down, loving to slumber... shepherds you have no understanding; they have all turned to their own way; each to his own game, one and all." In an era of extreme narcissism, the enemy of our souls would want parents to care more about gaining a following than watching over a family, about partying and posting about friends rather than investing in and discipling their children. This passive parenting creates a gluttonous, egocentric mindset that worships the god of self at the expense of the health of the next generation. It's a modern form of child sacrifice. May we be culture shapers who have an ear to the ground, a finger on the pulse of the nation, leaders who recognize that building our own kingdom is futile; unless the Lord builds the house, we labor in vain.

Parents, you are capable. You are equipped. You are called. You have everything it takes to step out of the culture of the experts and place your finger on the pulse of your precious children to see what God wants to do in and through their purposeful design. Who are they? How do they learn best? What are they passionate about? Do they know God? Do they walk in his fruit, his character, his wisdom? These are the starting points for both a familial and a cultural revolution, and this is restructuring, this reset, that will yield not just temporal fruit, but eternal dividends.

It's time for an honest assessment, a relational X-ray. If your children display an orientation that is more powerfully connected to their peers than to their parents, that is a form of relational dysfunction. There is a gap, a hole, a fissure in the foundation somewhere. If children are drawn like a magnet to their friends but repulsed and even embarrassed by their parents, that is not a culture of honor or respect being developed and discipled in their little hearts. Their obedience to the Fifth Commandment, to honor their mother and father, promises to bring length of days in the land of blessing. If we allow these malformed behaviors of disrespect and dishonor to stand as the norm in the culture, we will continue to see the same struggles for respect, self-government, and conscientiousness exhibited in every realm of the marketplace. Remember, we will turn out onto the world—through our training and investment—a brat, a bully, or a blessing.

CHAPTER TEN

Toxic Trait # 6: Truth Suppression

"The American school system is sick," Neil Postman once wrote. "Its methods are based on fear, coercion, and rote-memory testing. What is more, the subject matter it teaches becomes obsolete almost as it is taught." And this modern "knowledge explosion demands that students learn how to use their minds and talents while the schools are strenuously engaged in teaching them how to stifle their intelligence and creativity. That the nature and purpose of education must be changed clear: the unanswered question is how."

This quote sounds like it could have been a headline story in an alternative education magazine published last week; however, Postman actually penned these words in 1969. Why does the content seem eerily contemporary? Because nothing has changed in traditional schooling in the 50 years since Postman first addressed the educational crisis in 1969. Nothing! Traditional education continues to operate on a system of fear and coercion, of the amassing of irrelevant and obsolete data that has no practical life application. Traditional education continues to stifle creativity, to dull intelligence, and to drive an entire generation to intellectual stagnation. Educators know this truth instinctively. Parents recognize it, and students, of course, experience it daily. But this truth is stifled, stymied, buried in smoke-and-mirrors programming that has our entire nation running in circles. What are the results of this intellectual stagnation and how do we break free of its grip?

Proverbs 4 details a fathers careful instruction to his son, teaching him insights and precepts, the foundations of practical wisdom. "When I was a son with my father, tender, the only one in the sight of my mother," verse 3 says, "He taught me and said to me, 'Let your heart hold fast to my words; keep my commandments and live.'" This timing here is vital. Fathers, teach your children while they are tender, moldable, while they still care. As a professor for 20 years, I have seen many students cross the threshold of tragic disinterest in their father's instruction because their dads were focused on some other worldly gain during the impressionable season of their children's youth. Remember, attachments are formed from ages 0-6, and worldview is distilled from ages 0-13. Dads, there is a moment in time, a window of opportunity, a season of influence. Pour into your children while their hearts are open and pliable. You set the course. You steer the ship. Dads determine destiny. By your own design, you will thrust upon the world a child who is a bully, a brat, or a blessing. Choose well.

One of the key arenas where dads can begin to bring healing (outside of presence, of course, for the fatherless generation desperately needs healing in this arena) is the area of play-based learning. When we look at the social science research concerning how moms and dads play with young children, we see a distinctive difference in focus between mothers and fathers. Mothers are naturally didactic, which means they are oriented towards teaching. Watch a mom with her young child, and you will often see this trend. Moms naturally teach letters and reading and song memorization. Dads, as the volume of social science research demonstrates, are often oriented more towards play.

They wrestle, race, and throw kids up in the air. This is a unique sociological distinction we see across the globe in parenting studies, and it's one that could bear a significant impact on the extraordinary numbers of boys who have never had the opportunity to learn in accordance with their own methodology and style. God has designed the family to work in tandem; each parent brings a strength and a style that contributes to the order and health of the whole, the family unit. Many of the students we work today with have come from schools where the teacher was a female (or now, one of a number of other confusing pronouns) and failed to understand the differences in how men and women learn. As a result, boys have been expected to learn in the same way girls learn, which is a disservice to both boys and girls. More fatherly influence creates a grace for unique learning styles that will help all children succeed.

Instead, though, this high pressure, one-size-fits-none methodology has been a cog in the American school system machine for many years. Swiss psychologist Jean Piaget (1870 - 1980) studied how a child's brain learns. As one of the most famous developmental experts in history, he explored developmentally appropriate practices in education, creating what became known as the Stages of Cognitive Development. He found that these stages—sensorimotor, preoperational, concrete operational, and formal operational—were experienced by all children around the globe in the same order, though not always at the same rate. He was particularly fascinated by (and, I imagine, frustrated with) what he termed the "American question." As he traveled the world observing parents and looking for behavioral patterns in children, he saw a unique distinction in American parents. They wanted their children to grow up quickly. Instead of play-based learning, the approach applauded by the rest of the globe, American parents were in a terrible hurry to get their children, especially their young children, to look smarter and work harder. This all-work-and-no-play mentality is a consistent theme across generations in America, a national peer pressure of sorts that has played out with detrimental effects. When we look at the comparative global analysis of our academic performance as a nation, it's clear that this push for early childhood scholarship has not put us ahead. In fact, we are among the lowest performers in many key academic arenas, despite our rush toward "formal" education. We will talk in a later chapter about the damage this relentless push has had on early education.

Parents, let's pay the price and do the research. Take an honest assessment of your family, and if your kids constantly prefer their friends to their parents, as we talked about in the last chapter, the balance is off, no matter how normalized the culture has made this orientation seem. If they have not learned self-government at home, under our watch, the lack of this fruit of the spirit, this MIA self-control, will be evidenced in full force in the peer-driven environment. They won't respect other adult authorities because they haven't learned to quiet their souls, and they won't respect themselves, not authentically, because they haven't learned the boundaries of self-government that provide the margin they need for healthy development. This leadership track begins at home.

A parallel of this leadership vacuum is explained by the prophet Jeremiah. "My people have committed two evils," Jeremiah 2:13 says. "They have forsaken me, the fountain of living waters, and hewn out cisterns for themselves, broken cisterns that can hold no water." Scholars note that Palestine had three sources of water: fresh running water, also called living water; well or cistern water; and runoff water. The last of these is the least clean, often filled with silt and mosquitoes. The nation was being chastised in this verse for trading the best water for a broken cistern. The Bible calls this "covenant infidelity," and it's pictured here as a response that is ungrateful, unnatural, and foolish. How did this happen? Jump back a few verses, and it's clear that the nation was in a state of apostasy: the priests did not see God, the experts of the law didn't know God, the shepherds transgressed against God, and the prophets were driven by the voice and desires of the enemy. In other words, the nation's godly leadership had fallen away. Today, unlike the day of Jeremiah, many parents are awake. Many pastors are awake. We see the error of education's ways. Will we be courageous enough to become part of the solution, or will we continue to exchange the living water of God's presence for the stale, infested, broken substitute of the world system? Tragically, this has been the course of choice for many modern parents: They have exchanged a relationship with their children for some other perceived treasure, living water for the stale substitute.

We find these tragic exchanges all throughout American culture. The state pulls funding and cultural support away from thriving Christian institutions and pours it instead into abortion providers, morally deficient schools, and bastions of secular humanism. Should we then be surprised that 1 in 5 students in America say they are cutting or burning themselves on purpose? Should we be shocked that the leading cause of death for Black and Hispanic youth in America is homicide, or that our country has one of the highest rates of abortions in the developed world? Are we bewildered by the fact that America's 15 to 24 year olds are anxious and depressed or that the Christian faith has been rendered irrelevant to government, education, politics, medicine, arts, and entertainment? The dissection of moral absolutes from the public sphere has caused complete and utter anarchy throughout the system. Because we have removed the discussion of right and wrong, good and evil, true and false, from the public conversation, our young people have no moral compass to guide their decision-making process. We have, as Romans 1:25 says, exchanged the truth of God for a lie.

This is one of the many reasons that freedom of speech must be protected in our generation, as speech is the potential purveyor, the vessel, of truth. We all have the right to choose for themselves life or death, blessing or cursing. We were created with a free will. And, we also have a nifty little clause called the First Amendment that should (in theory) protect our freedom to talk with hurting and confused people about their life decisions so that they can make their own fully educated choices. As grownups in a democratic nation, we should be able to express (without the threat of physical harm or social media cancellation) the psychological, emotional, and physiological dangers of living outside the protective boundaries that are inherent to the Christian worldview. Instead, though, our financial systems fund morally averse programming while punishing the Christian institutions that teach abstinence, value, human dignity, and personal worth—the foundational personal values that can actually protect against rampant promiscuity and violence in the first place.

Parents, when you send your kids to the public schools, or even to private schools where God has been compartmentalized into a little box, you pay more than a financial price; you pay a spiritual price. And let's not miss the price tag: For every kid in the California public school system, the state spends $17K a student, over 3% of the taxpayers' income, which equates to over $80 billion in expenditures per year in California alone. When you free your child from the confines of public school, you topple the idol, the false god of money that drives much of the public school agenda. Dagon crumbles down powerlessly to his rightful place. Think about it this way: a public school exit is a loss for government indoctrination centers and a win for your children.

I always find it interesting to make comparisons to other parts of the world and how they have wrestled with the encroaching, truth-crushing pluralism that has spread like a flood across the globe. Though you might not expect a liberal, socialist country like the Netherlands to serve as a glowing beacon of religious freedom, we might have something to learn from a similar battle the Dutch people faced. When national education was introduced in the Netherlands in 1800, citizens were offered a standard secular curriculum. But in 1848, the religious community protested the lack of religious compulsory education in the state system. These religious groups then fought for their right to have fair representation on the scholastic home front. After a long debate, the Dutch government decided that the best way to fairly represent all of its citizens would be *to fund all education equally, religious or secular.* The program was formalized in 1917 and continues to this day. Now, I know that state funding always comes with strings attached, which is why I don't recommend that parents partner with charter schools. The government is not your co-parent. But imagine with me for a moment a land where dissident voices are permitted to have their own opinions. Imagine a state where differences in thought shared publicly and professionally in the public square have the freedom to do what they were designed to do: to foster civil discourse and personal growth. Imagine a classroom where you have the ability to become an objective and informed citizen by reading media sources that fairly and accurately represented *both sides* of a public debate. Can you envision a nation where you wouldn't be called a "hater" simply because your views are different from someone else's views?

Unique to the rest of the world, America's governmental system was established to be "of the people, by the people, for the people." Collectively, we are Caesar. We are the voice that elects the rulers who are intended to represent the views and ideals of the public they serve. Today, however, we are witnessing the sobering evolution of a government that is of the government, by the government, and for the government. We have allowed an uncircumcised Philistine to step into the Valley of Elah uncontested and demand that we bow to his ideologies. We have allowed politicians, lobbyists, and entertainers to rewrite truth that has been foundational to our nation's identity for hundreds of years. If we don't address these issues as individuals

167

and as a nation, if we keep plugging our ears and hiding away in our safe spaces, we will not get better. We we will only become more embittered, more vengeful, more divided. This faulty foundation has been established, built up, erected, brick by brick, day by day in America's classrooms, where students spiritual senses are numbed, where their minds are dulled, where their opinions and their faith are crushed, tested, mocked, and twisted. It's time to speak up.

It's clear that there is an overt, ongoing attempt to silence and marginalize Christians in every sphere, starting with education. Collectively, as Americans, we have allowed the foundation of the faithless, fear-mongering system to be poured in a slow-curing cement: We buried our heads in the sand 60 years ago when the Values Clarification Movement swept through our nation's public school systems, outlawing discussions on right and wrong and effectively reducing our nations classrooms to chambers of moral relativism. We crossed our fingers and hoped for the best when the Bible was booted out of the school system. We stood by limply when law after law undermined parental authority, increasing the power of the state. And perhaps most befuddling of all, Christian families have continued to send their kids and their financial support to the very institutions that continually berate, undermine, and oppress the Christian faith! Two generations of students have spent 7,200 hours a year being indoctrinated in belief and behavior: They're not allowed to pray, to talk about God, to share Bible verses, or to disciple classmates. In some cases, they aren't even allowed to have a Christian group on campus after school—unless the club is directed by a non-Christian leader. You can't make this up.

Compartmentalizing our faith has become an accepted way of life. An entire generation—two generations, really—has been desensitized to the outlawing of the Great Commission. And this ongoing religious discrimination has fostered a culture of indignation that bristles or melts with any opinion different from its own. Anyone who dares to speak a divergent view is quickly ushered off campus to a cancel-culture holding cell, while the poor innocent "victims" of this dangerous divergent-thought-exposure are ushered into safe spaces to color, blow bubbles, and watch videos of frolicking puppies until their minds return to an appropriate state of numbness.

As Christians, it is the element of free speech, the ability to speak in grace and truth, that we must protect. Without it, we can't instruct, train up, disciple, and certainly, we can't fulfill the Great Commission. When the rulers of the day commanded Peter and John to stop speaking and teaching in the name of Jesus in Acts 4:18-19, what did Peter and John say? Did they back down? Did they allow the gospel to be silenced? Marginalized? No, they said, "Judge for yourself what's right in God's eyes: to follow God or government." If we, as a nation, hope to preserve freedom of speech and freedom of religion, if we desire to see our posterity possess the freedom to engage in civil discourse, then we have to step up. We must stop hiding in our safe spaces to block out the noise of dissidence that fuels critical thinking. We must speak up against unreasonable and unconstitutional demands. We must require that the government release its citizens from Huxlian thought control. It's time to restore our country to its rightful representation of a government of the people, by the people, and for the people.

Human development through the ages showcases a generational pendulum swing: each successive generation responds in a sometimes overly dramatic fashion to the needs and failures of the previous generation. The Builder generation was prone to the practice of hoarding because their parents went through the Great Depression and lost everything. GenXers created the term and practice of work-life balance because their Boomer parents were always working, determined to provide materially for their families in a way they themselves were not provided for in childhood. GenZ desire relationship over wealth, becoming known as the "debt-averse" generation. These swings are a natural part of the growth and development of individuals, of families, of nations.

When we look at the models of the past, we saw a natural integration of children into the adult world of work. However, as the Industrial Era took over and started training children to be cogs in a machine, the education system focused on what we call one-size-fits-none education. We lost that individualized edge as well as that connection to the family business, family apprenticeship, and slowly, opportunities for family discipleship. Remember Lev Vygotsky's scaffolding approach and how absent this ideology is in most modern homes? The false esteem taught in the school system has undermined an authentic sense of self and has segregated ages, robbing our culture of the generational interdependence that was intended to provide both scaffolding and purpose at every age and stage.

I wrote in *The Multigenerational Marketplace* about how the youngest working generations often crumble when corrected in the workplace. This stands in stark disparity to Hebrews 12, that God disciplines those he loves as a father the son he delights in; thus, we should, in the same way, be ready to receive correction, admonition, coaching, as part of our personal growth and development. Children are arrows. What's propelling them forward, determining their trajectory? Years ago, our kids took an archery class at one of our homeschool academies, where they were taught to hold the bow steady and aim at the target. In dramatic contrast to this visual, many kids today are limping through life with bent bows and broken arrows because no one has trained them, mentored them, discipled them. The public school system has emasculated men, weaponized women, and created a generational rift that pushes families even further apart.

In his leadership address to Timothy, Paul provides a number of examples of self-government and intergenerational mentorship. He says that leaders are measured by their home life.

This is not a popular message, but with the extraordinary rate of lawlessness and anxiety in the youngest generations today, it is a truth that must be addressed. Husbands are to "manage their children and households well." Many men have been taught that kids are the wife's responsibility, and a sobering number of Christian fathers tell us that they have never prayed with, read with, or trained up their children in the ways of God (what the Bible calls making disciples). Often this is a generational pattern of disconnect in the family line. But what if you didn't get this training as a child? Paul makes provision for this in his letter as well. In 1 Timothy 4:7, he says, "Train yourself for godliness." As adults, even young adults, our training is our responsibility. Bootstraps up. Let's go. If you're a parent, make disciples, starting in the home. If you're a young adult, start by leading yourself well. Train yourself. Reach out to someone in your circle who can mentor and disciple you—and pour out what you learn to someone younger than you. In this way, linking together families and generations, we will break off the spirit of lawlessness and "constant friction" Paul describes, and we will experience peace, purpose, and "what is truly life."

One of the clear and present dangers overshadowing the public school system right now is the suppression of truth. I am fascinated by parents who win little battles with the school board and think, "Hurrah! Our school is safe now!" They send their children back into the dungeon of indoctrination because they win a tiny, insignificant battle. It's like the devil hands them a lavender-infused iced latte, and they think, "Well, at least I'll be cooler." No, it's still Hell! The location, the content, and the company have not changed. Children are still being taught lies about their identity, their purpose, and their destiny, yet these parents rejoice because they think that winning back the in-person classroom experience means the battle is over. No, the battle is raging. The stakes have never been higher. And their children are a living sacrifice on the altar of convenience.

The first chapter of Romans details the chain reaction that begins when people suppress the truth even when it is evident, even plain, to them. Their thinking becomes futile, and their hearts become darkened. They worship temporal gods instead of the eternal God. And then, Paul says, God gives them over to "dishonorable passions" and a "debased mind." Verses 29-31 offer a lengthy checklist of the deeds of darkness, and we can certainly see each one of these alive and active in the world today. As Dr. Henry Morris notes, they "wind up so distorting their lifestyle that they become unable to tell what gender God made them," he says. They have "rejected the truth that God has openly displayed for everyone to see" and "plunged into a foolish and damaging lifestyle that warps their intellect and emotions beyond repair." As a result, Morris says, they can find pleasure only in those who "live, think, and love as they do." People become so confused, so disoriented, that they lose their orientation in all senses of the word. Only through bringing up a generation in the truth of God's word—instead of the lies and deceptions of the public school culture—will we rescue the generation that is described so aptly in the first chapter of Romans. This is an all-hands-on-deck moment, parents.

Parents often tell me that they are not capable of teaching their own children. Actually, the truth is more along this line: certified teachers are not capable of teaching your children. Did you know that a recent National Education Association study shows that 2/3 of America's students are reading below grade level? In fact, the most recent results from the Program for International Student Assessment (PISA) show that American students display widening disparity in achievement when compared with 79 other countries. According to the National Center for Education Statistics, US math scores ranked #30 in the world. That's thirty, 3-0. Number thirty in the race. You don't get a medal for coming in 30th, friends.

The study also found that American students were not

motivated by an intrinsic desire to succeed. In fact, the students who did succeed were motivated by one factor: Financial payment for correct answers. In other words, American students have not developed a lifelong love of learning. They don't pursue knowledge for the altruistic betterment of the world. They have been taught, conditioned, to think of education as a carrot, a means to an end. Congratulations, America. Between our exclusive ivory towers and our morally bankrupt public schools, we're now training up a generation of students whose only motivation for success is financial gain. In fact, a Pew study just a few years ago showed that one of the chief life goals for our nation's youth was becoming famous. I shudder to think what the Pilgrims would think about our academic acumen, let along our biblical literacy, in the modern education sector.

But parents, don't despair. There is hope! Where to start? Read. Read the Bible together. Read the classics. Walk and talk together. Do life together. The last section of the book *A Thomas Jefferson Education,* DeMille includes a list of 100 classic books for kids and young adults (adults too!) as well as discussion questions. You couldn't ask for a richer environment for learning! This, I'm sure, is why school districts like the one I described in Chapter 3 are cutting the classics out of the curriculum and replacing them with "identity and relationship" nonsense. Readers are leaders. Reading gives us power, purpose, hope, inspiration, courage. Slaves were never allowed to learn to read. Why? Because reading makes a person full, wise, aware, revolutionary-minded. Reading gives us vision and power. We willingly shackle ourselves and our posterity with the bonds of slavery when we allow reading to become a cultural relic replaced by the artificial blue light of a screen. It's time to take it back, parents.

In his book *The Disappearance of Childhood,* Neil Postman notes that when a student learns to read, he learns a peculiar way of behaving, including the unique feature of physical immobility. Self-restraint is a challenge not only to the body but to the mind as well. Sentences paragraphs, and pages unfold slowly, he says, in sequence, and according to a logic that is far from intuitive. In reading, one must wait to get the answer, wait to reach the conclusion. Patience is required.

"To learn to read is to learn to abide by the rules of a complex logical and rhetorical tradition that requires one to take the measure of sentences in a cautious and rigorous way, to modify meanings continuously as new elements unfold in sequence," Postman says. "The literate person must learn to be reflective and analytical, patient and assertive, always poised, after due consideration, to say no to a text." These are tremendous skill sets! Screens, on the other hand, fail to draw out depth, to promote deep thinking or critical thinking. They simply entertain. Remember, learning requires interaction.

Given the importance of reading, and the knowledge that students spend 65% of their social time on a screen (with less than 1/3 reading at grade level), it is not difficult to see why we have a maturity crisis on our hands. As Erik Erikson said in *Identity and the Life Cycle*, "We have learned not to stunt a child's growing body with child labor; we must now learn not to break his growing spirit by making him a victim of our anxieties."

Learning to trust the growth sequence and to be fully present in the educational process, both emotionally and physically, is an increasingly lost art. DeMille summarizes that education hinges on two key components, a mentor and the classics. Mentors "meet face to face with the student, transferring knowledge through the force of personality and individualized attention. Classics were created by other great teachers to be experienced in books, art, music, and other media." The parent-directed method of education provides the opportunity for development in both of these critical arenas.

In her book *Teaching Squirrels,* my friend Dr. Kimberlee

Mendoza says fellow educators get frustrated when she tries to convince them of the need for making teaching fun. "The youngest generations have grown up with constant exposure to video games, phone games, Wii games," she says, "and (yet) we make no effort to make learning the slightest bit enjoyable." Laugh a little, Dr. Mendoza suggests. Find the joy. Let's not take ourselves so seriously all of the time. And let's make our homeschool classrooms environments of wonder, joy, and fun.

Remember, as Dr. Achor has shown, a positive environment activates the neural pathways of learning. Pleasant words "promote instruction," as King Solomon put it. Oh, but we are often a serious bunch as Americans. Recall Piaget's "American Question," where he wondered aloud why Americans are constantly in such a hurry for their kids to grow up. Ironically, this push for high brow toddler academia hasn't worked. The US is still one of the lowest academic performers in the world. We are consistently dispersing the wrong content cocooned in the wrong methodology.

The anti-fun mindset Dr. Mendoza experienced from her audiences is felt most severely at the beginning and end of the compulsory education spectrum, mostly often, ironically, in the early childhood range of 3 to 5. When we first asked parents to use play-based learning in parent-led PK classrooms, they looked at us in shock. The shock quickly turned to skepticism and then to disappointment, as though play-based learning were an assault to one's intelligence. "Make learning fun," we reiterated. But the high brow academia kept trying to get a foothold in the doorway. "My kid needs to know more, do more, achieve more," parents kept echoing, their stress levels rising.

Then, suddenly, the breakthroughs started happening. At first, in many of our classes, when young children were presented with a blank sheet of paper, all they could ask was, "What do I do?" Or "What should I draw?" They were paralyzed by the freedom of choice. The creativity muscle had atrophied due to lack of exercise. But within just a few weeks of experiencing freedom, students began to think, to dream, to create at new levels.

Once they got outside the boundaries of groupthink and perfectionism—those paralyzers of productivity—their minds literally opened up. DeMille describes the same observation in *A Thomas Jefferson Education.* A child who has been told for 7,000 hours what to create and how to create it suddenly finds himself lacking the ability to create at all. Parents, the scientific literature tells us that kids *need* to create; they need to play, and their play is naturally, organically didactic. I think sometimes our rugged American individualism causes us to want to micromanage results, to roll up our sleeves and try to make things happen. But instead of always making things happen, perhaps sometimes we just need to let them happen, to give margin and movement for organic growth.

In her book *Quiet,* Susan Cain writes of the "Cult of Personality" that has taken over our nation's school system, "enshrined in high school syllabi," a world where students are "increasingly skilled at shaping their own online and off-line persona." In these environments, students are whisked away from reality to "inhabit a world in which status, income, and self-esteem depend more than ever on the ability to meet demands of the culture of personality," Cain says. And the pressure continues to mount, causing increasing havoc in the identity of the next generation. "The culture to entertain, to sell ourselves and never to be visibly anxious keeps ratcheting," Cain says. "How did we go from character to personality without realizing that we had sacrificed something meaningful along the way?"

We see this development especially among the young, where the focus on personality, peer-influence, and the deism of me-ism can create emotional incentives that fuel addictive behaviors. This cult of personality wars against authenticity and prevents the establishment of true peace, both internally and externally. "Depart from evil, and do good," Psalm 34:14 says. "Seek peace and pursue it." Instead of seeking true peace, though, the system has trained students in a learned orientation toward conflict. There is a clear and overt addiction to the drama of relational conflict, and driven by the low esteem that stems from constant comparison and identity confusion, the youngest generations often view the world with a painful skepticism.

In their book *Attachments*, Dr. Tim Clinton and Dr. Gary Sibcy explain that the brain releases pain-killers (endogenous opioids) during times of extreme stress. In one study, after participants reviewed 15 minutes of a violent movie, their brains released the equivalent of 8 mg of morphine. In a non-desensitized culture, where people struggle with "emptiness, tension, irritability, and an internal sense of unrest," the author's note, there is a tangible drive to "reactivate that neural morphine." Like a child who has grown up in an unstable home, children begin to "crave the chaos that a turbulent environment brings."

Clinton and Sibcy say (and Beuchner would no doubt agree) that these are the foundations that compel us to one extreme or the other—attachment or withdrawal. "As we become increasingly aware of our need and how truly vulnerable we are, our attachment system flips on," they note. And because of our rugged individualism, it's easy to think we can fix it on our own. But life's a big deception, Clinton and Sibcy say, "is that we can achieve all this freedom, peace, and contentment apart from a personal relationship with God through Jesus Christ. So we cram our lives with everything we think might give us purpose, value, and meaning," they explain. But as we honestly evaluate our lives in the light of truth, we realize "how empty, shallow, and purposeless life is when lived selfishly and alone."

In his book *Already Gone*, Ken Ham makes a plea to churches to return to the truth of God's word. He describes a cultural parallel from the gloriously innate cathedral in

Westminster, where I once stood and sang a Beatles song to my future husband (equally befitting content to Ken's point). Here, in the honorable cathedral, a dissenter is buried among the saints. There in the midst of the bodies of Geoffrey Chaucer, David Livingstone, and the veritable Charles Dickens—in the very same room where the first third of the King James Old Testament and the last half of the New Testament were translated—lies the body of none other than Charles Darwin. Pause for a moment to reflect on that odd, sobering, confusing combination of the consecrated and the common. Ham calls this physiological juxtaposition "a powerful example of the short road that the Church has followed into irrelevance."

Darwin, whose evolutionary theories struck at the very heart of religious thought, is thus not only honored by the church but is also buried within its foundations. "It is symbolic indeed," Ham quips. Only a century ago, the Westminster Cathedral was considered to be the third seat of learning in England after Oxford and Cambridge. This placement elevated the voice of the cathedral, its personified actions declaring a version of truth to the trusting culture outside its gilded doors. Just as the intellectual elite have blurred the line between clarity and confusion, sacred and secular, so too, our modern education system mutes the holy heroes of our past by entombing them alongside cultural icons who echo the popular voice of the day. This blurring of the lines has taken on a life of its own.

The crisis of truth suppression in the public sector has so many branches, so many roots, so many realms of entanglement in our collective identity and our relationships that it's difficult to categorize its full impact. However, perhaps this erosion of trust is evidenced nowhere more powerfully than in the cultural perception of males today. David Blankenhorn explains in his book *Fatherless America* that the culture of men has been under attack in America for decades. We are warned to avoid the "Old Father" and embrace the "New Father," he says, "the improved version of a dad who looks a lot more like a mom." One after another, Blankenhorn details scholarly journals and books that intend to help women "effectively produce changes in male behavior," to make men more like women. High school and junior high school textbooks explain to children that our relational problems stem from "male resistance to needed change," that men must accept and embrace androgyny, that men are the problem. These scholars try to convince our nation's youth that men are holding back the socio-cultural development of our nation by "dragging their feet regarding a less gendered society...free of negative and distorting personality characteristics and internal blocks to self-esteem." By this, they mean to decry what they call "male bravado."

Blankenhorn's book, one of my all-time favorites, feels like it could have been written yesterday, but, like Postman's timeless observations, it's a warning siren that's been blaring for a long time. Here we are, over two decades later, with the school systems and their subtle weapons of mass destruction pounding out the same timeless tune. And that, my friends, is how we arrived at the ridiculous notion of toxic masculinity. It was preached in the academic journals and taught surreptitiously in the androgynous classrooms. It was rolled into research projects and speech topics and self-reflective writing prompts that taught 6th graders all about their white guilt and the oppressive natures from which they could never escape. Like the theory of evolution, this base of anti-male, anti-authoritarian, feministic fodder has been at the root of public school doctrine for many years. The rhetoric has already inflicted significant damage to the minds, hearts, and worldview of millions of children.

Many of the parents we work with today are what I call "reluctant homeschoolers." They didn't grow up dreaming of educating their own children. They didn't have visions of staying home all day, teaching their children to cook, reading classic literature by the fire, or turning their kitchen tables into biology laboratories for the dissection of crawdads. But when the public schools pushed these parents in areas where they had drawn a line in the sand, they stepped up. And now they are dealing with life in all its rawness and fractures, all its ups and downs, mountains and valleys. But they're staying the course.

As Frederick Buechner says, the gospel is bad news before it is good news. In the same way, our human condition as parents is often bad news before it's good news. We have to deal with the raw realities of who we are, where we came from first. It's darkest right before the dawn. And then, instead of allowing that weight to crush us, we rise up. We step up. We stare truth in the face. William James said that not everything that is faced can be changed, but nothing can be changed until it is faced. Once we face the suppression of truth head on, once we acknowledge the stagnation of the human intellect, pulling apart strand by strand the toxic teachings of the public school system, we will be poised for a level of influence that will sweep through the next two generations like an academic tornado.

Now that we are fully aware of the suppression of truth in the public school system, there is only one plausible response. We must expose the lie. Who cares the mandate of the whistleblower? The local church is the agent of social change, and parents are the activators of that change. If parents and the local church work together for the sake of the next generation, I have no doubt in my mind that we will turn the tide and redeem two generations. But a price must be paid. And many parents over the last five decades have been unaware or unwilling to take that step—until moment. During that time of stagnation, a great and terrible exchange has taken place for the hearts and souls of our nation's young as their lives have been poured out on the false altars of convenience, wealth, and popularity. It's time for the wise and willing to bring light to the darkness, to illuminate the deception, and to shift the culture once and for all. Let truth reign.

CHAPTER ELEVEN

Toxic Trait #7: Cultivating Communism

I love my country. I grew up in small-town America before the days of full-fledged, anti-American sentiment began sweeping through the public sector. Every year, as our family celebrates our nation's independence, I am reminded anew of my gratitude: I'm grateful for the freedoms of religion, speech, press, assembly, and petition that are protected by the Constitution, but I'm also thankful for a freedom that many Americans are unaware of: the freedom of educational choice. When we look back at the foundational documents that are still driving modern "compulsory" education in the United States, it's fascinating (and sobering) to see the focus. Much like the Values Clarification Movement, these doctrines actually served to undermine the freedom of thought, creativity, innovation, and entrepreneurship through "forced" education. The goal of these archaic educational programs was to create a compulsory training ground that molded a generation into submissive, passive rule followers, cogs in a government machine.

The Founding Fathers did not make any constitutional provisions for a government-controlled education system. As we saw evidenced in Chapter 4, attorney Kevin Novak has provided in great detail the documentation explaining that the civil government literally has no jurisdiction, no constitutional authority, to operate a school. Thankfully, parents, you have the freedom in America to choose how and where your child is educated. If you're tired of sacrificing your educational liberty at the feet of secular humanism and anti-American sentiment, it's time to liberate the huddled masses yearning to breathe free, America's school children.

One of the relative newcomers to the indoctrination engine of the public school system is the spirit of false pacifism, that warrior-crushing, male-bashing, Jezebel-ian spirit that rips the green army men off the Target display shelves and replaces them with fluffy pastel unicorns. In our modern, left-leaning school systems, students are often taught to be pacifists who "live and let live," eschewing even honest verbal confrontation. But evil must always be fought, and the freedoms upon which our nation was founded must always be defended, even with our very lives. Happily, there are still some vestiges of freedom alive in our country. I love, for example, that we still have a day called Veterans' Day on our calendar, an ode to battle that commemorates World War I. WWI was called "the war to end all wars," and Veterans' Day, originally called Armistice Day (armistice means truce), was designed to celebrate the anniversary of the end of that war. A 1968 Congress who failed to understand the importance of the day and hour (the 11th hour of the 11th day of the 11th month) tried to change the day of celebration to October, where it teetered awkwardly out of place until 1975, when it was restored to its rightful place of 11.11.11 remembrance. Veterans' Day still exists, at least for now, because soldiers and civilians fought to honor its memory.

In government schools, ironically, most students are no longer taught to honor the flag or the freedom for which it stands. The pledge of allegiance has been buried under perverse pledges to political agendas. In just two generations, the left-leaning K to college system has turned our youngest citizens from patriots to pacifists, from capitalists to socialists. If you've watched students stomping on a flag or high school athletes refusing to put their hand over their heart when the national anthem is played, you have witnessed the shift. Countries that teach their young to dishonor the memory, mission, and vision of their own country create a sense of chaos, like a self-abusive teen who feels trapped in a mind and body she loathes.

What a powerful contrast at one of our homeschool academies last year, where I walked into a classroom and saw local veteran heroes being honored and America's true heritage being celebrated! In a particularly poignant moment, a massive American flag was being moved into the auditorium, and, at the unexpected sight of our nation's symbol of freedom being wheeled out in front of them, students instinctively stood up and began singing our National Anthem. This might seem insignificant, but an automatic response like this is indicative of deeply rooted beliefs, the evidence of a worldview. These homeschoolers had been taught to honor and respect the symbol of the flag and the republic for which is stands. Sadly, many of their public school counterparts have been taught to hate the flag, to live not as one nation united under God, but as many sub-nations divided against one another.

Our worldviews, these looking-glass self-amalgamations, all work together to create our sense of self, our identity. This is true both corporately, in our national identity, and individually, in our own personal identities. Of course, it's no surprise that one of the most influential leaders in identity development today is the public school system, working in close partnership with mass media. The identities being peddled today are a far cry from the collective ideals narrated by our founding fathers. The United States of America was forged on the construct of religious freedom. Not only did the Pilgrims come to this land in pursuit of religious freedoms, but Christian education was fully embedded in their thoughts, their language, their teachings, their social life.

Historian Dr. Daniel Boorstin notes in *The Landmark History of the American Peopl*e that when the Pilgrims came to America, they saw education as a path to discipleship. Even when the Pilgrims founded the very first American university, Harvard Bible College (now Harvard University), their goal was a biblical foundation through education. They wanted to make sure that the Bible was protected and passed on to a literate mass, one who could understand it. Why? Because the Bible was the center, the anchor, of all of their relationships and research, their teachings and traditions, their laws and regulations, and their family life. Back then, the main forces of socialization were family, church, and education that supported, undergirded, their Christian values. Today, for our youngest generations, that is rarely the case. Instead, today's most powerful influencers are social media, music, friends, and a school environment that undermines Christian values.

Proverbs 14:27 says that the fear of the Lord is a fountain of life that turns us from the snares of death. Similarly, Proverbs 9:10 says that the fear of the Lord is the beginning of wisdom, and knowledge of the Holy One is insight. For the Pilgrims, the fear of the Lord was central to their teachings, and the Bible was at the epicenter of their educational process because the Pilgrims knew that without an understanding of the scriptures, without an anchoring to the truth of God's word, every aspect of life in the new world of America would be colored by a faulty paradigm. The Pilgrims were determined to instill in the next generation a foundational mindset of faith. Regent University history professor Dr. Elizabeth Youmans notes that colonial parents understood that their divine mandate to educate their children in the word of God was a "generational duty." The founding fathers were called "people of the book," and this family practice stemmed from their regular training in the local church. Dr. Youmans says that the Pilgrims' pastors were very intentional about discipleship; they regularly taught families how to reason justly with the Bible in the civil realm.

American statesman and founding father Samuel Adams said that "divines and philosophers, statesmen and patriots must all lead their children in the study and practice of the exalted virtues of the Christian system." Noah Webster, who spent 20 years writing the nation's first dictionary, said that the Christian religion is one of the first arenas in which all children under a free government ought to be instructed: "No truth is more evident to my mind than that the Christian religion must be the basis of any government intended to secure the rights and privileges of a free people." Then Webster made this mic drop statement: "Education is useless without the Bible." Let me say that again in the indelible words of Noah Webster: Education is useless without the Bible.

Now, let's reason with the data before us. Students in our nation's government monopoly schools are not only among the lowest performers across the globe academically, but they are also the most depressed, anxious, noncommittal, suicide-ideation prone students in the history of our nation. Why? Perhaps quite simply because "education is useless without the Bible." Though they might have the occasional faith-filled teacher who writes scriptures on the board and leaves out the author, Jesus, for fear of losing her job, most public school students are not taught through the lens of God's word. As the Department of Education notes plainly on its website, public school students are *forbidden* from learning from a Christian worldview.

In fact, a comparative analysis between the Christian goals of our founding fathers and the secular goals of the today's public schools show modern education to be on a trajectory directly opposite to that of our founding fathers. Why does that matter? Let's recall Plato's admonition: the two most important considerations for every civilization are, in essence, the character of the teachers and the content of the lessons. The manner in which we train up the youngest generations today will be the direction, the trajectory, of our nation tomorrow.

The Pilgrims would have answered Plato's question by saying that they taught their children the truth of God's word in the spirit of Deuteronomy 6:6-9: "These words that I command you today shall be on your heart. You shall teach them diligently to your children, and shall talk of them when you sit in your house, and when you walk by the way, and when you lie down, and when you rise." This verse commands a ubiquity to the teaching of God's word, that the teaching happens everywhere at at all times of the day, in the house and in the streets, when we are going to sleep and going about our days.

This, of course, implies having time, intentional time, together as a family. Teachable moments require accessibility. Because of their devotion to the Bible and the generational duty of discipleship, the Pilgrims were a biblically literate population; their decisions about every aspect of life were informed through the lens of the biblical worldview. Parents, how would you answer that question right now, whether about your own children or about the children of our nation? Who is teaching them, and what are they being taught?

I've been working with the next generation for 20 years, and based on the fruit that I'm seeing coming out of the educational system, it appears that we are living in the modern parallel of 2 Chronicles 34. In this ancient-but-oh-so-relatable era, King Josiah is clearing out the land of every idol when suddenly, Shaphan the secretary discovers the book of the law in the forgotten rubble of the temple. The book of the law was not passed down from the parents, as Moses had commanded. Instead, it was buried, forgotten, overrun by cultural cobwebs. When Hilkiah the priest reads the book of the law aloud, Josiah tears his robes and cries out that his nation's forefathers have not acted in accordance with God's law. Because the fathers had not discipled their children, because they had not carried on the

Deuteronomy 6 mandate to teach God's word to the next generation, the guiding wisdom of scripture was buried for almost 60 years. The parallel is striking to today's generation, and we will return to this topic in a few chapters.

Today, unlike anything I've seen during my time on this planet, there is a fierce driving force dedicated to separating us from our history. We see it in the attempts at revisionist history and the vehement removal of statues and monuments, the marbleized testaments to men and women who fought and sacrificed and labored a lifetime to protect and preserve the very freedoms we enjoy in our country today. Not even King David, whom God called a man after his own heart, would have passed the litmus tests of these haters! They take personal offense at anything that goes against the grain of their politically correct, woke doctrine. In my city, for example, the local Christopher Columbus statue was toppled by City Council after a 4-1 vote, and a neighborhood venue called Discovery Park was renamed after being deemed "offensive," though, ironically, the park was actually named in honor of NASA's space exploration program, not the discovery of America.

This attempt to crush the imperfect biographies of history is ridiculous to the root. Our founding fathers were in process, just as we all are. Virtually every leader in the Old and New Testament displayed some type of questionable judgment or behavior. Romans 3:23 reminds us that all have sinned and fallen short of the glory of God. If we expected perfection of these early historical figures, then we must expect it of ourselves too. The reality, though, is that we all see through a glass dimly. This convoluted mindset of political perfectionism makes the bearers so focused in on one mindset, one historical paradigm, that they fail to see all the good the individual also did for our nation. It's ironic to hear so much pseudo-moralizing from groups that wanted to strip morality out of the public sector in the first place. Statues are being toppled. Buildings are being renamed. Schools are severing themselves from their historic roots in an ultimate example of publican-to-sinner hypocrisy.

I recently received a call from a dad who went to drop off his kids at a local elementary school. When he told the principal his kids wouldn't wear a mask, the principal sighed, pulled out a cardboard box from the school district, reached inside, and handed the dad the district's mandatory alternative for mask-free children: a government-issued face shield covered with the politicized image of a rainbow. The parent said he recognized the agenda right away: You refuse to wear a mask? Then your children will be a walking advertisement for the rainbow flag that flies outside the county's public school district headquarters. This dad knew the shield was yet one more example of state monopoly systems pushing an agenda, so he took his kids by the hand, placed the rainbow shields back on the principal's desk, and walked out the doors of the dysfunctional government school. He and his wife filed a private school affidavit and became a homeschooling family that same day. It's that simple. And the following week, the principal of that same school decided he was done being a puppet for the public system. He left his post of 10 years and started a private school in his church! Today's parents (as well as some teachers and administrators) are fed up with the bullying, experimental injections, and overt Marxist indoctrination that has become the norm for public education.

Parents have seen it with their own eyes now. They walked into their kids' rooms and heard with their own ears government teachers on Zoom, teaching classes that are paid for by our tax dollars, who were promoting anti-family, anti-American, anti-Christian agendas. They saw the root of division sprouting up in pro-marxist, critical-race-theory-driven ideologies. As former Focus on the Family president Dr. James Dobson once said, "If you have your kids in a public school in California, it's time to get them out." If we don't change the methodology and content of education in our state, we will face grim consequences in just one generation. As the saying goes, America will never falter and lose her freedoms from the outside. If she is to be destroyed, it will be from within.

Now, I realize this concept offends the segment of parents who believe their children are called to be salt and light in a dark world, but let's consider in real time what it's like for a 7-year-old child to face off against a hardened career atheist. Third-person syndrome prevents us from seeing the weakness in that argument, but there is a reason why it's illegal to evangelize to anyone under the age of 18 in communist China. There's a reason that Jesus said in Matthew 18:6 that it if someone leads one of his little ones astray it would be better that he have a millstone tied around his neck and be drowned in the depths of the sea. Why? Because children are vulnerable. The student becomes like the teacher. Children need someone to defend them, protect them, train them, stand up for them. Since a child's worldview forms by the age of 13, we have to make every year intentional.

Some parents become eternally optimistic about the potential longevity of change in the system when they see one tiny victory in public school. In California, for example, parents won what they perceived to be a major victory when the school district postponed an earlier medical mandate for all all students. Parents rejoiced, completely missing the point. It was a postponement, not a cancelation. And even if students are not being inoculated, let face it; they're still being indoctrinated. Again, how many changes have actually taken place in the public system in the last 50 years to reverse any of these toxic traits? Zero. There have been virtually no long-term changes in government education despite the thousands of parents who have gone down to the local school board and stomped their feet to express frustration over a grievance. Nothing has changed. Evolution still reigns as a fact rather than a delusional opinion. Moral relativism still rules. Kids are still cogs in a machine. The fear of man is still elevated over the fear of God. Yes, I know the cute little saying, "As long as there are tests, there will still be prayer in school." However, in a "free" country, our prayers shouldn't have to be whispered in closed, fearful circles under the threat of expulsion.

In this chapter, we address another toxic trait of traditional education: this oddly ignored but culture-shaping force of anti-patriotism, which influences not only our national identity but also our personal one. Let's look at some of the foundations and the fruit of that root. We saw anti-patriotism rearing its ugly head on the international stage at, of all places, the US Olympics. In widely circulated photos, the US women's soccer captain, refused to stand during the national anthem at games. While the team did stand at the Olympics, only four of the eleven put their hand over their heart. Eight members of America's team refused to take part in this symbol of commitment to their country, America. Rapinoe told Forbes in 2021 and Today News in 2019 that she hasn't stood for the National Anthem since 2016 and doesn't ever intend to do so.

This disease of anti-patriotic globalism is widespread today. The International Olympic Committee has debated this topic for the last 18 months, deciding if, how, and where athletes can express opinions. In 1968 Tommie Smith and John Carlos, two American medalists, were expelled from the Mexico City Olympics for raising the "Black Power" fist at the podium. While the IOC still holds to the ruling that athletes can't express opinions at the podium, gestures are now being allowed after athletes leave the call room. Now hold on, super star athlete. Aren't you at the Olympics representing, ummm, your country? And who is footing the bill for these athletes? For most nations, though not America, an athlete's Olympic experience is sponsored by government funding. This necessarily begs the question: Why would a nation send athletes to the Olympic Games to represent a country they're ashamed of? And where on earth did this depth of insolence originate?

Anti-patriotism is another one of the twelve toxic traits of traditional education. Waving the flag has a whole new meaning today, as does kneeling. But this really shouldn't surprise us. Whereas students once recited the pledge and sang the Star Spangled Banner in their public school classrooms, we now see an opposite trajectory: patriotism is scorned, the national anthem is banned, and children are allowed, even encouraged, to show utter disrespect to the memories of those who shed their blood for the precarious freedoms we now enjoy. Should we then wonder how a US Olympian could embarrass us on the world stage by being ashamed to be an American? The seeds of dishonor were sown, sprouted, and harvested in the fields of public education. Listen to these examples.

In 1943, the West Virginia State Board of Education versus Barnette declared that "the free speech clause of the First Amendment prohibits public schools from forcing students to salute the American flag and say the Pledge of Allegiance." While we respect the freedom of speech, of course, we must take into consideration the disrespect for our nation's symbols that have emanated from cases such as these. This disregard has a trickle-down effect from the classroom to the courtroom: From NFL players to high school students to Olympic athletes, the banner has been banned across America. In 2018, high school students in a California school called the Star Spangled Banner "outdated and offensive." The student leader wrote that the Star Spangled Banner is no longer reflective of American ideals. "As our culture shifts to one that is more diverse and accepting of all types of people, so must our traditions," she told the school newspaper. In June 2020, The *Wall Street Journal* reported that 16-year-old Liana Morales, who was selected to perform the national anthem for her school, refused to sing the song because of the line "the land of the free and the home of the brave." This line, she said, gets to her because "people in prison are being treated as slaves. If I stand there and sing it," she said, "I'm being complicit to a system that has oppressed people of color." To be clear, what Liana is saying is that she can't sing a song commemorating our nation's successes because America is inexorably linked to oppression. These are the direct teachings of CRT, which we unpack in a later chapter.

In September 2019 *The Anchorage Daily News* announced that their public schools would no longer be required to play the national anthem or the state song. Though some of the school board members said the songs would instill more unity and patriotism in the students, the winners of the vote said that students needed to stop "wasting time" on this fluff content and focus on improving academics and closing achievement gaps. One member, Alisha Hilde, said, the national anthem "does not advance student learning, help kids get jobs or get into college." Another speaker, the president of the NAACP and a US Army veteran, said, "The purpose of attending public school is not to show patriotism, love for, or devotion to one's country, but to learn the fundamentals of education: reading, writing, math, etc."

Hmmm. The irony is palpable here. It's tragic that an Army veteran, who once fought for the rights of citizens, would deny students the opportunity to ground themselves in the rich history and appreciation of our nation's successes, to celebrate the great American accomplishments that are recognized the world over. But again, this is the focus of the public school classroom, to undermine our spirit of nationalism, to turn the tide toward pluralism, socialism, and ultimately, communism. One public school teacher, Katie McIntosh, told NPR why she doesn't believe patriotic songs belong in the classroom. America's diversity, she said, means we shouldn't just sing about America. "Why aren't we representing other countries? Why aren't we singing the national anthem of other countries? We are diverse and we accept everyone." Seriously. Again, you can't make this stuff up. Parents, these are the teachers who are speaking into your children's lives. "The Star Spangled Banner may have survived bombs bursting in air, Fox News writer Todd Starnes noted, "but it may not be able to withstand the rampaging mob of politically correct inclusivists." Parents, it's time to wake up to what's happening in your school district!

A program called The National Anthem Project was founded in response to a study that showed that 2/3 Americans didn't know the words to the Star Spangled Banner, and 3/4 said that when they did learn the song, they most often did so in school. Critics of the National Anthem Project said, and I'm not making this up, that the Star Spangled Banner is "musical propaganda" that "forwards the limited claim of nationalism to the exclusion of building international and local affiliations and identities." In other words, the national anthem teaches a protection and preservation of a national identity. Ummm, yes. That is the goal of every nation's national anthem! This anti-border, anti-nationalist, anti-patriot, anti-truth nonsense must be stopped!

Why does it matter if we raise a generation of patriots or a generation of communists? Well, in case that answer isn't obvious, America is a pacesetter. America is a leader. America influences international belief and behavior. As Well Versed World founders Dr. Jim and Rosemary Garlow put it, "America is the world's role model." Nations literally make decisions based on what America does and does not do. Now, for those who have grown up in the culture of pluralism, I realize that sounds like an extraordinarily ethnocentric worldview, but because our founding documents are built on the word of God, there is inherent power in the core of our national identity. If you grew up with a leftist education on politics (as I did!), be sure to check out the work Rick and Kara Green are doing at the Patriot Academy to help counter the anti-patriotic political activism sweeping the nation.

There is a powerful connection between believing in a nation's purpose, as well as in one's individual sense of purpose. These foundations are intertwined. Both individually and collectively, we need a sense of unity, of shared beliefs, of direction and hope and purpose. This is true both individually and collectively. If our youngest citizens are told over and over that their nation and even their own lives, in fact, are not worth fighting for, we will all ultimately experience the grim repercussions of that teaching. As Postman notes in *The End of Education*, "To be nowhere means to lie in a barren culture, one that offers no vision of the past or future." What a perfect description of today's American schools! We cover up and criticize history, make it irrelevant, stir up animosity for our founding fathers, and find ourselves stuck in the perpetual present. A society that neglects the foundations of healthy identity, both individual and national, will reap a harvest of passive, desensitized consumers devoid of purpose and direction. A system that undermines its historical roots and alienates its citizens will ultimately be robbed of the confident assurance of purpose, power, and vision. A house divided against itself, Mark 3:25 says, cannot stand.

In his book *Live Not by Lies*, Rod Dreher outlines the onset of what he calls "soft totalitarianism" in America. Whereas overt totalitarianism is a recognizable "political authoritarianism with an ideology that seeks to control all aspects of life," soft totalitarianism uses an unexpected port of entry: the utopian constructs of help and healing. This Dreher calls "therapeutic control," an addiction to comfort that taps our human need for harmony and happiness. It plays on our sense of justice and masquerades as kindness to humanity, the "cult of social justice" as Dreher puts it, that demonizes its dissenters. The roots of cancel culture are clearly identified here: You don't agree with us? We cancel you. This is the opposite ideal of free speech, civil discourse, even critical thinking! Marxism, as Dreher puts it, is a "highly theoretical, abstract set of doctrines" that took Russian intellectuals by storm because its evangelists presented Marxism as a secular religion for the post-religious age." Sound familiar?

First, we wiped out religious roots in the American school system, creating a void, and then we began teaching a new religion to fill that void. Marxism was first taught at the universities in Russia, as it is in America, where it trickled down through reading groups, often disseminated to the larger culture by students. Again, we see the same predictable pathway of influence. Students graduate from their secular schools and become Marxist influencers in neighborhoods, churches, traditional education, medicine, and politics. Dreher note emphatically that at the time of the totalitarian uprising, Russian parents should have spoken up. They should not have remained silent when their children came home spouting Marxist ideals. Parents should have known that this new "political faith" their children were preaching would mean a total collapse of the culture, but tragically, parents looked the other way. They did nothing. Mom, Dad, this is our wake-up call. In the same foreboding footsteps, our public schools are training up social revolutionaries who want to flip our country from capitalism to communism. Take notice.

At its root, Dreher says, Marxism teaches that class inequality—the rich exploiting the poor—is the true reason for all the world's misfortunes. The rich are the bad guys, and the poor are the good guys. This unhealthy relationship with money and wealth has seeped into American churches, homes, politics, and, certainly, schools. The rich are bad (unless they're celebrities, of course; then the bad genes somehow pass over them). The poor are the oppressed good guys who have done nothing to merit a life of poverty and failure. Never mind if they are addicted to drugs and sport multiple felonies on their records: they are the good guys. End of story. This concept of rich-versus-poor should sound familiar, as it closely resembles the foundations of Critical Race Theory—one victim, one oppressor, and zero chances to rise above either label. It's a hopeless, victim-minded, intellectual entrapment that denies the power of neural plasticity, tenacity, potential, and even forgiveness.

A parent in one of our academies grew up in pre-1990s communist Poland. When she came to California and trustingly placed her children in the "capitalist" government's national school system, she couldn't believe what she she saw in her children's books. "I recognize these history books, these stories, this doctrine," she said. "These public school textbooks are teaching communist principles to the youngest Americans." Of course, she knew she had to sever the tie. She unenrolled her children from public school and became a homeschool parent. It seems impossible to many of our immigrant friends, especially those who grew up under communist regimes and fled to America for freedom, but when they see the evidence up close and personal in their child's textbook, they reach the same conclusion as Dreher does: Through its soft-totalitarianism approach, the public school system is quite literally cultivating Communism.

There is a powerful interconnectedness between national and individual identity. When we look at individual identity, it is our connection with our early years that provides a sense of security and safety. When I was a child, I read Psalm 139 for the first time, and the words of verse 13 pierced my heart: "You knit me together in my mother's womb...I am fearfully and wonderfully made...my frame was not hidden from you when I was being made in secret, intricately woven in the depths of the earth...all the days ordained for me were written in your book before one of them came to be." As a child who thought she was an accident born to an unwed teenage mother, this Psalm gave me a glimmer of hope toward purposeful design. Our past gives us purpose. Today, 51 million kids across America are told daily in government schools that their lives are the result of a cosmic accident, that they're just taking up space on the planet. Should we be surprised at the level of hopelessness, depression, and anxiety that characterizes our youngest generations? If you have a child under the age of 25 in your realm of influence, today is a great day to read that passage aloud together. Remind your children of their purpose, their destiny. Remind them that their lives are ordered and ordained by the creator of the universe. Let's restore a sense of hope in the next generation beginning with a heart connection to their identity in the kingdom.

When Moses stood before the Pharaoh who had enslaved his people, he uttered the famous cry, "Let my people go!" For the last two years, America's parents been rallying around this cry to the government schools: stop enslaving our people; stop teaching hypersexual curricula; stop masking our children; stop dumbing us down; let my people go. Parents, this a "we the people" moment in American history. Because the truth is that we are already free. We are not forced by law to endure the prison sentence of government schooling. We don't have to put our children on the big yellow prison bus and send them off to be incarcerated and indoctrinated eight hours a day. We are free to choose where and how and with whom we educate our children. We don't have to bow our knee to secular content or ineffective methodology. We are already free. As Eleanor Roosevelt once said, "We can either curse the darkness or light a candle." We can either complain about the blackened soul of our nation, or we can turn on the light, be the change, make a difference. If we want to overcome the toxic traits of anti-patriotism and anti-purpose, we need to be diligent in training up our children. We can't leave that to someone who does not share our values, our convictions, or our wisdom.

As Postman pointed out, there is a difference between education and school, quite literally, *institutionalized* learning. Gatto said that institutions lack a conscience because they "measure by accounting methods," not by human compassion or dignity or purpose or direction or divine calling. As parents, we care about the Psalm 139 call, the days ordained for us and for our children, their unique wiring and giftedness. Our children are not a number. They are a reward, a heritage from the Lord. An impersonal government institution is incapable of that level of personalized care. Many parents know this deep down, but their own personal fear of failure, their erroneous sense of inadequacy, keeps them from stepping up to the plate. God cares about this incongruence of the heart and the mouth, of the human conflict between beliefs and behavior. He calls it out in Psalm 50, "What right have you to recite my statutes or take my covenant on your lips? For you hate discipline and you cast my words behind you." Though the language we speak certainly has an element of power, our words themselves must also stem from a foundational congruency with our beliefs, our foundation of faith. James says that he who doubts is unstable in all his ways.

But even in this stern calling out, God offers grace to those will turn to him. "Mark this then, you forget God," the Psalmist notes in verse 23, "to the one who offers Thanksgiving…to the one who orders his way rightly, I will show the salvation of God." Hope reigns, and this is a generation that desperately needs hope. They need answers. They need godly instruction. Many are stumbling along blindly in the forest of folly, and the more foolishness they exhibit, the more bitter they become, creating the circular effect described in Proverbs 19: "When a man's folly brings his way to ruin, his heart rages against the Lord." The fool blames God for his own stupidity, always ascribing consequences, but rarely blessing, to the Creator. This verse is especially poignant for GenZ, as the most common reason 18-25s say they don't believe in God is because they believe a good God would never allow the presence of pain. They don't understand God's judgment, his discipline. They falter because they believe that God would never allow such consequences that sin brings. However, this verse reminds us that it's actually our own folly that ushers in the consequences we experience. The fool projects the blame onto someone else instead of taking responsibility for his own family and recognizing the natural repercussions of his actions (these same patterns are evidenced in children who have not experienced godly discipline in the home. They are far more likely to project blame than accept responsibility). If your mind and mouth are a bit out of alignment right now, call on the Great Physician, the divine chiropractor, to help you order your way rightly. He is ever able and willing to turn a heart, to re-order a life, or to transform a household. Today is a great day to retrain ourselves and our posterity in the foundations of this great nation. Today is a great day to help our children understand their purpose, their intentional design, both personally and nationally.

Parents, our children need to understand that their ideas have consequences. They can learn even from childhood to take responsibility for their actions. Teach them to ask for forgiveness when they've done wrong and to give generously out of their own forgiveness well to those who wrong them. These small steps toward discipleship will help turn a generation away from narcissism, blame, and projection and back to personal responsibility. And the same is true for us, parents, when we look around at this current generation, we must ascribe blame to its proper place. We all need to do some soul searching here. What is the fruit we see in our own children's lives, and how can we best set them up for success in a world that is increasingly determined to destroy their faith? The Great Commission was outlawed in the public square because good men and women did nothing. A generation of adults were complicit in the removing of absolutes from the public sphere, and the youngest generations are paying the price. It's time to stand up, to speak up, and to take back the culture.

Patriot Academy Founder Rick Green says that the average span for a nation to hold true to its principles is 250 years. We are poised right at the precipice of that hour. Our nation is at a crossroads, and unless we turn the sphere of education, we are in a clear and present danger of the extinction of our faith. Let hope arise in your heart right now. People may try to remove

Jesus from the history books. They may try to topple statues of the men and women who came to this country to worship Jesus freely. But you can't remove Jesus from America's history no matter how creatively you try because our very calendar is a living testament to his birth. The birth of Jesus, His life, death, and resurrection are the center point of history, He is the singular event that forever altered the world. He cannot be moved. He cannot be supplanted. His name is above every other name, and our job as Christians is to make his name famous.

I am fully confident in God's ability to complete this rescue mission, to help parents step up and begin discipling their children, and to see this generation turned away from spiritual apathy, away from emasculation and pacifism, and toward a firmly rooted, transformational focus on the kingdom of God. And I am fully convinced that the local church is the answer to this national crisis. I am praying for churches across our country to step boldly into the current flood of parents who are seeking refuge from the public system and give them hope and practical opportunities for change. Parents and pastors, it's time to rise up for the sake of the next generation. We can turn this trajectory, one heart, one church, one family at a time. We are the land of the free because of the brave. History matters, education matters, and family matters because all of these facets form our sense of identity, both personally and collectively.

CHAPTER TWELVE

Toxic Trait #8: The Death of Discipline

Our great-grandparents would likely be shocked if they walked into the door of a local public school today (if they were even allowed on the property). Gone is the collective sense of reverence and respect that my grandmother experienced as a teacher in her one room schoolhouse. Gone are the hymns and the prayer books, the acquisition of knowledge through the lens of the biblical worldview. Gone are the ink wells and quill pens too, of course. But perhaps the most overt loss, the most concerning transformation in student behavior, is the death of discipline. Since the next generation is no longer held firm by an anchor of truth, a belief in one moral right or wrong, what remains is only "your truth and my truth." Without a moral code of accepted behavior, no one can be held accountable for wrongdoing. Discipline is a dead word.

Of course, many of the system's teachers know that there is a right and wrong. There is good behavior and bad behavior. There are brats and bullies. Everyone seems to be aware of this at some level, but like the Emperor's New Clothes allusion we talked about earlier, most people pretend not to notice. A teacher in our local school district recently explained to me the strategy she is is expected to utilize for "discipline" in her public elementary school classroom. When a student who lacks emotion regulation gets mad, the teacher is supposed to see the wave coming and tell the other students to "evacuate" the class. The teacher remains in the class with her hands in a heart shape over her eyes, telling the child, "You are loved. You are safe." I am not making this up. Meanwhile, the child storms through the classroom like a tornado ravaging the space, venting his frustrations, and spewing his pent-up anger on the innocent victims of his drive-by-style hostility. It's a free-for-all that tragically reinforces the worldview of chaos: the death of discipline.

One of the key distinctions we see in students across the nation today (one of the first early markers evidenced in the Alpha generation) is a lack of self-government, self-control, emotion regulation. Of course, while it may seem obvious that a generation growing up in the venting culture of social media may have learned some negative habits for emotion regulation, there is another vital piece to the puzzle. Many have not been required to demonstrate discipline at home, nor have they been discipled (root word = discipline). Parents, when actually present, have become buddies, friends. There is a time for friendship when our parents are fully-trained adults, but age 2 is not that season. Proverbs tells us as parents must not to be a "willing party to a child's death" by failing to discipline him or her. Children need both nurture and admonition, Paul warned us, especially from a father. Proverbs 16:32 says, "He who is slow to anger is better than the mighty, and he who rules his spirit than he who takes a city." Parents, you are not alone in the journey of teaching self-government. As Paul told Timothy, God has not given us a spirit of fear but of power, love, and self-control. The Holy Spirit is here to partner with us, to help develop character and the fruits of the spirit in our children.

Dads, you are also vital in this mix. I love the story of the dads in Louisiana who got together to combat violence at the local high school. After 23 students were arrested for violence within a three-day period, a group of 40 fathers named themselves Dads on Duty and took over the school. As the *New York Post* noted, the dads rely on "tough love and good old humiliation" to keep the kids in line. Moms, be honest: Would you ever dream of using "good old humiliation" to keep kids in line? Well, it worked for Dads on Duty. Student violence dropped to a near-imperceptible level.

In the modern school system, all the "negative" emotions of shame, guilt, and embarrassment—the consequences that are naturally birthed from the fruit of stupid ideas—have been stripped away, sterilized, and repackaged as unhealthy. Thus, students never learn that their ideas have consequences. I try to imagine what it will be like for that fifth grader who swirled around the room like a tornado of terror when he's an adult. Imagine the first time he is turned away for a job, and he explodes in rage, toppling the cup of pens in the Human Resources office, kicking through a computer screen at a supervisor's desk, being led away in handcuffs because no one cared enough to teach him to control his responses as a child. Imagine when someone cuts him off on the interstate or bumps into him in the grocery store. Imagine this terrifying young tornado attempting to start a meaningful life with a spouse and children. He has been trained by the system to expect his future spouse to shape her hands in a heart emoji like his teacher did, so that his behavior will continue to be excused, justified.

It's impossible to picture any level of personal or professional success for this kid, because if someone does not intervene in his life, Tornado Tommy will forever be captive to his out-of-control emotions. From childhood to adulthood, life is full of opportunities where we must learn to manage our emotions before they manage us. Teaching children that there are no consequences for their behavior contributes to the greater social crises of immaturity and even criminality. The tornado-kid evacuation drill is, in fact, a perfect training ground for future criminal behavior.

In I Timothy 4, Paul warns his disciple Timothy that the road of faith will soon become less populated, as many will be deceived and fall away. "In later times some will depart from the faith by devoting themselves to deceitful spirits and teachings of demons, through the insincerity of liars whose consciences are seared," he says. The public school system teaches these same lies, these same doctrines, these same deceptive and empty philosophies that are leading away an entire generation of children. I was talking with a friend this week about a new educational movement that teaches that children are born good and if we just show them enough respect, they will magically become mature, wise citizens.

I hope you see a big warning light flashing over that ideology. If you've every seen a mom trying to reason with her tantrum-throwing two-year-old in the line at the grocery store, you understand the futility of the exercise. Like the damaging teachings of Dr. Spock two generations ago, "new" methodologies are always being espoused, and some of these are to the great detriment to both parent and child (not to mention the culture who inherits the child). Parents, we have to filter our own training and ideologies through the biblical worldview so that we won't be captive to counterfeits. May we not devote ourselves to the deceiving teachings and doctrines of the day, but may we instead be rooted and grounded in the truth of God's word, which includes hundreds of instructions on parenting.

One of my academy team leaders, Ebey Sorenson, works with parents in the early childhood years, helping them break through this developmental dysfunction daily. "Whenever we make the child the center," she says, "we lead them towards selfishness and entitlement" (hear Ebey's full interview on the Communication Architect podcast). There is a push in secular education today toward socio-emotional learning, which sounds on the surface like a positive and helpful tool for identifying feelings, thoughts, and emotions. But, as she notes, "If there's no biblical solution introduced for how to handle and manage those emotions, then it's humanistic." We will unpack SEL in a moment, but for now, suffice it to say that the solutions and philosophies that are ringing the loudest in the ears of the culture are from secular authors who don't, won't, can't point back to God's word. Parents, we need to filter every teaching through the truth of scripture so we don't run the risk of becoming captive to a vain philosophy of man. As Fellowship Church Pastor Ed Young says in his book *Kid CEO: How to Keep Your Children from Running Your Life*, we need to dethrone our children from the command center of the home.

Correction, and our response to it, actually has more than a personal impact; it has a social impact. "Whoever heeds instruction is on the path to life," Proverbs 10:7 says, "but he who rejects reproof leads others astray." When we as individuals fail to embrace correction, coaching, direction, or reproof, those around us are also led astray by our rebellion. We have both a personal and a collective responsibility for raising emotionally regulated children. The secular worldview, put forth daily by media and public education, is the promotion and preservation of self. This view is fostered by self-esteem movements that, at their extreme, lead to narcissism. Dr. Jean Twenge says GenZ are marked by narcissism without a balance of empathy for others, an unfortunate fruit of growing up as the kid CEOs of the home and the classroom. This buffered protection of self and a twisted desire to preserve one's own way often leads to what scripture calls *eritheia*, the Greek word for strife, a "contentious political; maneuvering" for power. We've all experienced a child (or an adult) demonstrating this maneuvering for power. But self-service is not a Christian ideology. God's ways are higher. The biblical worldview is built on loving and serving others, not on worshipping the self. As believers, we have an extended responsibility of stewardship, not only for ourselves and our children but also for those around us. Traditional education undermines healthy discipline with its self-proclaimed tornado-student evacuation zones that protect the villain and vilify the innocent.

One of the relative newcomers to the public school's behavioral scene is a philosophy called PBIS, Positive Behavioral Intervention Systems. Now, this might sound like a relatively benign approach at first, with its promise to help participants "learn the secret to helping students replace a problem behavior with a positive behavior." PBIS is a three-tiered program that identifies "universal supports" (because the public system is not allowed to believe in a universal morality), provides practices for at-risk students, and offers formal support for major offenders. Let's look a bit closer at PBIS and its actual, stated mission. "To improve equity...especially for students from underrepresented groups." If the terms "equity" and "underrepresented" are not familiar terms for you in light of educational methodology, take a moment to look them up, and you'll quickly see the agenda layered within the PBIS approach.

We see similar ideologies expressed in a movement called "respectful" parenting. Like its socio-emotional "health" counterpart being taught in the public school classroom, it sounds good on the surface. Respect is good. Socio-emotional health is good. But let's look beneath the surface layer to find out what's being espoused. The heart of this movement is avoiding both rewards and punishment to get children to comply. Heretofore, as we all learned in child development class, parenting techniques fell into three categories: authoritarian, authoritative, and permissive. But "respectful" parents are apparently coloring outside of those lines. Dr. Justin Coulson, author of *21 Days to a Happier Family*, believes that the trend is tied to an age where people question authority rather than complying with the norms.

He believes the elevation of egalitarianism and kindness have played a role in the rise of these types of parenting techniques.

And this happiness factor is clearly a driving force across the generational swath. When Yale psychology professor Dr. Laurie Santos offered the university's first ever "happiness" class, the highest number of students in Yale's history, 1182, signed up. The pursuit of happiness has become a topic of extraordinary focus, especially when we consider the rates of anxiety and depression in the current generation. But we often want "happy" without effort in the same way we want weight loss without caloric reduction.

One author shares advice on her blog for parents whose children are hitting them, and the parents just don't know how to respond to this behavior. She calmly advises them not be punitive, for she rejects teaching that a child's behavior is "bad" or needs to be addressed through fear. Again, these sound good at the surface level, but let's look at some of the commonly recommended titles in this genre and reflect on what they're avoiding: *No Bad Kids: Toddler Discipline without Shame; The Secret to Turning a Toddler's No to Yes; and How to Raise Decent Children without Spankings or Time-Outs.* These titles have several elements in common. They clearly presume that children are born good and can be reasoned into self-discipline. They also seek to avoid punishment, fear, shame, and guilt. And they use humanistic, arm-of-the-flesh methodologies to avoid dealing with the real issue, the root of sin that is embedded in the heart of man. Mom, dad, your child hitting you is not okay, and you won't be able to reason him or her out of this behavior.

Conversely, let's look at the biblical worldview of nurture, admonition, and fear. The Bible is crystal clear on sin, rebellion, and corporal punishment. "Folly is bound up in the heart of a child," King Solomon said, "and the rod of correction will drive it out." Proper biblical correction is swift, meaningful, and preserving of the relationship. Additionally, the Bible is also clear on the natural existence of hierarchies. The parent is in charge of the child. The husband is in charge of the home. God is in charge of the world. The child is not in charge of any of these domains. As part of the "gentle" childrearing movement, the word "fear" has been softly and cautiously translated into "respect" in the verses where we are told to fear God, that the fear of the Lord is the beginning of wisdom. I remember being taught in school that this word "fear" just means respect. Now, it can mean reverence, but not always. Reverence doesn't make as much sense when you consider Matthew 10:28, where Jesus said that we are not to fear man, who can harm only the body, but instead to fear God, who can throw both body and soul into hell. The word here, *phobeo,* is used in other scenarios like Matthew 2:22, when Joseph learned of the rise of an evil ruler threatening his safe passage; in Luke 1:30, when Mary is told she will have a supernatural implantation of a human being in her womb; in John 6:19, when the disciples saw Jesus walking toward them on the water and thought he was a ghost. Did they have "great respect" for the creature they thought was about to attack them on the waters? Not likely. News flash: The word *fear* often means, well, *fear*.

If you've ingested any of these toxic trainings, consider refocusing with the only known antidote: a healthy dose of the word of truth. And in the places where your existing worldview contradicts the Bible, ask God to help you, to mold you, to shape you into his image. Parents who have been raised in the "like" culture of social media will naturally want their children to like them. But your children won't always like you your decisions; they won't always understand your logic or your actions. Your ways are higher than their ways. That why you're the parent. They are called to respect you and love you biblically, but in the moment, sometimes the correction hurts.

In what is perhaps one of the most famous parenting verses in all of scripture, King Solomon tells parents to "train up a child in the way he should go, and even when he is old, he will not depart from it." Founded on the Abrahamic covenant, the concept here involved dedicated teaching in "the way," meaning a moral orientation that points children to a right relationship with God. Deuteronomy 6:6-9 makes it clear that this investment comes through time and an intentional focus on the content of our conversation (as well as nurture and discipline, of course), Social science research shows that a child's worldview is developed by age 13, roughly by the age of junior high. That means their lens on life is fashioned mainly by those who pour into them from ages 0-12. Every day, every hour, our children are confronted with a system of teachings that quite literally "trains them up," not in the way of the Lord, but in the ways of the world. Recently, parents in our city celebrated a perceived victory from the government school system, a postponement on certain medical mandates. But, friends, this one temporary change does not alter the trajectory of the classroom content! Even if children aren't being inoculated, they are still being indoctrinated. Even if they aren't being masked, they are still ingesting Marxism, evolution, CRT. It's almost as if the system uses a form of virtue signaling to garner the trust of the public. "See, you can trust us now. We stopped one of the twelve toxic traits!" Parents, if we are to turn the tide on the most atheist generation in the history of our nation, it starts with us and our willingness to invest in our children. Our actions (or lack thereof) today will determine the course of our nation tomorrow. Discipline's death sentence will be based on our parental judgment.

We've talked before about the generational pendulum swing, how each successive generation responds in a sometimes overly dramatic fashion to the needs and failures of the previous generation, like Builders hoarding useless items because their parents went through the Great Depression and lost everything, or GenXers creating work-life balance because their Boomer parents were always working, and GenXers wanted relationship more than the material possessions their parent thought were the driving force of happiness and stability in a home. These swings are a natural part of the growth and development of individuals, of families, of nations. There is a unique dichotomy in this pendulum swing today, with some men feeling like they need to be home with the kids more and some feeling like they need to model the world of work more. We really are still figuring ourselves out as individuals and as a nation, but this topic of training and the dad differential is of vital concern right now. The toxic wave of anti-male teachings flooding the public system has turned even some of our most ardent, androgen-infused humans into powder puffs.

There is most certainly a reigning confusion about the workplace in the pendulum swing. When we look at the working models of the past, we see a natural integration of children into the adult world of work. As we talked about earlier with Uri Bronfenbrenner and Lev Vygotsky, parenting was more of a natural discipleship process, a model of scaffolding that was naturally supported by the rhythms of the broader culture. How do we restore the essence of that movement from a cultural perspective without adapting the negative segments of the past that failed to balance the need for individuation? Training needs to be intentional, focused, and oriented toward the values, norms, and culture of the family. For example, a local homeschool family I respect is training up their preteens to run the family business. The son goes on business calls with his dad and watches him interact with other professionals. This is mentorship. This is the model we use at CVCU, getting our students around great leaders, giving them an opportunity to be sharpened by other people in their field, where they can watch and listen and learn from both our successes and our mistakes. This used to be a natural part of the discipleship or apprenticeship component of child-rearing. If you're new to homeschooling, by the way, this is model used by the Institute for Excellence in Writing, that we learn to be great communicators by being around great communicators. We learn to emulate excellent writing by reading the works of excellent writers. It's a macrocosmic view of the mentor-driven model in one subject area, English (check it out at IEW.com).

"We have heard with our ears," Psalm 44 says, "our fathers have told us, what deeds you performed in their days." Our fathers have told us. This means fathers shared the good news of the Bible with their sons. There was a transference of information and, in this verse, wisdom, from the older generations to the younger. One of the saddest experiences I have in working with Christian parents today, in a culture where youth atheism is rampant, is the absence of the dad conversation. More often than I would like to admit on paper, when I ask dads about their spiritual investment in their children they say, "That's just not my personality. Mom is the spiritual one." Or they list off all the other ways their children are probably exposed to biblical teaching. "They go to church, to Awanas, to youth group." And that's great. But dads are taxed with the responsibility of giving testimony to their children. Dads are called to spiritual leadership of the home, to disciple and train up the next generation in the "nurture and admonition" of the Lord. No matter the personality, the age, or the job title, dads carry a mantle of authority and responsibility.

"Oh, Timothy," Paul exhorted, "Guard the deposit (the sacred trust) given to you. Avoid the irreverent babble and contradictions of what is falsely called 'knowledge,' for by professing it some have swerved from the faith." The word knowledge here, *gnosis,* literally means science. A clear and accurate understanding of science is a vital foundation for our mindsets. If we don't understand how we were created, with purposeful design, with vision, with destiny, then we will live a life without purpose, without intention, without vision. Romans 1:20 says that God's nature, his character, is revealed in the natural realm, the created realm. The enemy's plan is to dissect us from that, to segregate us from the light of truth, so that our mindsets shift. Our students need good science, real science, like the lessons taught in Apologia and the Institute for Creation Research.

Former Focus on the Family President Dr. Dobson has said in no uncertain terms that the public schools in California are "indoctrinating students in a godless, anti-Christian agenda disguised in progressive curricula." Christians, he says, must "flee" public schools. Lieutenant Colonel Ray Moore, founder of the Exodus Mandate, adds, "If we don't change the way we do education, we will lose our country." If this seems a bit alarmist, I would encourage you to read over a few of the textbooks chapters in your child's science book, history book, literature book (or now, since literature has been removed, look in the "identity and relationships" book). Look at how history is being taught, how literature is being taught, how writing, creativity, and self-expression is being taught, and compare these values with the ones the Pilgrims brought to our nation. Compare them to your family values. Most importantly, hold them up in the light of scripture, and see how they fare. Is education just accidentally overlooking our Christian heritage, or is it being purposefully dissected it from the annals of history? I think we all know the answer.

Prayer and Bible reading were removed from public schools in 1962 and 1963, clearing the way for Values Clarification to sweep through the system. From there, we quickly spiraled to cases like one in the Third Circuit Court, where judges determined that a first grader who was asked to share his favorite story in class could not read his story of choice because it came from the Bible. Under a similar ruling, a 2nd grader in Palmdale, California was visited at his house by the sheriff after he dared to bring Bible verses to school in his lunch bag to share with his friends on the playground. When Jesus gave his followers the Great Commission, he said that we are to make disciples of all people, baptizing them in the name of the Father, Son, and Holy Spirit, and teaching all people to obey all that he has commanded us to do. But the reality is that we are not even allowed to talk about any members of the trinity in the public sphere now. How can we make disciples if we can't even make conversation?

The Pilgrims held that the Bible was central to educational culture. By contrast, today's state system marginalizes the God of the Bible. A friend of mine wrote a book and was contacted by a local charter school who wanted to use it. "Could you take Washington's prayer out of this book so we can use it?" the charter asked. "Can you write an edition without prayer?" No. Why would they want to rewrite history? Because it changes the paradigm, the mindset, the narrative. The authentic version of the book models Washington as a man of faith. The edited version dissects his faith from his presidential leadership as if it were a cancerous tumor.

Let's return briefly to our overarching question: Who is teaching the children, and what are they being taught? Public schools are prohibited from promoting or observing religious holidays and from permanently displaying religious symbols like the Ten Commandments. These documents and celebrations are outlawed, and this ruling is ironic for two reasons. First, the Ten Commandments form the basis of law in the United States. Applying them will help even nonbelievers become law-abiding citizens. Second, a reminder of the Ten Commandments might actually help kids to learn the form of self-government and personal responsibility that they so desperately need. This is a win-win. However, these highly beneficial addendums are severed by the state. According to the National Education Association, teachers are not allowed to organize or participate in religious activities, including prayer. Teachers can mention all religions with a broad-brush stroke, but they may not show favor to one specific religion over another (oh, unless it's a flag of an anarchist movement. Or the religion of secular humanism. Or New Age teachings. Then that's totally okay). So, in a sense, you can have a form of godliness, but as 2 Timothy 3:5 warns, you will absolutely be required to deny its power. You can talk about Jesus in public school as long as he is presented as equal in power to Buddha, Mohammed, Confucius, Zeus, or Satan. Are you hearing what I'm saying?

In the book of 2 Corinthians 6:14, Paul told the church of Corinth, "Do not be unequally yoked with an unbeliever, for what partnership has righteousness with lawlessness? What fellowship has light with darkness?" These mandates of separation, removing the religious from the common, make people feel like we are offering some utopian, non-partisan approach to education. This is one of the great deceptions. We are protecting individual rights and freedoms, absolutely. But the challenge is that you can't teach in a vacuum. If, truly, what was being taught in the system was not an adherence to any religion, any "sectarian" point of view, as the state likes to term it, then why not just fly the American flag instead of the rainbow flag? Why the inclusion of aggressive sexual education agenda? Why the constant lobbying for alternative lifestyles? Because every school, every district, is selling a worldview, and more often than not, that worldview is not congruent with the worldview of the public that school serves.

If you went to public school 20 or 30 years ago and find yourself thinking, "Well, it wasn't that bad back then," you're absolutely right. It wasn't as bad. The seeds of these toxic traits were just starting to take root. The system has grown progressively darker over the last 20 years. Go to SaveCalifornia.com to see some of the examples of the sexual "education" and experimentation agenda in California, even in elementary school. It is alarming, sobering, grievous. We can say, "Well, no weapon formed against me will prosper." True, but if we are standing knowingly, willingly, in front of the firing squad, we are asking for trouble. If we are throwing a child into the deep end of the shark-infested waters and expecting him to swim (or worse, to convert all the sharks), we are fooling no one but ourselves. When the devil tempted Jesus, audaciously quoting Psalm 91:11 to the son of God, he told Jesus to throw himself off the cliff because God would send angels to his rescue. What did Jesus say in response? Do not put the Lord your God to the test.

"Blessed is the man who walks not in the council of the ungodly," Psalm 1:1 reminds us. What does it mean to walk in the council of the ungodly? It means we take their advice, we listen to their teaching, we sit at their feet. Friends, this is what our children are doing every day in the public school system. They are walking in the council of the ungodly. Let's look at the fruit, the impact, that post-Christian education is having on the culture. According to the National Alliance on Mental Illness, GenZs have "crisis of mental health," including anxiety, depression, suicide ideation, self-injury, and a crippling fear of failure. According to the *Journal of Pediatrics*, almost 60,000 girls between the ages of 10-18 tried to poison themselves in 2018. Well-adjusted, happy 10 year olds don't try to poison themselves on purpose. The Center for Disease Control says teen STD rates in the US are running at 8,000 a day, 3 million a year. Add to this the tragedy of 57 million abortions globally each year (half of the world's total death count from all causes—*if* we counted abortion as death—112 million lives). We will talk about this more in Chapter 13. And, as we've noted more than a few times, GenZs are the most atheist, unchurched, disconnected, confused generation in the history of our nation. Again, the top reasons for their atheism should concern us deeply: They can't believe a loving God would allow evil and pain, and they believe science and the Bible contradict. The fears of the Pilgrims have been realized: We now have a biblically illiterate generation.

In his Farewell Address published in the *American Daily Advertiser* in 1796, George Washington warned the American people of the dangers of dissecting biblical principles from "Reason and experience both forbid us to expect that national morality can prevail in exclusion of religious principle." It is impossible to govern the world without God and the Bible. And it is impossible to raise a biblically literate generation when the Bible is forcibly removed from the public sphere and notably absent in the conversations and study life of the home culture. These gaping holes in content leave behind gaping holes in character. If we are to counteract the cultural death of discipline, it must be through the access point of spiritual renewal. Paul told Timothy to observe his beliefs and behaviors, as they would influence his own life as well as the lives of those around him: "Watch your life and doctrine closely. Persevere in them, because if you do, you will save both yourself and your hearers."

King Solomon said, "These teachings are the way to life." A return to biblical literacy, to family solidarity, to the anchor of truth and moral absolutes—this is our pathway to peace, to restoration. The very last verse in the book of Malachi says that God is sending the spirit of Elijah to restore the hearts of the fathers to the children and the children to the fathers or else he will strike the land with a curse. It's time to right that wrong, to break off that curse. Truly, the most anxious, depressed, atheist generation in the history of our nation desperately needs redeeming from the curse. Lord, thank you that you are thawing out the hearts of distracted, disconnected parents right now. Thank you that you are bringing restoration to a fatherless generation. Parents, let's make sure we are the ones who are training and discipling our kids to be self-governing, productive, followers of Jesus. It's going to take intentionality, time, courage, and hope. It's going to take difficult conversations. It's going to take separating ourselves from the council of the ungodly and leaning into the wisdom of scripture. Let's do whatever it takes, mom and dad. The next generation desperately needs resurrection from the death of discipline.

CHAPTER THIRTEEN

Toxic Trait #9: Embedded Evolution and Radical Racism

"Learn not the way of the nations," Jeremiah 10:1 says, "for the customs of the people are vanity." We don't hear the word *vanity* much in common culture today. The word vain, *hebel,* means empty, unsatisfactory. Certainly, we have all met people who typify this adjective, whose appearance may be radiant but whose minds are vacant. The "customs of the people" means their manner, their statute, their ordinance. The vacant-minded not only model their own mental vacancy and disconnect from logical, critical thinking; they expect others to bow to their ordinances, their statutes, as well.

However, this is not the intended path of the Christian. Believers are to walk in the ancient path, the eternal highway. Philippians 3:16 says that we are to walk by the same rule and mind, pay attention to, what is of greatest importance, explained in verse 14 as pressing on toward the mark for the prize of the high calling of God in Christ Jesus. Galatians 5:25 says that we are to walk in the spirit. As parents and leaders and concerned citizens of this great nation, we must pay careful attention today to any "ways of the nations" that may be trying to encroach on our beliefs or behaviors. Instead, we must resist the customs and vanities of this world, walk in the spirit, and keep our eye focused on the prize of the high calling that propels us onward.

One such work of vanity is a subversive teaching that is no stranger to the American education system. In fact, through lectures, textbooks, museum displays, even state standardized testing, the gospel of evolution has been poisoning the waters of America's education system for over 50 years. Evolution is the original gangster of the rebel public classroom, one of the very first markers of religious dissent that now carries the record for the longest running cultural influence in the public school classroom.

Parents fought with great energy and vigor the first few weeks of evolution's school board acceptance in 1968, when the theory began burrowing its roots into the classroom culture of our great nation. That year, when the US Supreme Court overturned the laws that had previously banned the teaching of evolution, parents expressed their dissatisfaction to the school boards. They made phone calls. They stomped their Birkenstocks (it was the 60s). They talked to local newspapers about their dissatisfaction concerning the swift and aggressive change from creationism to evolution.

But gradually, oh so gradually, parents began to step back, to reassure themselves that maybe the teaching of evolution wouldn't make that much of a negative impact on their children. For awhile, both creationism and evolution shared a spotlight in many schools, but in 1987, the Supreme Court ruled that giving equal time to evolution and creationism was unconstitutional. Since that time, evolution has been taught authoritatively as fact, virtually uncontested, on the impressionable grounds of the public school classroom. And as with the other traits, we now see the fruit of that educational toxicity evidenced in the generational beliefs and behaviors of the youngest students.

Honestly, though, mom and dad, this probably doesn't surprise you, right? We all know that evolution is being taught and has been taught as fact in America's public school system for the vast majority of our lives. We accept it as the norm. We tell ourselves that we will explain the differences to our kids. We convince ourselves that our children will somehow reflect rather than absorb this anti-creation ideology that is so lucidly at odds with the Genesis account of creation. When we started our first "reluctant homeschooler" support campuses, one of the striking behaviors we saw in the classroom was that students as young as 7 could not wrap their heads around the idea of creationism being "real" science.

As they read Apologia science textbooks aloud, as the teachers tried in vain to convince the children that the Bible was real, these very young, very impressionable students from Christian homes wrestled with the concept of being created as a human instead of a monkey. As second graders, most of these children had only been in public school for two years, four years if they attended preschool, but already, they had a fully formed worldview on evolution over creationism. Parents, we must remind ourselves of the importance of this topic. Do you remember the number two reason that today's youngest generation says they don't believe in God? Because, they say, "science and the Bible contradict." Hmmm. I wonder where they came up with that idea.

On this subject, I interviewed a specialist in the field, Dr. Brian Thomas, a paleobiochemist with the Institute for Creation Research in Dallas, Texas. He holds a Ph.D. in paleobiochemistry and a Master's degree in biotechnology and is a science writer, editor, and research associate for the Institute for Creation Research (as well as a professor at CVCU). He is the author of several books including *Dinosaurs and the Bible, Creation Basics and Beyond,* and *Ancient and Fossil Bone Collagen Remnants.* He is passionate about helping the next generation think critically and scientifically about God's design of the created realm, and you can learn more about his research and writings at ICR.org.

As a paleobiochemist, one of his specializations is analyzing the tissue of recently excavated dinosaur bones and assessing the findings in the light of creationism. On the manipulation of the meaning of science, Dr. Thomas explains, "When people say science, they do not mean observable, measurable, repeatable, like actual science. They mean science as the story of evolution." This calls for discipleship and apologetics-oriented conversations, he says. "We need to train ourselves and our kids how to think about the difference between storytelling and actual science." Every area of culture is affected, Dr. Thomas says, when we supplant the historical accuracy of Scripture with pop-culture pseudo science.

Dr. Thomas recently took a group of our CVCU students on a Flood-based tour of the Grand Canyon, which means the tour centered on assessing the physiological evidence that underscores the existence of a catastrophic, worldwide flood. Now, I am not the type of person who needed proof in the created realm, as even from childhood, I saw in the beauty of the natural world the character and nature of the God I did not yet know. But seeing the evidence of Noah's Flood in the Grand Canyon was quite an extraordinary experience, both for me and for my students.

As I stood on the canyon floor, looking out across a 277-mile chasm flanked by ancient rock walls, I marveled at God's ability to trade beauty for ashes, hope for despair, beauty for catastrophe. The Grand Canyon is the result of a global catastrophic flood designed to wipe out humanity, and yet the majestic presence left behind is a testimony to both God's sovereignty and his grace. It's a Romans 1:20 showcase: God's very character is perfectly exemplified in the work of his creation so that we are without excuse.

This is a difficult concept for our youngest generations to understand because the lack of parental discipline and biblical literacy have left them profoundly confused. Remember, the most common reason GenZ say they don't believe in God is because of the existence of suffering, of pain—which most certainly took place in the tsunami of Noah's flood. They don't believe a good God would allow for the existence of bad thoughts, bad people, bad experiences. They have had almost no teaching on free will.

The lack of biblical foundations from childhood have left America's children floundering and fault-finding, much like the well-known actor who said she believed in God until she actually read in the Bible that he was a jealous God. That aspect of God's character personally offended her, so she determined to rewrite his nature into something that she could respect, something more palatable to her Hollywood tastes. Like the Israelite's waiting for Moses's return, she created her own god. However, when children are taught the truth from childhood, their worldview is fashioned around the truth of Scripture rather than the arrogance and cynicism of adulthood. In the light of truth, we are clearly able to see his nature: He trades our sin, our darkness, our despair for his glory, his majesty, his beauty, his perfection. And that element of exchange is perfectly exemplified in the Grand Canyon.

When a group of elementary school students fresh out of public school got to meet Dr. Thomas, a "real live dinosaur expert," they were so engaged that we had to extend the lecture time just so he had the opportunity to answer all of their many questions. Many of them had already been taught uncontested evolutionary theory for five, six, seven years—some for as long as a decade. It takes months to unlearn the teachings even for elementary school students, who kept returning incredulously to the idea that God could have made them *ex nihilo*, out of nothing. With rare exception, their ten-year-old brains continued to cling to an imagined connection with distant primate relatives.

Why does it matter? Because beginnings matter. Origins matter. Genesis matters. Since the day evolution took root in the public school classroom, students have been incessantly indoctrinated in micro-evolutionary theory, convincing them their past has no purpose and their future has no hope. If we don't believe the creation account, despite the overwhelming natural and theological evidence for its legitimacy, that leaves the remaining 65 books of the Bible stacked on a faulty foundation. This shift is actually quite a shocking reversal from the laws on the books just forty years prior to that moment of evolutionary unleashing in 1968. On March 13, 1925, the state of Tennessee enacted a law called the Butler Act. This act *prohibited* public universities and K to 12 schools from *denying* the biblical account of mankind's origin. Let me say that again.

The law *prohibited* the teaching of evolution because of its contrast with biblical origins. But, in the midst of the Values Clarification Movement, the law was repealed, and evolutionary theory has been preached as fact in public schools and universities across America with a ferocity ever since. Our origins matter, and what students are taught to believe about themselves and their purposes on this planet dramatically impacts the way they behave toward themselves and others.

But evolution is just one of the many toxic traits being proffered by today's public school system. In 2009, I wrote a book called *Emerge* where I documented the impact of media voices on identity formation. My graduate school research at Regent University had opened my eyes to the insidious influence of media on the mind and heart. Through songs and news and social media, these modern "false prophets" declare their version of truth. The end result was the culmination of false esteem that undermined an authentic sense of self and segregated ages from one another, robbing our culture of the generational interdependence that was intended to provide both scaffolding and purpose at every age and stage.

And this divisiveness has continued in one of today's hottest topics: Critical Race Theory. CRT is getting a lot of new press today, but the concept itself is not new. It's been a featured philosophy under several different monikers over the last five decades. Postman was already talking about it in 1996 in *The End of Education.* It has flown under the radar in many unique titles, but the final analysis is always the same: There is one class of people who are obsessive oppressors and one class of people who are the forever-victims. From these two vantage points, CRT continues to segregate mass segments of society and pit them against each other.

Moms and dads across the country are up in arms right now over CRT and its poisonous offspring, common core and the culture of victimhood. But, parents, the CRT train left the station five decades ago. To call schools "public" is a misrepresentation of the driver, the captain. The public is not steering this ship, friends. The government school system is driven by a larger, darker agenda that has nothing to do what you or I want as parents. Instead, government monopoly schools continue their work of chipping away at traditional values. We invited CRT specialist Kevin McGary to speak to our students at CVCU (catch the follow-up interview on my podcast, The Communication Architect). As he says, the proponents of Critical Race Theory are "fusing a demonic gospel with the purity of the Gospel of Jesus Christ." The answer to this cultural crisis? "We have to get reacquainted with the word of God."

When his daughter was accepted into a college that he knew had the propensity for teaching these and other falsehoods, McGary and his wife determined to called their daughter *every single day* to talk through the classes and give an opportunity for deprogramming any false teachings that might have planted a seed in their daughter's heart. This uncommon level of commitment, along with a childhood full of training in biblical literacy, kept their daughter protected from the onslaught of anti-Christian teachings that came against her like arrows every day.

"Discipleship," McGary notes, "is earnestly and sincerely sharing your life with another brother or sister. But you must begin in your own household." If we don't get this right in the home, then we won't get it right in the church, and if we don't get it right in the church, we won't get it right in the culture. Everything hinges on our ability to communicate the truth of God's word to the next generation. If we are distracted by lesser things, we will lose the larger battle. Let me say that again, parents: If we are distracted by lesser things, we will lose the larger battle.

It's time to put our finger on the pulse of the culture and proclaim the truth to the nations and generations. This requires a compelling combination of grace and truth, of compassion and straight-up fire. Jeremiah is often called the weeping prophet because his heart was so broken over the rebellion of his people. But he didn't just cry in his closet about them. He also spoke the truth to them.

When the people complained that they felt like God had deserted them, Jeremiah reminded them over and over that their greed, their slander, their deceit, and their refusal to know God was what was keeping them bound, oppressed, broken, sick, fruitless. Their actions had consequences. Their health was not restored because they perpetually consulted the wrong physician. They preferred false prophets to the truth of God's word. "They bend their tongue like a bow; falsehood and not truth has grown strong in the land; for they proceed from evil to evil," Jeremiah 9:3 says. "They have taught their tongue to speak lies…Heaping oppression upon oppression and deceit upon deceit, they refuse to know me, declares the Lord."

How did an entire nation turn from truth to lies? "Behold, the lying pen of the scribes…the wise man shall be put to shame," Jeremiah says. "Behold, they have rejected the word of the Lord, so what wisdom is in them?" When national leaders, celebrities, denominations, or systemic influencers like monopoly school systems reject the word of God, exchanging it for a lie, the trickle-down effect is sure and swift.

In just under six decades since the Bible was removed from the US school system, we now have the most atheist generation in the history of our nation. Again, the leaders have rejected true wisdom, so what level of wisdom is left? We must all be careful today not to sip from the fount of folly that is so ever-present in modern culture. The voice of godless prophets calls out like a siren from the airwaves day and night.

Just as Jeremiah warned his people, those who reject the truth of God's word will bear the fruit of that folly and rebellion. Like Jeremiah, we are called to speak the truth that will set them free. As McGary notes, "We must develop and maintain discipleship relationships and networks, and we must hold our government leaders accountable" for the lies being tolerated in the school system.

In Jeremiah 23, these false prophets are described in contrast to true prophets: "They speak visions of their own minds, not from the mouth of the Lord. They say continually to those who despise the word of the Lord, 'it shall be well with you,' and to everyone who stubbornly follows his own heart, they say 'no disaster shall come upon you.'"

Don't we hear this all the time? It's for your safety. Just trust the system. Listen the experts. They know best. It will be well with you if you follow our vision, our way, our agenda. No, parents, these experts are false prophets! They don't know what is best for your child. They don't love your children more than you do. And most importantly, you—not they—have been given the mantle of authority in your child's life.

Who among you, the prophet asks, has stood in the council of the Lord? "If they had stood in my council," verse 22 says, "then they would have proclaimed my words to my people, and they would have turned them from their evil ways, and from the evil of their deeds." The false prophets of the world's system take council together with the spirit of secular humanism in the public school system, and they proclaim the same drivel, the same doctrine, the same lies. But God says his word is "like a fire…like a hammer that breaks the rock in pieces." The truth of God's word confounds the lies of the modern day prophets of secular education, and it's our responsibility to be the carriers of that word to the broken and confused generation that has been swept away by these false prophets of the day.

If you're a parent, make disciples, starting at home. If you're a young adult, start by leading yourself well. Train your mind, master your emotions, guard your heart. Reach out to someone in your circle who can mentor and disciple you, and then pour out everything you learn to someone younger than you. Our children need to hear the truth that will set them free. We have to break off this public school fruit of peer-orientation that has kept our youngest generations living under a ceiling of immaturity and dysfunction. They will continue to be bound by the victim-versus-oppressor mindset preached by the false prophets of critical race theory until we the people, we the parents, step up.

When Jeremiah was persecuted by Pashur the priest, placed in the stocks all night for boldly speaking truth, he momentarily considered embracing the ease of silence, but he says it's impossible because the word of God is like a fire in his bones. He can't hold it back. "If I say I will not mention him or speak any more in his name, there is in my heart as it were a burning fire shut up in my bones," Jeremiah says. "I'm weary with holding it in, and I cannot."

How about you? Is the word of truth a fire, a flood, a radiant, undimmable, unstoppable force inside of you? Do you feel compelled to speak up and let that river of truth wash over a generation that desperately needs to hear the good news? There's someone waiting on the other side of your obedience, friend. God's word will prevail. It will accomplish his desire. On our Grand Canyon trip, two of our team members came across a hiker alone in the wilderness who was dying of kidney failure as the dark of night set it. Though they gave him practical help, they also provided him a more vital lifeline: They led him in the prayer of salvation right there on the canyon floor. In the same way, there are souls all around us dying in the darkness of the cultural canyon, confused and alone in the public school wilderness. It's our job to keep watch, to speak up, and to set the captives free.

The teaching of evolution embedded in curricula as fact in the public school system for almost 60 years how has trained up four generations with increasingly persuasive appeals to believe that they have no purpose, no direction, no hope. There is no ultimate meaning in life, no higher reason for existing. This leaves students feeling unanchored, unmoored from the foundations of faith that, in the past, helped to provide a sense of direction and vision. A typical public school science textbook today, for example, etches its philosophy of hopelessness on the young human psyche by denying the direct, intelligent design of living systems. By contrast, curricula like Apologia and Institute for Creation Research show the scientific foundations for intentional design in DNA, for even our likes and dislikes, our genetic predispositions. Science should be inspiring. Nature is a teacher. King Solomon told us to look at the natural world and learn a lesson of application to humanity. But embedded evolutionary theory has effectively disabled the foundations of faith in the current generation.

As if functioning in a diabolical partnership, just as evolution has spawned a division between humans and the God of the universe, the teaching of radical racism has birthed a new level of division and distrust amongst students. A generation that was once the least likely in history to walk in racial division, a generation who embodied Dr. King's words, that a person should be judged by the character of their heart and not by the color of their skin, is now a generation caught in the undertow of divisiveness taught by the preachers of CRT. We are, as Ken Ham once put it, one race, one blood. The human race desperately needs carriers of unity and not division in order to sustain humanity's ultimate mission. The teaching of CRT is one of many subversive curricula elements designed to create division, to fracture unity. For together, we accomplish more. We dream bigger. We go further. Limiting our human potential by limiting our relational resources is a strategy of destruction marked by the characteristically insidious infiltration of the one who comes to steal, to kill, and to destroy.

As Gatto says, "Government monopoly schools are structurally unreformable." They are doing exactly what they were designed to do, to create cogs in a machine, to dull our academic curiosity, to segregate children from intergenerational influence, and to indoctrinate the next generation in a Marxist belief system. From decades of evolutionary indoctrination to modern twists on Critical Race Theory, today's public schools are leading a generation astray. Parents, we don't need to mend them; we need to end them. It's time for a public school exit.

CHAPTER FOURTEEN

Toxic Trait #10: Desensitized and Devalued

As I mentioned in the first chapter, my mom got pregnant with me as a teenager. She faced many dramatic challenges and lived an isolated life separate from mine until her latter years, but I am forever grateful for an extraordinarily courageous decision she made: She did not abort me. She was 17 years old, a senior in high school, and I'm sure there was tremendous pressure on every side, from her family, from her friends, and, of course, from the father—who just so happened to be her high school science teacher. Abortion was already a prevalent conversation topic in the newly post-Christian culture: Within a year of my mom getting pregnant with me, Norma McCorvey, the infamous Jane Roe, would bring her case to the state of Texas, demanding the right to abort her child. This was the beginning of the cultural genocide, and thousands upon thousands of children, sobering numbers of lives that we will unpack momentarily, have been taken since that moment.

It should be no surprise to anyone reading this book that one of the ten toxic traits of the public school system is a devaluing of the oldest old and the youngest young, which is systematically accomplished not only through generational segregation, but also through the direct and coercive pro-abortion rhetoric being taught in the public system. As a grateful human who was not aborted, and as a parent invested in the health and well-being of the next generation, I recognize the hand of the enemy in today's public school system with regard to the devaluing of life. It is promoted both through the applauding of abortion and the general desensitization toward the value and dignity of a human life at any age. What is often overlooked, though, is that abortion is a symptom of a larger cause, an underlying issue that desperately demands healthy public dialogue. It's almost as if we've somehow forgotten that abortion comes from pregnancy, which, in the vast majority of cases, stems from a willful decision to engage in sexual intimacy outside the context of marriage. These are the very behaviors being promoted and celebrated in the public school system! But instead of focusing on this first issue as a culture, instead of helping men become protectors instead of predators, instead of helping women find their value and worth in their identity in Christ instead of Hollywood's hypersexual culture, the public dialogue is clouded by smokescreens.

There has been a great deal of public press on abortion in recent years. On January 23, 2019, New York Governor Andrew Cuomo signed into law a bill that legalized abortion up to the time of birth (and, in some cases, after birth). The legislation, called the Reproductive Health Act, allowed not only for late-term abortion but also for non-doctors to perform abortions for any reason, including "age, economic, social, and emotional factors," according to the New York Right to Life Association. Less than a month later, the Senate voted down a bill that would require doctors to provide medical care to a child who survived an attempted abortion. The Born-Alive Abortion Survivors Protection Act would have mandated that doctors would care for the surviving baby as they would any child of that "gestational age," but according the *Washington Post,* the bill was voted out 53 to 44. Then-President Trump tweeted that this was a murderous position akin to "executing babies after birth" and that the decision would be "remembered as one of the most shocking votes in the history of Congress." After the defeat, the bill's author asked the Senate floor a piercing question: "Are we now a nation that tolerates infanticide?"

In contrast to RHA's terminology and the defeat of the Born-Alive bill, a number of states then introduced dialogue surrounding the "Heartbeat Bill," first introduced the previous year by Iowa Governor Kim Reynolds. In 2018, she asked on National Public Radio, "If death is determined when a heart stops beating, then doesn't a beating heart indicate life?" Questions and accusations quickly ensued, with a few key issues emerging. Central to the emerging themes was the absence of "the recognition of personhood" for the unborn. When, legislators asked, is an unborn child considered to be human? And how do we categorize the loss of life if the life isn't human? This crass cultural conversation could only be possible after decades of devaluing paved the way for this manslaughter of millions. It could only be possible through the daily indoctrination, year after year, that emanates from public school classrooms across the nation. These conversations deny the individual design and sanctity of human life and instead defend arguments like "my body, my choice," political dogmas that offer protection to only one of the bodies within the abortion equation. Let's look at the significance of the impact and the definitions on a statistical, scientific, and spiritual level.

In 2016, the University of North Carolina, Chapel Hill conducted a groundbreaking study on the rate of death by abortion by ethnicity titled, "Induced Abortion, Mortality, and the Conduct of Science." Three important findings emerged. First, abortion disproportionally destroys the lives of Black and Hispanic babies in the US. Second, and the focal point of the study, abortion is not listed as a "cause of death," nor are the aborted recognized with a certificate of death. More on this in a moment. And third, coupled with data from the World Health Organization, the findings show that abortion is the leading cause of death over all other conditions, with 56 million abortions worldwide per year. Let me say that again. Abortion is the leading cause of death, globally, with 56 million abortions per year. To put this in perspective, WHO says heart disease kills about 9 million people worldwide per year, strokes kill 6 million, chronic obstructive pulmonary disease 3 million, lung cancer 1.7 million and diabetes 1.6 million. About 140 million babies are born each day around the world, 385,000 per day.

Let's compare those leading numbers once again: The leading killer, heart disease, takes 9 million lives per year, while abortion takes *56 million lives per year*. According to the World Health Organization's "Key Facts on Induced Abortion Worldwide," in 2016, there were 56.9 million deaths worldwide AND there were another 56 million abortions worldwide per year. This means that of the average 112 million deaths per year worldwide, a staggering 50% of those are from abortion.

Now that we have a sense of the quantifiable impact of abortion, let's look at the second finding mentioned in the study, the "cause of death" delineation. In the UNC report, the authors point out that there is "no credible scientific opposition to the fact that a genetically distinct human life begins at conception and that an induced abortion is a death. Yet abortion is not reported as a cause of death in the US vital statistics system." These mortality patterns, the authors go on to say, have "profound implications for public policy." According to the report, IF death by abortion by ethnicity were reported as a cause of death in US vital statistics, the deaths would be categorized as follows: 64% of Hispanics die from abortion in America; 61% of Blacks die from abortion in America; and 16% of Whites die from abortion in America. As the UNC study authors note, "As a cause of death, we found abortion to be highly consequential, with large racial and ethnic disparities." In fact, Bishop EW Jackson told CNS

News that he was deeply disturbed by the Center for Disease Control's data on abortions and that in any other arena of life, that type of disparity "would be considered as proof of racism."

Again, this idea that abortion is a "leading cause of death" has been vehemently disputed in the mainstream media, but it's important to note that the dispute has absolutely nothing to do with the accuracy of the numbers. Rather, the argument purportedly concerns a fuzzy line of semantics. Abortion is not reported as a cause of death because the mainstream medical community does not define "personhood" until birth, and this, the UNC report summarizes, is somewhat of a lie of omission: "The science community is not appropriately engaged in this crucial public health problem…the logical and most cost-effective way to achieve that goal is to formally consider abortion as a reportable death," the report notes. *"The exclusion of abortion as a cause of death, in spite of conclusive science to the contrary… may be the ultimate example of science denial"* (italics mine).

Heather Boonstra, the director of public policy for the Guttmacher Institute, says that abortion is not listed as a cause of death because it is a "medical process," not a departure from the realm of the living: "Abortion is a legal, constitutionally protected medical procedure in the United States. It's not considered a cause of death by CDC, WHO, and other leading authorities." This is the same tune that emanates from the public school classroom, day in and day out. LA journalist Bethania Palma summarizes these thoughts by noting the implication of the pseudo-political tone of the word "death": "Stating that abortion is the leading cause of death worldwide (as opposed to a medical procedure) is a problematic pronouncement, because *that stance takes a political position, one which is at odds with the scientific/medical world. The medical community does not confer personhood upon fetuses that are not viable outside the womb"* (italics mine). Thus, in short, though we do have 56 million abortions occurring worldwide every year, the lives being taken are not considered "human" by public schools or the scientists who graduated from these schools and now create our nation's public policy. In the secular system, there is currently no conference of personhood on a child prior to birth. In school, students are taught that a baby inside the womb is simply an unformed blob of tissue. The devaluing of life is a subtle—and here, not so subtle—attack on the inherent value of a child created in the image of God. In contrast to the mainstream science definition, The American College of Pediatricians says it wholeheartedly defines life and personhood not only prior to birth but from the moment of conception:

> "The ACP concurs with the body of scientific evidence that corroborates that a unique human life starts when the sperm and egg bind to each other in a process of fusion of their respective membranes and a single hybrid cell called a zygote, on one-celled embryo, is created. As physicians dedicated both scientific truth and to the Hippocratic tradition, the College values all human lives equally from the moment of conception (fertilization) until natural death. Consistent with its mission to enable all children to reach their optimal physical and emotional health and well being the College, therefore, opposes active measures that would prematurely end the life of any child at any stage of development from conception to natural death."

This power quote brings us to the definition of life and personhood. Scientifically, the basis for distinguishing the differences in cell types has two criteria: cell composition and cell behavior. But this scientific model is not taught in the public school classroom, not as it relates to the practical and pragmatic applications of abortion and not as it relates to the field of science in general! Instead, science has become a catch-all classroom filler for teachings on gender fluidity and the practices of promoting perversion. But listen to the actual, non-political science: These are "universally agreed upon definitions," Dr. Maureen Condic notes in the journal *Human Life International*. "Human embryos from the zygote stage forward," she says, "show uniquely integrated, organismal behavior that is unlike the behavior or mere human cells...the cells do not 'generate' the embryo...they are produced by the embryo as it directs its own development to more mature stages of human life. *This organized, coordinated behavior of the embryo is the defining characteristic of a human organism*" (italics mine).

Condic goes on to say that "the conclusion that human life begins at sperm-egg fusion is uncontested, objective, based on the universally accepted scientific method of distinguishing different cell types from each other" and on ample scientific evidence (thousands of independent, peer-reviewed publications). "Moreover, she notes, "it is entirely independent of any specific ethical, moral, political, or religious view of human life or of human embryos. ...a neutral examination of the evidence... *unequivocally indicates that human embryos from the one-cell stage forward are indeed living individuals of the human species; i.e., human beings*" (italics mine). In both the ACP's definition and Condic's findings, we see a common denominator, a defining characteristic for life: the cell's composition and behavior. From the very first cell of life, prior to any cellular multiplication, the zygote itself drives the process of growth and development. All reputable parties agree that pregnancy begins at conception, but the school system, like many other government institutions, fails to mention these well-established foundations of the beginning of personhood. As a result, the rate of abortion amongst our youngest citizens is extraordinary, as are the emotional and physiological consequences. In 2019, according to the Department of Health and Human Services, 90.5% of teen births occurred outside of a marriage relationship. About 350,000 US teens under the age of 18 become pregnant every year, with 82%

of these pregnancies being "unintended." Of these, 14% end in miscarriage, and 31% end in abortion. The question that falls on deaf ears in the public school classroom is that of personhood: Is the aborted baby a human?

Judeo-Christian literature is replete with examples of personhood prior to birth: In Genesis 25:21, Rebekah feels her twins, Jacob and Esau, struggling within her. She inquires of the Lord as to why they are wrestling around, and he tells her that two nations are in her womb grappling with one another. The twins wrestled in the womb for leadership, and, in fact, Jacob came out holding his brother's heel, an action he had to initiate prior to his departure from the womb. These babies had purpose and destiny, and certainly the qualities of humanness, before birth. Hosea 12:3 says of Jacob, "in the womb he took his brother by the heel," and as an adult he wrestled with God. John the Baptist not only leapt but "leapt for joy" in his mother's womb when he was greeted in utero by the presence of Mary, who was carrying Jesus in her womb, but Luke 1:15 also says that John was filled with the Holy Spirit "even from his mother's womb." David says in Psalm 22:10, "From my mother's womb, you have been my God," and Psalm 58:3 says the wicked are estranged from the womb; they go astray from birth." These are not just poetic utterances; they are clear examples of the establishment of personhood prior to birth. Isaiah 46:3 says, "Listen to me, O house of Jacob, all the remnant of the house of Israel who have been borne by me from before your birth, carried in the womb."

In these examples, we see the concept of personhood clearly established in utero. From a developmental perspective, even the very first human cell of life, the zygote, contains the DNA, the blueprint design, of a human being's entire development process through the lifespan. This concept, yet unbeknownst to him, underscores King David's proclamation in Psalm 139 that God's eyes saw his unformed body in his mother's womb and that all the days ordained for him were written in his book before one of them came to be. Does the definition of personhood matter? Does the absence of a death certificate or the cataloguing in vital statistics listings matter? Yes. As the UNC report summarizes, "The appropriate role of science is to inform the societal dialogue with objective information...*refusing to acknowledge abortion as a death undermines the role of science and the value of transparency so fundamental to a free society*" (italics mine).

Definitions matter. Our words shape our worlds. When science hides behind semantics and refuses to acknowledge statistics, that same "science" impedes our understanding of the social crises that we desire to help eradicate. The next generation will continue to flounder while schools waiver on the vital nature of our very existence, our purpose, our identity. Information is power. The willful absence of information is manipulation of the truth.

Dr. Martin Luther King is often quoted in the government school system, but just as teachers dissect the prayers of Washington and Lincoln from the history books, so too do they conveniently leave out Dr. King's poignant teachings against abortion. King saw abortion as the disruptor of the dream, saying that his people cannot win if they "are willing to sacrifice the lives of his children for comfort and safety." How can the Dream survive, he asked, "if we murder the children? Every aborted baby is like a slave in the womb of his or her mother. The mother decides the fate." His granddaughter, Dr. Alveda King, says, "if we hear the cry of mercy from the unborn and ignore the suffering of the mothers, then we are signing our own death warrants." Our students have never read these King quotes in their modern history textbooks.

Like many of our current social crises, abortion is a symptoms of a much larger issue, an arena where we have a tremendous opportunity to speak words of life and hope into the next generation. Yet again, the public school classroom creates the perfect storm here by promoting promiscuity, severing parents from the conversation, and then promising to "sweep away" the offspring birthed of that tragic decision! From aggressive sexual education curricula to a lack of parental discipleship, the next generation is desperately lacking in hope, guidance, discipleship. The multiple-partner modality has been celebrated in mainstream media in increasing measure; the vast majority of music, movies, and sitcoms celebrate the "casual sex" relationships that have become the norm for the two youngest generations.

The viral state of abortions, STDs, and suicide rates is indicative of a culture that has lost its sense of value, its personal worth, its connection to the core. In addition to abortion statistics, the US leads the developed world in youth violence, homicide, incarcerations, teen pregnancy, and self -injury. Dealing only with the presenting problem, the end result, is ineffective in the long run. Instead, we have to focus on the root issues: the lack of value, dignity, and self-worth that drive our nation's youth to this place of devaluation and destruction. We have a cultural crisis on our hands, and the 56 million annual abortions are sobering symptoms of a systematic problem. If a Christian parent sends her children away to be discipled in a secular classroom, and that child is "trained up" to believe that abortion is perfectly acceptable because an unborn baby is simply "a blob of tissue," then that child exhibits a worldview not of value and sensitivity but of devaluing, desensitization, and destruction. The student has become like the teacher.

In 2019, California became the first state to require all of its public colleges to provide abortions on all public college and university campuses. Then-governor Jerry Brown demanded that these abortions be provided to students free of charge. In October of 2021, CA became the first state to require its public colleges and universities to offer abortion medication under a law signed by Governor Gavin Newsom. Of course, Planned Parenthood applauded the decision, saying that California must strengthen legal protections for abortions. In response to neighboring Texas imposing stricter ruling on abortions, Gavin Newsom announced that he wanted California to become an abortion "sanctuary state" that would offer abortions to women from other states and "combat misinformation about abortion," even, CalMatters reports, helping cover the costs for the abortion, transportation, lodging, child care, food and lost wages. As if it wasn't bad enough that CA was dragging its own youth down, the state government had to stretch out its talons to the surrounding states. You can't make this content up.

Newsom stressed that he wanted to make sure state schools offer "medically accurate, culturally-relevant and inclusive abortion education" with a focus on data collection that would measure schools effectiveness in "sexual health programs" and the impact that Covid has had on abortion services. The governor and the government schools place an extraordinary focus on the access and availability of abortion to our nation's youngest citizens, which should give any thinking parent great cause for concern. Newsom is joined on his mission by local school boards. In what *Education Week* called the first such school district stance of its kind, the Los Angeles County School Board passed a resolution to "stop the bans" on abortion. *Education Week* called the move "unusual." The LACSD sad that "anti-choice state laws" banning abortion are "a violation of women's freedom and reproductive rights," the district noted. "This is an anti-choice movement that will particularly impact women of color and low-income women," the Los Angeles resolution reads in part. "The district will support legislative advocacy in an attempt to fight back against this unconstitutional attempt to gut *Roe* v. *Wade* and punish women." Ironically, the school board ended its quote with a piercing construct that belies its blindness: "Our children are counting on us to be our absolute best selves."

Did you catch that? "Our children are counting on us," the

district said. Well, let's talk about that, LA County. Which children are you referring to? The children you are literally seeking out and targeting for abortion? Or are you speaking of the children who will carry the burden of grief and guilt as a result of their coerced decision to destroy not one life, but two? By the way, LA's 50 Planned Parenthood centers, conveniently located within walking distance of public school classrooms, will be funded by a $10 million grant from LA County and another $6 million donation from Planned Parenthood. As *Education Week* notes, it's not that school districts don't push political agendas, "but those are generally tackled as they set curriculum and manage schools, not as separate endorsements of belief." That last statement is a powerful reminder that these mindsets and methodologies are at work in the curricular choices, the day-to-day teachings and influences of the classroom culture. And that is perhaps the most dangerous route of influence. As C.S. Lewis quipped, the surest road to hell is the gradual one.

The CA State Constitution requires California to spend 40% of its tax revenue on public schools. Did you catch that statistic, mom and dad? In California, a whopping 40% of our taxes go to fund the public school system. Each public school student receives $17,000 a year, which, by the way, is the average rate of many private, non-government funded schools in our county. The National Center for Education Statistics says that on average, 80% of public school funding goes to salaries and employee benefits. And yet, despite our forced personal funding of these government indoctrination centers, they and their employees continually fail to represent the ideals, interests, or values of the public that they are supposed to be serving.

This coming year, California has a projected surplus of $31 billion dollars. Is our governor planning to spending that money on increasing academic support to rescue the next generation from its pathetic global math and science rankings? Is he spending it on reading programs to pull CA's students up from the sobering rates of illiteracy? According to the World Population Review, California has the lowest literacy rate in the nation, a statistic squarely blamed on the State of California and the Department of Education. No, instead, this surplus will likely continue to fund political programs like Planned Parenthood, further evidence of the government school system taking on decisions and responsibilities that belong to the parent—not to the state. If, as the Associated Press reports, Newsom will be forced to spend at least another $11 billion on public education, we can easily speculate what his agenda will be. As the dedicated driver of the abortion sanctuary state, he will make sure his ungodly agenda is drilled down firmly and fatally into the most populous state in the nation through the unguarded gateways of the public school classrooms.

We've already established the idea that public schools are unreformable, so to expect a government institution to stand up for truth and life would be hopeful, but perhaps naive. Believers are called to defend the rights of the poor and needy, to speak up for those who cannot speak up for themselves, as Proverbs 31 exhorts. We are also called to preach the good news to the poor, to proclaim liberty to the captives and recovery of sight to the blind, to set at liberty those who are oppressed, as Luke 4:18 (and Isaiah 61) remind us. This means we speak up for the unborn, and simultaneously, we care for the wounded, frightened mothers who don't yet realize that the entity within their womb is a living person created in the image of a loving God. The spirit of the Lord is upon us to proclaim the good news, the gospel.

Throughout history, great men and women have responded to cultural crises by allowing a holy discontent to serve as a catalyst for behavioral change. As sociologist Anthony Giddens once remarked, Christianity is a "revolt against the ruling social order of the day." Believers are called to act wisely into the conversation of our culture. In the book *The History of Christianity*, Collins and Price write that throughout history,

Christians being motivated by social ills have made significant progress, from the Salvation Army to the YMCA, even to Sunday School, which was started in the 1800s to address the educational needs of children who had to work 16-hour days Monday to Saturday in unconscionable conditions.

In 1879 D.L. Moody became increasingly frustrated with how isolated seminaries were from the common people, so he worked to train communicators who could carry God's simple message to the masses who needed it (the Moody Bible Institute still bears his name as a legacy of his work). William Wilberforce brought a bill before parliament in 1787 to end the slave trade. In 1833, one month after his death, the House of Commons voted to free the slaves and abolish slavery. Sometimes we plant the seeds and don't see the harvest, but we must plant the seeds all the same—if not for us, for the future generations.

G.I. Williamson writes in the *Westminster Catechism* that most of modern life in society is ruled by the concept of religious neutrality, taking no stand for or against a particular religion. But Christians, he says, are "finally beginning to realize that Christ has been denied" (and, thus, the Great Commission thwarted) "under the innocent-sounding claim of neutrality or tolerance." This, he says, is why Christians must labor together: "to build Christian schools to educate the next generation, to break them free of the indoctrination of neutrality." For the believer, he says, "all spheres of life and activity must manifest open loyalty to Jesus" (p. 203). In 100 years, what will be said of our generation's response to the annual destruction of 56 million lives? Of 50 Planned Parenthood clinics erected on the grounds of Los Angeles County schools? Of 51 million students being shipped off daily to the lowest educational bidder, the public school?

Clearly, the hidden hurt of America's abortion crisis is embedded in a much larger struggle. So, we must begin, as Stephen Covey would have encouraged, with the end in mind.

Using the gifts and talents of writing, speaking, researching, filming, and singing, we must educate the next generation on their value, their inestimable worth, in the sight of God. We must share the accounts of history that remind us of both the hurt and the hope of mankind. We must teach our daughters and our sons to protect what is precious, what is holy, what is pure. We must disciple our children.

We must also be prepared to address the hypersexual hypocrisy flooding the classrooms and the airwaves: from movies to sitcoms to songs, uncommitted relationships are championed and celebrated. The heartbreak of the hookup culture has been normalized, meme-ified. Cause and effect relationships between hookups, disease, and desertion are underrepresented (if they are represented at all) as the exception, not the norm. Mass media, peer dependency, and laissez-faire parental approaches have co-labored to birth a generation of hurting, hopeless, and increasingly isolated young men and women. Giving an unwanted baby up to adoption instead of sacrificing it on the altar of abortion is, of course, the better option. But let's face it, the unwanted baby is still a symptom of a larger issue. Abortion is not the cause; it's the effect. Abortion is the fruit of a hypersexual culture and the classical conditioning of the public school system, including the culture of peers. Let's not forget that behind every stand-alone pregnant woman is a man who has, in one way or another, failed to take responsibility for his actions. Behind every pregnant woman is a man who should have been leading as a husband, a father, but instead has become a chronic cohabitator, a perpetual adolescent—the modern version of a deadbeat dad. Our young men must learn to take their place as protector instead of predator. But this behavior of honor is not taught in the public system.

As I write this chapter, the Christmas season is upon us, and I think of a young girl, carrying a baby under significantly controversial circumstances. Mary was mocked, rejected, and ostracized though she did no wrong to find herself in such an extraordinary situation. The savior of the world was, in a sense, dependent on the recognized sanctity of human life.

Desensitization and the general devaluing of the youngest young and the oldest old will have significant influences on the culture in general. Rejecting both sides of the age spectrum will bear increasingly negative fruit in the lives of all generations. America's children need an education revolution. They need a clear understanding of the sanctity of life, their own as well as others, and they need an older generation to share with them the tremendous worth they carry in God's sight. Of course, these teachings do not come through the government school system. The closest it can approximate is a false sense of esteem that teaches a superficial value in fleeting characteristics like beauty and youth. Instead, the next generation needs an anchor of truth that will carry them firmly into their future without guilt, without fear, without regret. Parents, what we tolerate today, our children will embrace tomorrow.

CHAPTER FIFTEEN

Toxic Trait #11: Manipulated Mindsets

When the religious leaders of the day were offended by Jesus, he noted in John 8 that they sought to kill him because his word found no place in them. "If you abide in my word," he said, "you are truly my disciples, and you will know the truth, and the truth will set you free... Everyone who practices sin is a slave to sin...so if the son sets you free, you are free indeed."

Many students and parents tell us today that they never felt they had the freedom to leave the traditional education sector. All their lives they had absorbed the message that they are incapable of breaking free, trapped in a system, doomed to failure. It is a grandiose, global form of classical conditioning, a malevolent mindset.

What is a mindset, and how is it formed? A mindset is an established set of attitudes or beliefs, and these mindsets are developed through exposure, through an ongoing focus on something we personally place value on or something that is thrust upon us, as in the case of public school students. And out of that mindset will flow our actions. That's the belief-to-behavior pattern. This means that the ideas we hold to, whether these are offenses, fears, or allegiances, these all illuminate what's really in our hearts.

We really don't hear that word "allegiance" very often today. It's typically associated with the school pledge we used to say in class prior to the plague of political correctness that raged through our nation's public schools. We used to pledge allegiance to the flag of the United States of America, but that action is increasingly uncommon in America's schools today. An allegiance means loyalty or commitment to a cause. And in John 8, those who found no place for Jesus and his word in their hearts were loyal to another cause, not the cause of Christ. A mindset is a great litmus test for where our allegiance lies.

To understand these allegiances, it's vital that we are keenly aware of the subtle (and not-so-subtle) influences bombarding us daily. Even outside of the public school classroom, we are confronted with hundreds and sometimes thousands of persuasive appeals each day—messages that are designed to sell us a belief, a behavior, or a worldview. And these "virtual" influencers, along with their persuasive images, can be quite powerful. The late Neil Postman once said that the image is all-commanding, that the image and instancy had been raised "to an exquisite and dangerous perfection." The screen and its indelible image, Postman said, has become children's most accessible teacher and the most reliable friend, a virtual peer whose bias was shaping the world in frightening ways. And even if you unplug the television, close your laptop, turn off the phone, and shield your eyes when passing roadside billboards, it is difficult to escape the realm of influence entirely, especially when companies are spending billions of dollars a year trying to influence our behavior, and social media influencers are spawning and spinning their collective creative energies to convince us to subscribe to their point of view.

In 1 Corinthians 15:33, Paul writes, "Don't be deceived: Bad company corrupts good character." As we will see in this chapter, the company we keep, whether physical or virtual, bears heavily on our beliefs and our behavior. Our mindset is tremendously impacted by the influence of others, which is why a wise man is cautious in friendship. Our mindsets, our beliefs, our paradigms, drive our behaviors. Way back in the 1890s, William James was one of the first psychologists to recognize that goal directed-behaviors (decisions) were always preceded by a cognitive representation, a thought. Though it seems obvious to us right now, basically, he saw that actions are always preceded by a thought process; what we believe determines how we behave. As the *Journal of Integrated Social Sciences* notes, mindsets are cognitive biases that are built on access to information, past experiences, and personal relevance, that is, how much value we ascribe to a certain experience.

A mindset is a way of thinking about objects or actions that influences our decision patterns, whether that's something simple like what we want to eat or something more complex like how we choose to interact with other humans. One of the most well-known modern researchers in the field of mindset is Stanford University professor Dr. Carol Dweck. She coined the terms "growth mindset" and "fixed mindset" to help people see beyond the limitations of some of our belief-to-behavior patterns. Dweck found that people with fixed mindsets believe that their achievements are based on innate abilities, and because of this, they are often reluctant to take on challenges. People with growth mindsets, on the other hand, believe that they can learn, change, and develop needed skills, and so they are more likely to bounce back from life's inevitable setbacks. They recognize that hard work can help them accomplish their goals, so they are less likely to get stuck or to resist challenges.

These mindsets begin in childhood: If we were constantly praised for being smart or talented (or dumb or clumsy), for example, we can tend to remain stuck in a mindset that relies on a "fixed" set of traits. If those around us don't expect us to succeed, we can literally develop a mindset that prevents us from excelling! In fact, parents, if we encourage our kids' efforts, acknowledging their persistence and hard work (rather than fixed traits like intelligence or beauty), we will support their development of a *growth mindset*—better equipping them to learn, to persevere, and to get back up on the horse when they come tumbling to the ground. Our mindset can affect our decisions in business, in relationships, in parenting, and in the larger social sphere. We—and our children—were created to be dynamic not static, to grow and stretch and develop, not to remain stuck in faulty patterns that can bear a negative impact on our personal and professional relationships across the lifespan.

The public school system creates a fixed mindset of dependence on approval. Through its maddening methodology, we learn to crave the acceptance of an authority figure, which severs us from our own intrinsic drive for curiosity and makes us slavishly obedient to the praise of others. Gatto gives the example of a roomful of students raising their hands with great enthusiasm —not enthusiasm for their excitement about the material or its application, but enthusiasm for the possibility of pleasing the teacher with a correct response. And, as we've seen, the questions most teachers ask in traditional education are not reflective. They don't center on exploring students' thoughts and drawing out stored up knowledge and experience. Instead, the questions focus on knowing what the teacher is thinking. If you become proficient at reading the teacher's mind and know precisely what answer she wants you to give, then you can most certainly win that coveted gold star. This mindset teaches us to replace our own drive for knowledge with the superficial praise and approval of an authority figure. It doesn't teach us to think deeply or to discover what interests resonate with us personally, individually. Instead, this methodology teaches and reinforces a hive mindset. You must think like we think. You will be rewarded only if you mirror my thoughts, my answers, my agenda. This tragic fruit is evidenced in the manipulated mindset surrounding communication: civic discourse is now scorned.

Matthew 15 provides a glorious example of mindset. Jesus and the disciples have just arrived in the district of Tyre and Sidon, a region in Lebanon, when a woman approaches them, crying out for mercy. The Bible calls her a Canaanite, a term that dates back to a heritage of Noah. In this context, it means she is a non-Jewish, pagan woman. She is an unbeliever. But despite her pagan upbringing, she has apparently heard of Jesus, and she pleads with him to heal her daughter from demonic oppression. The disciples want to send her away, as they often want to send the children away, but, ignoring their request, Jesus says this: "I was sent only to the lost sheep of Israel," in other words, woman, your healing is outside my jurisdiction. But he's not insulting her; he's testing her. Watch what happens.

She kneels before him, and he pushes back again. He says, "It's not right to take the children's bread (what belongs to the Jews) and throw it to the dogs." Ouch! Even though he gives the word "dog" an affectionate twist, *kynarion,* meaning little doggie, cute or not, dogs were scavengers, and his response could have seemed very derogatory. But this woman is no snowflake. She doesn't get offended. She doesn't run off and complain on social media that Jesus hurt her feelings. She has a resilient mindset. She has a growth mindset. She knows the truth and she is holding to truth despite the perceived opposition.

The Canaanite woman again asserts herself: "Even the dogs can eat the crumbs that fall from the table," she says. In other words, despite my spiritual and socioeconomic status, I know you can bless me with something, even a little overflow from the royal dining table. And Jesus tells her, in essence, "Yes! That's faith right there! Your request is granted." The Bible says her daughter was healed at that moment. Clearly, this woman had a mindset of tenacity, of hope, of faith. And this faith, as Hebrews 11:1 so poetically defines it, "is the substance of things hoped for, the evidence of things not seen." Faith is a mental scaffold, a lens that sharpens the picture of possibility and gives us the courage to take action. Faith is a system of ideals that guides our actions; our belief determines our behavior. We need a measure of faith to rise above the fray of modern education, to turn the tide for the next generation.

I grew up in a home of scarcity: there was never enough. In this void of love, of hope, of trust, of food, of freedom, I didn't have the faith, the mental scaffolding, to hope or dream or envision a better future. I was stuck in a mindset of scarcity, so I clung to what I knew, what was familiar, and as a result, I stayed wounded, broken. Growing up in that kind of environment, it was easy to focus on the lack rather than the provision, to set my eyes on the waves rather than on the master of the waves. But God sent mentors and role models to help me break free of the mindset of scarcity, to help me learn to become a victim instead of a victor. These mentors taught me about God's exchange policy, how he trades His beauty for our ashes, His hope for our despair, His purpose for our pain. They gave me a glimpse of the ideal life while I navigated my real life. This is one of the reasons it is vital, moms and dads, to surround ourselves with mentors who have good fruit in their marriages and in their families. If your entire social circle consists of parents who complain that teenagers are sassy and toddlers are brats, you will start to adopt that mindset. Bratty will seem normal.

It takes examples like this to break free of limiting mindsets. One of the most common concerns we hear today is parents don't feel capable of teaching, discipling, or in any way inspiring their children. They feel like others are more capable that they are. These identity struggles can run deep and can take time to mend. Even after I became a follower of Christ in college, I still struggled with a victim mindset, a less-than mindset. I didn't doubt that God *could* bless, but unlike the Canaanite woman, I didn't know he wanted to. Hebrews 11:6 says, "Without faith it is impossible to please God, because anyone who comes to him must believe that he exists AND that he rewards those who earnestly seek him." In other words, it's not enough to believe in his existence. That's an incomplete mindset. Why? Because we also need to believe in his goodness. In fact, James 2:19 says, "You believe there is one God, good." Congratulations. But that's not enough. Who else believes there's one God? The demons. And they tremble.

The healthy mindset here, faith, is believing in God AND in his goodness. It's believing that we can do what God's called us to do. It's believing that we are more than conquerors, that we have the ability in him to rise above the labels and lies of the culture to become what he has called us to be. This is the mindset the next generation needs! They need to understand their purpose, their value, their uniqueness. Romans 12:2 tells us, "Do not conform to the pattern of this world, but be transformed by the renewing of your mind. Then you will be able to test and approve what God's will is—his good, pleasing, and perfect will." The word transform, *metamarphaoo* in the Greek, is the image of total and complete change, like a caterpillar to a butterfly. Paul is basically telling a group of grown men, "Don't let anyone tell you that you are too young or too old to change." Our minds can be transformed, renewed, over and over throughout our lifespans.

Because of the prevailing snowflake culture, many members of today's youngest generations have a mindset of failure and fear. They are often traumatized by relatively insignificant events because they have not learned to overcome, to stand strong in the face of persecution or even ridicule. Their sense of self is underdeveloped, and they lack the general sense of resilience we talked about in Chapter 5. Lest we despair, though, there is hope. As a comparative analysis and a marker of courage under fire, we can take a page of advice from the book of Daniel. In the year 605 BC, a rugged, healthy, wise Israelite named Daniel was taken from his home in Jerusalem as a judgment for his nation's disobedience and unfaithfulness to God. He was sent to live in Babylon under the rule of King

Nebuchadnezzar. The king first tried to socialize Daniel and his captive friends by renaming them, changing their God-centered names to names of Babylonian gods: Shadrach, Meshach, and Abednego. The king was attempting to change their identity and connection with the one true God, affiliating them instead with the gods of King Nebuchadnezzar's kingdom. This is very similar to what happens in the public school system, where identity is attacked, challenged, marred beyond logical recognition. As a result, students lose their sense of self and their common sense.

Next, the king tried to indoctrinate the Israelite captives by reeducating them in the literature of the Chaldeans, who were both a regional group and a people known for their magic lore and dream interpretations. This literary influence bears a direct resemblance to the training students receive in the public school classroom. I wrote extensively in the book *Emerge* about the most popular textbook publishing companies and how they are literally peddling the literature of lobbyists. Their "Chaldean" literature is a reflection of the pluralistic culture where the only groups one is permitted to offend are white men and Christians. Third, the king attempted to seduce Daniel and his friends with an appetite for the king's foods, which Daniel and his friends refused. This seduction back in 605 B.C. is the same driving force alive today in the four deadly sins, which are certainly more prevalent across the entire swath of culture today due to the ubiquitousness of social media and advertising in general. These debilitating sins, the lust of the eyes, the lust of the flesh, and the pride of life, sway many a young heart that has been primed for hedonism and narcissism in the world of public education.

I think we could agree that Daniel experienced some pretty intense trauma. He could have been angry about his captivity, bitter about his sentence, indignant about being separated from his home, but what kind of response do we see instead? Daniel was determined to live a life set apart for God. He lived consecrated. He refused to eat the king's food or drink, and he kept his mind and heart stayed on the one true God even in the midst of total cultural indoctrination. As a result, Daniel's friends, Hananiah, Mishael, and Azariah, all had the courage they needed when the king turned up the heat. They refused to follow the rule of the secular authorities by bowing their knee to a false idol. When the king said, "Worship this image," they determined in their hearts that they would serve God over government. The men were thrown into the furnace for their refusal. Scholars say the governmental leaders called the men "ungrateful" for their refusal to obey the king. Unkind, selfish, ungrateful—sound familiar? But a miracle took place. Not only did God meet them in the fiery furnace, but they escaped the heat without compromise in their heart or the smell of smoke on their bodies. They were promoted in the province, and the king declared it illegal to speak against the one true God.

We can learn a great deal from Daniel's friends and their determination, their dedication, in the face of indoctrination. The cultural indoctrination sweeping our nation is embedded in everything from sitcoms to music to ads to flags being flown at local public school district offices. All these symbols are an attempt to create allegiance to a mindset, a paradigm, a worldview. Like Daniel and his friends, we must make an intentional choice about the kind of mindset we are going to embrace, and we must make a determined attempt to free the next generation from their addition to the gold star, to the social media like, to the applause of an unknown and unimportant audience.

An emotionally healthy mindset, as researchers have shown, means we use our challenges as a point of reference to understand life, and we also help others do the same. This is another example of the coherent narrative, making sense of life's challenges and finding purpose in the pain. Restorative resources can be found in a number of places, and even when they have been absent in early childhood development (such as infant-parent attachment), they can be later forged through what Siegel calls "two person governed self-regulation": Through these therapeutic alliances, he says, "experiences (external constraints) can help modify the synaptic connections (internal constraints) that enable the individual to achieve new levels of flexible and balanced forms of self-regulation." This measure of personal control, this intentionality to balance and regulate ourselves and our emotions, is a vital component of growth: "Self-regulation is a key to mental health," Siegel says. As the saying goes, healthy body, healthy mind. For generations that have lacked connection as well as awareness of the potential for transformation, these truths have been too long silent. It's not the existence of trauma but the response to it that makes the difference.

When I was a teenager, I had a very dysmorphic view of myself. I would look in the mirror and see every perceived flaw as magnified, and the longer I looked, the more hideous my visage became. So, I would live in a way that was congruent with that view, that I was worthless, that I had no personal value. Up until I was saved in college, my mindset was yoked to the lies and labels of the past, demonic strongholds that had to be broken and severed off my life. We must address this as a culture; we have to open a door of conversation on this because we have a whole generation of children that are experiencing similar frequencies of deception, whether that's exhibited in careless actions, self-injurious behavior, or suicide ideation. As I've said more than a few times in this book already, GenZs are the most atheist, unchurched generation in the history of our nation. Look up the rates on youth homicide, suicide ideation, self-poisoning, cutting, burning, addiction, anxiety, depression, the sexually transmitted disease rates among ages 14 to 25 in the United States. The numbers are all staggering. These are offshoots of a generation that has not been taught its value in Christ. When we know our value, our identity in Christ, we possess and operate in a different level of care for ourselves and others.

In 2009, I wrote a book that documented the impact of

media voices on identity formation. My graduate school research at Regent University had opened my eyes to the insidious influence of media on the mind and heart. Through songs and news and social media, these modern "false prophets" declare their version of truth. In Jeremiah 23, these false prophets are described in contrast to true prophets: "They speak visions of their own minds, not from the mouth of the Lord. They say continually to those who despise the word of the Lord, 'it shall be well with you,' and to everyone who stubbornly follows his own heart, they say 'no disaster shall come upon you.'" Don't we hear this all the time? It's for your safety. Just trust the system. Listen the experts. They know best. No, parents, those are false prophets. They do not know what is best for your child. They do not love your children more than you do. And most importantly, you—not they—have been given the mantle of authority in your child's life.

Who among you, the prophet asks, has stood in the council of the Lord? "If they had stood in my council," verse 22 says, "then they would have proclaimed my words to my people, and they would have turned them from their evil ways, and from the evil of their deeds." The false prophets of the world's system take council together with the spirit of secular humanism in the public school system, and they proclaim the same drivel, the same doctrine, the same lies. But God says his word is "like a fire…like a hammer that breaks the rock in pieces." The truth of God's word confounds the lies of the modern day prophets of secular education, and it's our responsibility to be the carriers of that word to the broken and confused generation that has been swept away by these false prophets of the day.

The book of Joshua provides a helpful visual of triumph. Picture the Israelites camping at the side of the Jordan, dreaming of the land they were about to inherit. The manna, the provision, ended the day Joshua stepped into the promised land and ate the fruit of his spoils. Joshua had the courage to envision the territory, to see the things that were not as though they were. When God said to Joshua those famous words, "See I have given Jericho into your hand," the city was actually walled off, shut up, with no one going in and no one going out. Joshua had to see his forthcoming victory with the eyes of faith. At its heart, the account is really all about taking ground. It's about conquering territory. It's about the rule and the reign of the kingdom of God, conquest after conquest as the Israelites spread out across their promised land. As you read, I want to encourage you to take ground in your life, in your own habits, in your family. Reflect on the influences that are shaping the way you think and act, and be intentional about making change where change is needed.

It's time for us to become territory-takers. We need to take back our families, our churches, our cities, our states, our nations. If you're a parent, make disciples, starting in the home. If you're a young adult, start by leading yourself well. Train yourself. Reach out to someone in your circle who can mentor and disciple you—and pour out what you learn to someone younger than you. We have to break off this public school fruit of peer-orientation that has kept our youngest generations living under a ceiling of immaturity and dysfunction.

Remember, as Proverbs 13:20 says, "A companion of fools will be destroyed." We will become like the company we keep. It doesn't take a modern-day Paul Revere to warn us of what's coming. We stand in the midst of a perfect storm: parental abandonment, social media ubiquitousness, and a stamp of governmental ownership on the minds, hearts, and bodies of the next generation. When the storm recedes, there will be a clear distinction between right and wrong, truth and folly, good and evil. When the sky is rolled back and the King of kings comes to call his people home, make sure you and your children are standing on the side of the sheep and not the goats.

CHAPTER SIXTEEN

Toxic Trait #12: Methodological Madness

I remember a reading program we had in our elementary school classroom, one that separated the men from the boys, proverbially speaking. Students were grouped into colors according to their reading level, and every student had to walk up to the color box in front of the whole class to pick our their next essay during our in-class reading time. I proudly walked up to the blue box to collect my "smart" essay, while my seat neighbor tiptoed up to the front of the class to retrieve his "dummy" red box essay as invisibly as humanly possible. There was no way out of the color assignments until you reached the end of your packet, at which point, you could move to the next color if you doubled up on the workload, read enough essays, and answered all of the reading comprehension checklist questions correctly.

I don't know if my red box classmates ever went on to achieve literary greatness; I only know that at the time, the cloud of shame and disinterest that hung over their prepubescent heads seemed to do little to motivate them to scholastic success. That's because a one-size-fits-none, hive-mind educational methodology does not promote academic interest. It doesn't stoke individual talent. Instead, it simply offers a psychological reinforcement for the smart kids, like a queen bee rationing out honey rewards drop by drop to her most loyal servants.

After years of being a student and then a professor, I saw clearly that something just wasn't right in America's classrooms. Shockingly ineffective methodology was turning smart students into passive, disinterested blobs who sat in the back of the room counting down the minutes to the end of school. The pervasive gold star system was driving students to crave the incessant approval of man at the expense of their own academic inquisitiveness and drive. Weak students slumped over in their chairs, developing insecurity complexes: While their midrange classmates were propelled forward, the malnourished learners were left behind. "Teach to the middle," we were told over and over in our instructional design courses. But teaching to the middle necessarily means leaving behind the best and worst students. Inspiration does not lie passively in the middle of the scholarship divide; inspiration requires individuation, individualized learning that creates a launching point for ingenuity and interest.

As a professor, I saw repeatedly the dark underbelly of a disconnected and dysfunctional system. Like a midlife medical exam measures the collateral damage from a lifetime of poor dietary choices, college professors see the cumulative effects of America's damaging K to 12 system in our university classrooms. We see the gold star addicts, the driven-but-unpopular overachievers, and the back-row dwellers whose parents (and their own lack of career initiative) are the sole reason they take up space in the college classroom. The only exception to the narrative is the swath of lifelong homeschoolers, who are, with rare exception, some of the only students in college who actually seem to enjoy the process of learning for its own inherent value.

Yes, the public school system is spewing out aggressively anti-Christian content across the classrooms of our country. Yes, the public school system is teaching pseudo-scientific theory as impregnable fact. And yes, the public school system is polluting the minds and hearts of the next generation with morally reprehensible content. But I want to give one more reason why our schools are broken. It has nothing to do with what's being taught and everything to do with how it's being taught. Methodological madness is one of the twelve toxic traits of traditional education.

While there are many overt attacks on students in the government school system, there are just as many little foxes that seek, little by little, to undermine parental authority, Christian principles, and even the spirit of innovation. We've already talked about the Values Clarification Movement, the fear-driven content, the anti-family culture where parents are not allowed in the public school space, the blatant hypersexuality, and the false esteem movements that are ultimately rooted in narcissism. There is a linear thrust to public school doctrine, a similarity of teaching methodology and content threaded across the nation, through each generation since the 1960s. This consistency of pressures and practices underscores a concerted, collective approach to overt indoctrination. Broad is the road that leads to destruction.

One of the most insidious training grounds in all of America, the public school system, uses a covertly malevolent methodology to slowly and subtly train up a generation in the way the government wants it to go. It's a visible attribute in students: As we work with them, we can literally witness the tangible fruit in their thought processes, in their sense of self, in their motivation. They have been classically conditioned by public education, and they have lost their connection to the elusive nature of freedom. Freedom can only be protected and preserved as it is defended and distributed from generation to generation. As former president Ronald Reagan once said, "Freedom is never more than one generation away from extinction. We didn't pass it on to our children in the bloodstream. It must be fought for, protected, and handed on for them to do the same, or one day we will spend our sunset years telling our children and our children's children what it was once like in the United States where men were free." That chilling statement should make us want to rise up, step up, and take back education for the next generation.

John Taylor Gatto, whom we've talked about in past chapters, lived in the trenches of academia as a former New York State teacher of the year. One of perhaps his most profound insights on the insidious ideological infiltrations of government schooling is methodology. Gatto noted that public schools train students to crave the approval of authority so they will work obediently as adults and never question why they're spending 40-50 hours a week doing something they care very little about. The public school system trains students to look down on their classmates, to believe the human race in general is subpar and in need of ongoing government intervention. Finally, he says, public schools train students to keep them from living up to the true, enterprise-adoring, pioneering American spirit that sets us apart in the world as innovative problem solvers, as entrepreneurs and out-of-the-box thinkers. Instead, today's students are trained to obey without question, and this same mentality then persists in adulthood, leaving a nation scattered with the hollow shells of dispassionate men and women who live only for the weekend, not for the purpose, passion, or impact of their industry.

Even as we look at some of the brand new educational programming emerging from the storm clouds of 2020, a common theme continues to resound throughout education, including the idea that 1) children need an expert to learn, and 2) the parent is not it. Some of the formats I see being developed today demonstrate an overt disconnect in this regard: research has contributed toward an upswing of programs and companies that profess to acknowledge the problem facing America's education system; however, they continue to overlook the developmental science necessary to understanding and applying the solution, choosing instead easy-way-out-approaches that deny all we've learned from great thinkers like Lev Vygotsky and Uri Bronfenbrenner regarding the vital need for scaffolding and mentorship in the developmental process.

Think, for example, about athletes. How effective would their training be if it were all delivered via a screen, without a personal role model, without a face-to-face coach, without the critical feedback and sharpening that is best delivered through F2F interaction? A cursory glance at education's founding documents tells us just how far the modern scholastic system attempts to pull students away from innovation and entrepreneurship--and how deeply this philosophy of conformity and groupthink is rooted in modern American education. The next generation needs an approach to academic freedom that is only accessible thorough discernment and systems thinking. The sterile, secular approach to education is void of true wisdom; therefore, it can never create a product that perfectly identifies both root and fruit. We were wired for interaction, for scaffolding, for mentorship.

The brokenness of modern education is also exemplified in its classroom policies and practices. Take school hours as an example: There is no rational reason for students to be trapped in classrooms for seven hours a day, five days a week. The Department of Education even notes on its website that three hours a day is sufficient for scholastic training. Three hours. The 7-hour day is a total and complete waste of time and energy for students, but, it should be noted, these unnecessary hours are what gives teachers the uptick in payroll needed for the categorization of full-time employment. And since 40% of our California taxation goes to public schools, and 80% of that amount goes to employees and their benefits, herein lies the challenge. In addition to daily hours, start times are also off kilter. The developmental science shows conclusively that students' scores and emotional health improve when they start school at 9am or later; however, most schools begin at 7:30 or 8am, not because it's better for the students but because teachers want to start early and end early, as their developmental clocks are set to the rhythm of adulthood. Educators and administrators in these broken systems continue to think from a myopic, generationally-centric mindset that caters to adults while discounting the needs and experiences of GenZs and Alphas.

If we want innovation, we must approach the solution from a whole-student, systems perspective. Habits of the heart and mind will leak into habits of the soul, spirit, and body. A healthy approach to educating the young must include processes that are attuned to the needs of how this generation learns best. This requires a classical approach with education coaches who ask open-ended questions that produce critical thinking skills, not a one-size-fits-all approach that measures knowledge through "multiple guess" assessments. As Sir Francis Bacon once said, "Reading makes a full man, speaking makes a ready man, and writing makes an exact man." In other words, we expand our imagination and innovation, our very connection to the world, by reading, and we hone our skills of preparedness and excellence through the time-tested processes of speaking and writing. None of these vital skills are truly measured or measurable in the myopic approach of online, non-systems-oriented education.

When I began graduate school and experienced for the first time the tangible differences between effective and ineffective educational methodologies, I began comparing the traditional system of education to the fruit I saw as a homeschooling parent, and I knew there had to be a way to build more effective educational systems. Chula Vista Christian University was launched to address three of the primary social ills of modern American academia: Ineffective methodology, sweeping secularization, and financial irresponsibility. In partnership with parents and the local church, CVCU offers flexible, affordable education that inspires self-directed learning through a biblical worldview. I knew that students would rise to the ceiling of the expectations set for them. I knew strong role models would drive strength of character. So, through the utilization of a tutorial, apprenticeship model, we were able to develop an innovate strategy using the proven success of one-to-one academic mentoring instead of a mass, one-size-fits-none educational shoebox. With this methodology, to date, we've now built 19 academic support systems, including one of my K to 12 favorites, Awaken Academy.

A thousand years ago, early universities depended on discourse for the transmission of knowledge (or, more accurately, data). Once the printing press was invented in 1436, scholarship began to lend itself to individual acquisition, so long as the leader was literate. However, the "sage on the stage" ideology, the culture of the experts, persisted, even while knowledge became increasingly available to the common man. In 2007, an emerging juxtaposition of technology and creativity sparked an idea for a few visionary teachers: they realized they could record their lectures for students to watch outside of the classroom walls. This created a new level of margin and headspace that offered the opportunity for deeper conceptual discussions within the classroom because students could, in essence, train themselves. This "flipped classroom model" became a popular buzzword in teacher training, but it has still been difficult for traditional educational institutions to fully embrace it and release their grasp on the expert culture. Why? I believe the obstacle lies within the larger academic visage of the culture of the expert.

When I taught in traditional schools, I often noticed that teachers and administrators overtly mocked the homeschool community. Homeschoolers were the regular butt of jokes, and if there were ever a crime or moral failure in the homeschool community, the news was widely circulated in the school as a proof text of the failure of the methodology. I found this scholastic stance odd, because we all knew rather instinctively that the longer a student had been homeschooled, the smarter, more self-assured, and driven that student was likely to be. But one day, I made a vital mental connection: If homeschoolers are highly successful, without parental certification, without "proper" training on the probability density function of the standard Bell curve, and without having survived hideously boring classes like instructional design, then what did that say about the teacher? For the teacher is a due-paying member of the culture of the experts, and the successful homeschooler is a threat to the job security and reputation of the expert, who must rely on fear-mongering to keep students on task.

This is a fascinating dichotomy, because educators know that homeschooling works. We all know that the number one predictor of a student's socio-academic success is an involved parent. And yet, teachers and administrators go to great lengths to preserve their own egos, to protect their own seat at the table even when they know students would be better served by a parent educator. The truth of the matter is that homeschooled students outperform traditionally-schooled students by at least 30 points and five grade levels on average—even if the parent who is doing the homeschooling didn't graduate from high school. Let that sink in. And unlike public school teachers, homeschoolers can't "teach to the test," because we don't have access to the test or its answers, and we would likely not waste valuable instructional time teaching to something so utterly meaningless in the first place. This construct completely shatters the lie of the expert culture, and it's easy to see why traditional educators would be offended and threatened by these findings. But it's vital to address these concerns right now because at this juncture, both the motive and the method of traditional education are highly questionable.

This culture-of-the-expert sociocultural conditioning is why so many new homeschool parents often get lured into the charter school movement. The charter school is a public school, and some parents don't realize at first that with a charter, they will be required to teach the same failing public school material at the same rat-race pace; they will just be doing so at home. They will still have to bow to the same measures of meaningless accountability, they will still have to complete the same time-wasting busywork, and they will still be forced to subject their students to the same non-scientific lies about the human brain and body that classroom-based public school students are exposed to daily. The content is the same, the methodology is the same; it's just a change of location. The charter is public school at home. Parents, I get it: The charter is "free." This is tempting. But free education (or free anything) always comes with strings. We know intuitively as Americans that freedom isn't free. When we boil down the essence of what we are truly trading out, the price of "free" becomes more lucid: a free ballet class in exchange for a yoke to the secular system, a free laptop in exchange for a secular humanist curriculum, a free "education specialist" in exchange for fear-fueled, rat-race-driven Marxist indoctrination.

Attorney Mary Schofield put it this way: It's as if the government stepped into the local church and offered to foot the bill for all of your music. The only catch would be that you had to remove any reference to Jesus, to God, or to Scripture. Instead, you would sing about positive messages that make people feel happy. If you accept the government sponsorship of your church worship experience, you are forced to exchange Christianity for secular humanism. You can sing about happy thoughts, but not Christian ones. You can quote secular poets, but you can't quote scripture, the living word of God that sets people free. This is exactly what happens when we exchange our freedom of independent homeschooling for a charter yoke to the secular education system! So, parents, think first about your values, about why you're teaching what you're teaching and the way you're teaching it.

Educators get trapped in this valley of decision too. They know they are part of the larger system, the problem, but they often delude themselves into thinking there is no way out. Teachers, I get it. I hear it all the time. "I'm just doing my job." Google that quote throughout history and see where it leads. Many good people have become complicit by being complacent. At some point, we have to decide whether we will be part of the solution or continue being part of the problem. We must "live not by lies." I am very heartened by the current cultural movement among traditional educators who are courageously stepping out of the sterile classroom environment and using their gifts and talents to tutor students. A one-to-one tutoring methodology, while not a replacement for the parent, is a far more successful model of education than the traditional classroom environments. Educators can use their creative abilities to break free of the system that is weighing down and holding back the next generation.

At CVCU, our educational methodology centers on an integrated ideology that features the capstones of coaching and mentoring, the flipped classroom model, studies that inform the research on three generations of learning styles (Millennial, GenZ, and Alpha), andragogical (adult learning) applications, and the parent-directed (aka homeschool) education movement. The goal of education in this viewpoint is not solely the pursuit of a piece of paper, the achievement of an ethereal degree. Instead, through their experience in college, students gain a career-focused, mentor-modeled, well-rounded education that prepares them to be workers and citizens of the modern world. Our professors recognize that they're doing more than simply teaching the students of today; they're training the culture-shapers of tomorrow.

Any experienced (and honest) academic will admit that, to be successful, the youngest generations need educational methodologies that differ vastly from the lecture-driven systems of the past. However, most aging scholastic vessels have grown so cumbersome and resistant to change that they are unable to fully access the creativity required to meet the academic and socio-emotional success of the next generation. Instead of embracing innovation, many traditional institutions of higher learning in America are weighed down by towering hierarchies and overly indebted building programs, investing millions of dollars into bricks and mortar instead of investing their capital into the most valuable resource of all: the next generation.

Today's highly ineffective methodology has dramatically impacted student success, as evidenced in a number of significant hurdles facing today's traditional education system: Illiteracy rates, falling retention rates, and crippling student debt are all rampant in America. Practical skill acquisition and job placement rates are suffering. Colleges and universities have failed to adapt to the new modalities of learning required by the current generation, who have been raised in the era of constant connectivity and instant information access. As a result, college dropout rates are soaring. Though high school retention and graduation rates in California have improved somewhat over the last decade, retention rates in California state colleges remain abysmally low. According to 2018 report by EdSource, only 47% of Latino students who begin college in California complete their degrees, only 38% of Black students, only 60% of White students, and only 68% of Asian students. Clearly, students are not being effectively served, mentored, or coached within their collegiate experience. As *Time Magazine* noted, these stats point to two significant challenges: a high dropout rate and a delayed completion rate—40% of students don't even finish their undergraduate degree within six years. The US higher educational system is pushing a one-size-fits-all model that is ineffective in meeting the needs of today's generation.

Furthermore, the sociopolitical environment of most modern schools and universities serves to undermine rather than nurture what students have been taught in the home and the church. Parents often make extraordinary financial sacrifices to educate their children in a biblical worldview K to 12, only to see them walk away from those values in college. A 2017 report by Campus Renewal found that almost 70% of Christian students attending secular universities leave the faith by the end of their freshman year in college. It's no wonder that, as Barna notes, Gen Z is the most "unchurched generation in history." Bad company corrupts good character. Luke 6:40 says that the student, when he or she is fully grown, will become like the teacher, and the evidence of this behavior modeling is played out today in a generation that has now been defined by its astronomical rates of anxiety, depression, suicide ideation, atheism, abortion, and STDs. That ultimately brings us back to Plato's question: "Who is teaching the children, and what are they being taught?"

Universities must take extraordinary care in the selection of professors who are not only academically qualified but who are, most importantly, grounded in the DNA of the faith, who inherently demonstrate the "guide on the side" model, who are committed to the local church, and who are "relationally warm" and spiritually mature—professors whose lives exhibit a harvest of good fruit. Though this approach tends to limit the pool of qualified professors, I believe it is a vital step in the mentor-driven model and a foundation for education reform, vital ingredients for the socio-emotional, relational, and spiritual health of the next generation. As Lieutenant Colonel Ray Moore once said, "If we don't change the way we do education, we will lose our country." CVCU has stepped up to this call in order to change the trajectory of higher education within our realm of influence. It is our goal to nurture the investment parents have already made into the next generation, protecting and equipping our most important asset: our children.

Modern educational institutions anchor on measurable outcomes. The challenge is that their goal is not always the same as God's goal. We have to know our end goal. If our end goal is to create critical thinkers, world changers, industry disruptors, then we need to create those environments that will encourage active learning, give students the freedom to ask questions, to stop stifling creativity and critical thinking in the name of conformity and groupthink. Neil Postman said there is a distinct difference between school and education. He published a fascinating study on inquiry in the traditional educational environment where he looked at the types of questions kids asked in school. The vast majority of questions asked by students, 93%, were administrative questions: how do I hold my pencil, how do I spell this word, how many questions can I get wrong and still pass? These are a far cry from learning that is built on critical thinking, on the why behind the learning.

In the traditional sector, "why" questions are squelched. Good behavior is defined as sitting quietly with hands in laps, getting along with others, and conforming to the behavioral norms of the classroom. This format is antithetical to true education because it silences meaningful questions and critical thinking. It subverts passion and industry disruption. Like its industrial era inception, it creates cogs in the machine. By contrast, let's look at the inquiry method of education, which was popularized by Socrates but modeled most effectively by Jesus and the manner in which he taught his disciples. Consider his use of parables and questions:

"Who do you say that I am?"
"Why are you afraid?"
"Why did you doubt?"
"Whose image is on this coin?"
"Do you still not understand?"
"What does scripture say?"
"Who touched me?"

Jesus could most certainly have given the answer to any of these questions himself. He could have lectured his disciples for hours on an infinite number of manifold topics. He could have called a messenger pigeon to drop a scroll detailing the answers on the disciples' heads. He could have commanded the skies to open, calling angels to storm down and pen the responses across the cumulonimbus clouds. But instead, Jesus chose inquiry, reflection, relationship. He chose the methods of inductive reasoning that would cause his followers to think, to reason, and, ultimately, to return to him.

As believers, our measurable outcomes are not simply academic. They are social. They are spiritual. They are relational. If we raise really smart kids who go to Harvard and earn a Nobel Peace Prize, but they walk away from God, what have we gained? "What does it profit a man," Mark 8:36 asks, "if he gains the whole world but loses his own soul?" These are vital questions for the current generation, who holds the dubious honor of being the most anxious, depressed, atheistic people group in the history of our nation. The traditional system is failing America, from values clarification to Marxism to the lack of critical thinking and the eradication of the arts, the seedbed of creativity and innovation. Instead of focusing on enhancing individual potential, the focus in traditional education for the last 50 years has been on how to make all people perform to a specific measure, how to create a system that fashions a product, something predicable, replicable, measurable. Students are taught what to think but not how to think. The school system favors rigidity and control over human behavior, but these markers are absolutely antithetical to the true heart of education. The traditional school system is a social construct with the singular goal of producing an outcome, a product.

Margaret Thatcher once noted the futility of this compromise of consensus, this molding of all minds into one conglomerate whole: "Consensus is the process of abandoning all beliefs, principles, values and policies in search of something in which no one believes," Thatcher said. "What great cause could have been fought and won under the battle phrase, 'I stand for consensus?'" Instead of a hive-minded whole, humans thrive when they are appreciated for unique differences that sharpen and shape us. And as adults, we don't make our decisions on the broad basis of public opinion or, definitely, public school opinion. Broad is the way that leads to destruction, Matthew 7:13 reminds us, and many will enter in. Traversing the broad way, the popular path, the road most traveled, is what has led us to the place we are today in American education and culture.

Ineffective methodology and sweeping secularization, however, are not the only significant issues affecting today's students, especially in higher education. Millennial college students were the first generation whose student loan debt surpassed the nation's credit card debt. In California today, there are 3.7 million student borrowers who owe a total of $141.9 billion in student debt. Moreover, California's students hold approximately one-tenth of the entire nation's $1.5 trillion student loan debt, a disproportionately high number of borrowers. Our youngest citizens are being sent out into the adult world carrying the unnecessary and overwhelming burden of educational debt, another statistic connected to their high levels of anxiety, depression, and "perpetual adolescence." Furthermore, of the percentage that actually complete their degree programs, many report leaving college with no sense of direction, no specific calling or goal, and no hands-on, job-related experience. In fact, 60% of American college students say they are currently employed in jobs that share no commonality with their college degree field.

Inattention to the student's individualized and generationally-specific learning needs is one root of the multifaceted problem. Most US colleges and universities today are built on Industrial Era information-dispensing ideologies that are now short-circuiting the educational prowess of America's youngest students. The vast majority of Millennials and Generation Zs are not auditory learners, students who absorb material by sitting quietly and listening to a lengthy lecture. Instead, most are kinesthetic or visual learners, students who learn by seeing, doing, and discussing. The educational model of the future must fan the flame of learning within the student, creating a thirst for knowledge and a lifelong love of learning.

To this end, CVCU is one of the first modern universities to be built almost entirely on the mentorship format, which allows for flexible, affordable education at a fraction of the cost of traditional private higher education. Because of this learner-driven model, which provides a "guide on the side" instead of a "sage on the stage," we are able to offer a financially responsible model of Christian higher education where students graduate debt-free. Instead of being encumbered by debt or restrictive scheduling, our students have the freedom to pursue their passion within the protective margins of affordability and flexibility.

GenZ and Alpha learners represent an entirely new style of learning. Both of their generations have been nurtured outside of the classroom in a learner-driven modality where every imaginable question is instantaneously answerable at their fingertips. In such a knowledge-based economy, the tutorial, discipleship-based methodology is the most rational response to the academic needs of this generation. Why would we send them backwards to a lecture-driven modality instead of capitalizing on their natural curiosity? As we discussed earlier, curiosity is one of the key attributes of intrinsic motivation. Students need to be given opportunities to develop practical skills that help them acquire the vital attributes of problem-solving and critical thinking. These come not through lecture but through laboratories. Students must be given the opportunity for self-government, independent learning, and local leadership. Their educational processes should include serving in field-based internships to gain practical, real-world experience before they earn their degree. Today's college graduates should have both the education and the practical skills to compete in today's complex and multifaceted world of work.

As I was writing this chapter, my son Ethan was having a conversation with his younger sister Cymone as she prepared for a CVCU class discussion on the voluminous American History text, *A Patriot's History of the United States*. Cymone asked Ethan a question about some seemingly random event in the early 1800s, and he proceeded to enlighten her—from memory and with great aplomb—on the major political occurrences over the span of 100 years of American history. They talked for 30 minutes about why these events mattered. Mind you, I didn't teach him this content. As a lifelong homeschooler, he was innately curious. He read material that fascinated him, including volume after volume of American and world history. The general education classes that are the bane and the bore of scholastic suffering for many traditionally educated students take on new meaning, purpose, and promise when they are steered by the correct educational methodology, namely an intrinsic curiosity that is fostered by living in the real world instead of being sequestered in the artificial laboratory of a common classroom. Homeschooling works.

In his book *Atomic Habits*, James Clear writes of the importance of accepting the fact that people are born with certain gifts, talents, and skill sets. "Some people don't like to discuss this fact," Clear says. "On the surface, your skills seem to be fixed, and it's no fun to talk about things you cannot control," he says. However, "the strength of genetics is also their weakness… (for) they provide a powerful advantage in favorable circumstances and a serious disadvantage in unfavorable circumstances." Modern, traditional education has ignored the individual gifts and talents of its students, forcing standouts and outliers into a statistically-valid, politically-correct mold that helps the state check off its measurable outcomes with the singular goal of receiving more funding. The state rewards conformity, mom and dad. Modern education does not cater to creativity. It doesn't stir up genius. Instead, like an Army tank, it steamrollers over any stroke of intellect that doesn't fit neatly into its standardized measurement checklist. Recognizing our human propensity for uniqueness, exploring both our strengths and weaknesses, and stoking the power of the misunderstood genius—these are the job descriptions best befitting a freshly inspired parent educator who is ready to step into a new methodology living and relating and learning in the real world.

Finding ways that we (and our children) learn best and teach best is part of our homework as parents, our formal preparation for the individualized instructional design methodology that homeschooling provides. There is no one-size fits all approach to education for every child, even every child in the same family. Once you feel like you have the perfect methodology figured out with one child, the second child will come along as an outlier to all your tried-and-true data. That's why we have to be flexible, open, creative. My friend Corie discovered that one of her children needed the sunlight on her back to be able to focus. Another friend found that her son needed music in the background to study most effectively. We each need unique stimuli to focus. The two youngest working generations possess the unique ability to study undistracted in a chaotic coffee shop. Older generations, like mine, often need total silence to focus. Likewise, we are also smart in different ways. When our CVCU paleobiochemistry professor took us on our Grand Canyon tour, we had 7-hour car ride with an SUV of students to talk about all the wonders of dinosaur DNA. Paleobiochemistry is not my field of professional expertise; thus, by the second hour of the trip, I was already beginning to question my intelligence. When the conversation inadvertently switched to neural plasticity and Knapp's relational stages, I suddenly felt "smart" again.

There will be times in homeschooling where you won't feel smart. That's okay. When our students are educated in the parent-directed, one-to-one tutorial system, they will naturally go further than their parents did. When my oldest child was in 10th grade, I realized he was venturing outside my realm of academic experience, so I needed to add some assignments that he could drive forward himself, classes he could own. I introduced him to mentors in his field that could keep fueling his curiosity and ingenuity. If your child surpasses your knowledge base in his or her particular fields of study, rejoice! Don't feel threatened or inadequate. Sometimes you can best help your children excel by stepping out of the way and letting that drive, that thirst for knowledge, take over. This, in essence, is what Jefferson meant when he said no one can be taught without their consent. We have to want to learn in order to learn. It's that simple. If we provide the mentors and the classics for our children, and for our nation's children, we will help them develop that flame of learning that will drive the scholastic process.

I firmly believe that if we can break free of the bondage of traditional, worm-dispensing ideology, if we can shake off the shackles of the expert culture, we will be perfectly positioned to train up a next generation of culture shapers and world changers. Parents, you can do this. It's time to break free of the system. "Lean not on your own understanding," Proverbs 3:5 says. "In all your ways acknowledge him, and he will direct your path." You don't have to have it all figured out, mom. Reach out to a mentor. Find someone who has characteristics in their family that you want in your family, and start asking questions. Step out in faith. Teachers, you can do this. It's time to use your creative gifts and talents to innovate new approaches that will disrupt the fractured field of education.

Pastors, it's your time to shine, to step up, to speak out. You can be part of the rescue mission! If your church is sitting vacant all week long, it's time to reclaim that space for a generational training ground, a center of educational discipleship. If just 50% of California's churches would open their doors to

224 students, we could shut down every one of the state's schools tomorrow. Pastors, be sure to check out the work we're doing at in San Diego at AwakenAcademySD.com (as well as several other churches across the nation), and click the Start an Academy link at CVCU.us for tips on getting your church off the bench and onto the field. The harvest is ready. It's time to undo the radical damage this ineffective methodology has done to the next generation. It's time to the block the sale of woeful wares being peddled daily in the public school system. It's time to break off the shackles of doubt in your own life. No matter what obstacle has kept you from freeing your family from the scholastic swamp, it's time to step up and take back education for the sake of the next generation.

CHAPTER SEVENTEEN

Let My People Go: An Escape Route from Egypt

A former student of mine who grew up in Communist Russia told me about her first time visiting an American shoe store. Yana's American host had expected her to be thrilled with the many beautiful choices of footwear towering in front of her, but Yana stood paralyzed in front of a wall of black shoes: tall ones, short ones, pointy ones, square ones, chunky heels, and skinny flats. She was totally overwhelmed with the freedom of choice at her fingertips, unable to process the idea of choosing one pair from the massive selection of black shoes. When she was a child growing up in Russia, she said, if you wanted black shoes, there was one pair of black shoes to "choose" from. There was no choice of style or finish, shiny or matte, no choice of toe, pointy or square. There was just a shoe, a black shoe. In America, there is freedom of choice. There are zillions of pairs of black shoes.

When I first started working with the new demographic of home educators, whom I called "reluctant" homeschoolers in 2020, I thought they would be thrilled with the level of freedom that homeschooling brings. After all, as a homeschooling parent, you can choose your reading list, your math books, your history readers, your science curriculum, your teaching methodology, your assignments, your extracurriculars, your time of day, and your method of assessment. Exciting, right? But like my Russian student, our reluctant homeschoolers were not overjoyed. They did not feel free. Instead, they stood paralyzed in front of the wall of curricula that I mistakenly thought would inspire them. Parents had become so accustomed to being told what black shoe to wear that the freedom of choice felt overwhelming. Many had never chosen a book, let alone an entire curriculum, for their children. They had never contemplated learning styles or given a homework assignment. The freedom that I thought would send them soaring instead left them drowning. The sea of choice was too choppy, too deep, too unknown. It look about a year for parents to start to relish that freedom.

We had to start with a life ring and some scaffolding—a little guided support that helped them learn to walk in freedom. They had to relax from the constrictions they had been living under their whole parental lives. Their choice muscle had atrophied. In the public school system, you've got one choice: Do what we say. Follow directions. Obey. In the homeschool arena, you have hundreds of great choices. Instead of being paralyzed by the prevalence of the proverbial black shoe, you will eventually find the freedom and appreciate the adventure in the choices that lie before you. Stay the course.

This freedom-versus-slavery mentality finds its way into many of the mindsets we work with in the new era of homeschooling. Most of the toxic traits of traditional education have been active in the public school classroom for 30 years, 40 years, 50 years. But there are also a few new seeds of destruction that have sprouted up in the soil of America's education system. What makes these seeds most dangerous is not only that they are disseminated by the trusted authorities of the school system; they are also watered by the fake tears shed by celebrities who pretend to care about the hearts and minds of the next generation. They are magnified in media, and they are so insidiously snake-like and ubiquitous that they have even slithered their way into the American church. We saw the outpouring of critical race theory flood directly from the school classrooms into the nation's pulpits last year.

In our county, Awaken Church was one of the few churches to stand up and speak out against this divisive rhetoric. Many churches, sadly, bowed their knee to the doctrine of the hour because they either feared man more than they feared God or because their own socio-political wokeness blinded them to the truthful application of God's word. The road to destruction is broad and well paved by overachievers. But in America, every traveler on the road of academic slavery is walking that pathway by choice. Because in America, we have options. We have the legal right to choose how, when, where, and even why we educate our children.

When Moses stood before the Pharaoh who had enslaved his people, he uttered the famous cry, "Let my people go!" And many parents in California have been rallying around this cry to the government schools: "Stop enslaving our people; stop teaching hypersexual curricula; stop masking our children; stop dumbing us down; let my people go." And that's fine. I'm not saying we shouldn't care or try to fight back. But the truth is that we are already free. We are not forced by law to endure the prison sentence of government schooling. We don't have to place our children on the big yellow prison bus and send them off to be incarcerated and indoctrinated eight hours a day. The government has no jurisdiction over private schools in California, which includes homeschooling, so if we choose that route, we don't have to bow our knee to their secular content or their ineffective methodology. We are already free.

Freedom is a mindset. A few chapters back, we defined a mindset as a cognitive bias, a systematic manner of thinking that influences our decisions, our actions. We talked about Dr. Dweck's two mindset delineations, the growth mindset and the fixed mindset. People who focus on innate abilities, fixed traits, are often reluctant to take on challenges. They get stuck. On the other hand, people with growth mindsets are more likely to take on challenges and less likely to get stuck in a limiting behavior. We need a growth mindset to get us through the challenges that undoubtedly lie ahead.

Understanding the foundations of our mindsets can help us move beyond the limitations of some of our belief-to-behavior patterns. Mindsets are formed through an ongoing focus on something we personally place value on. Where our treasure is, there our hearts will be also, there will our mindsets be also. And out of that will flow our actions. That's the belief-to-behavior pattern. But our mindsets are also powerfully impacted by social factors, the impact of the social system on the individual. Once we recognize this, we become better equipped to evaluate the influence of our social systems—and our children's social systems—and their collective spiritual, psychological, and sociological impact on our lives in the church, the family, and the culture. We learn, as Proverbs 13:20 says, "to walk with the wise" so we will grow wise.

As a nation, we have wasted an extraordinary amount of time and resources in the public sector trying to fix a broken system. This is a losing battle. Again, as John Taylor Gatto says in one of my all-time favorite quotes, "Over the years of wrestling with the obstacles that stand between child and education, I have come to believe that government monopoly schools are structurally unreformable. They cannot function if their central myths are exposed and abandoned." A central goal of this book has been exposing the myopic myths of public education through the analysis of the twelve toxic traits and their impact on the next generation.

Instead of focusing on reform, a better use of our time and energy would be strategizing what we can do to rescue parents who want out of government indoctrination centers. How can we help those who want to leave but feel trapped, hopeless, scared? What can the local church do to assist parents who believe they are unable to homeschool? How can we sponsor them, support them, come alongside them, and make what seems impossible possible for them? What can we do, individually and corporately, to help free the captives?

Instead of spending our time and energy on a structurally unreformable system of corrupt content and methodology, we would be better served as industry disruptors in the field of education. We would be better served envisioning new ways to inspire, to train up, to coach, to educate. Most of the families that are exiting the public system in our region are motivated by masks and medical mandates. But these are simply surface issues that belie the true heart of the public system. Let's remind ourselves of all that's happening in government schools right now:

- The promotion of critical race theory
- The peddling of revisionist history
- The devaluing of life
- The vying for control: state versus parent
- The promotion of anti-American sentiment
- The promotion of anti-male sentiment
- Control over thought and emotion
- The elevation of pseudo science
- The teaching of evolution as fact, not fiction
- The prolific promotion of hypersexuality
- The ongoing attack on gender identity
- The mockery of biblical events, beliefs, and behaviors
- The outlawing of the Great Commission

And this is just the content, which doesn't even begin to address the highly ineffective methodology that has students trained in sycophantic obedience to the approval, likes, and dislikes of someone whose opinion doesn't even matter in the long run. It's a broken system. It's time to rise up and be the change that the next generation needs. Freedom is protected and preserved as it is defended and distributed from generation to generation. So, sure, we may win the right to sit in a classroom without wearing a mask, but that will never stop the viral disease of anti-family, anti-purity, anti-science, anti-Christian philosophy that's spreading across the hearts and minds of the next generation.

And let's not be fooled by Christian schools, who are often not faring much better than their public counterparts. Many of them have copied the methodologies and ideologies of the secular system. They walk like a public school, talk like a public school, and think like a public school. They're like a secular textbook with an I ♥ Jesus bumper sticker slapped on the front cover. And why? Because most of the teachers went to secular schools and are simply parroting to the next generation of unsuspecting students the information they gained in their humanistic classrooms! One of my professors actually became an atheist while taking a philosophy class in his Christian high school. And, of course, many educational institutions from K to college that call themselves Christian don't even hire Christian teachers. Parents, do your homework! Praying with kids before subjecting them to feminist ideologies or worm-dispensing methodologies will not sanctify the classroom. It won't protect their little hearts from heresy. And it won't foster a sense of wonder and gratitude, two emotions that should fuel the transformative experience of learning.

That sense of wonder is notably absent in most traditional educational institutions, where Piaget's American Question is exemplified but never exonerated. And this pervasive thinking, this drive-faster, push-harder mindset is propelling a generation into performance anxiety. An article in *The Economist* called GenZ "stressed, depressed, and exam obsessed." As one teen said in an interview with Colorado Public Radio, "through all the work, all the pressure, all this testing and box-checking, (we) still don't feel prepared for the real world." This focus must change.

Institute for Excellence founder Andrew Pudewa was teaching a session for our Awaken Academy families recently, and he talked about how parents coming from public schools are literally afraid to help their children succeed. They have been conditioned to believe that helping a student get to a point of success would somehow undermine that success. Add to that mistaken belief the ongoing culture of the expert, which again, makes parents feel incapable of teaching their own children anything, and we have the recipe for confusion. Andrew sat with a small group of young students as they worked through one of the IEW workbooks, noting in particular one boy who seemed to be struggling with the assignment. Andrew patiently talked to the student, and little by little, he was able to discern that the student was lacking a sense of autonomy, efficacy. This element, as you will remember, is a key to intrinsic motivation.

So, Andrew gave the boy a small, manageable task: Cross the t and add the period and the end of the sentence. Simple. Remarkably simple. But as the young student was finally able to do something right in his own mind after toiling in frustration for 30 minutes, he was immediately unlocked. His countenance changed. His posture changed. And the student's father told us later that this specific moment was the turning point for their son. If we make the work too hard and we don't ever give our children, especially our young children, the ability to succeed, they won't develop intrinsic motivation because they will never develop a sense of efficacy.

Another curious intentional infringement of freedom has recently swept over private education, especially in California.

The state does not require teachers in private schools, which includes homeschools, to be certified or even degreed. After all, the research tells the story—even a student taught at home by a parent who never graduated from high school will still outperform students taught in traditional school by a certified teacher. However, because parents have bought the lie of the expert, they have somehow now been convinced that they need the state's permission, blessing, or signature to teach their children. Let's remember that this is the same governmental system that brought us the twelve toxic traits. And do we yet again want to bring ourselves under their submission? "Do not allow yourselves to be burdened again by the yoke of slavery," Paul said. Even the state does not require that private schools, including homeschools, hire certified teachers. And yet, there is a movement amongst parents to make sure teachers are certified and schools accredited. This is yet another example of how we willingly exchange our intellectual and familial freedoms for academic slavery.

The lie of the expert runs deep, and it is a threat to our personal and collective freedom. Remember, this education crisis didn't just take over American minds and souls overnight. This gradual decline of values and truth and integrity have brought us to where we stand today: at a national crossroads. As Neil Postman always said, it's up to those of who see the older, clearer waters to speak up.

The training of our children is our responsibility. We can delegate some of our subjects and content to a trusted member of our circle, of course, but just like a good organizational leader takes full responsibility for what's happening in the company, we have to take responsibility for what's happening in our homes. Genesis 18:19 is the first mention in scripture of training of children. A father will "command his children and his household after him, and they shall keep the way of the Lord, to do justice and judgment." It is significant, as Dr. Henry Morris notes, that this first reference stresses paternal instruction in the ways of God. Deuteronomy 6 tells us that this training should be ongoing, regular, a daily event that cannot be replicated by emotionally or physically absent fathers. God has delegated the training of children and the household first to the father. Fathers lead the way. And what will be the result? Isaiah 54:13 says, "All your children shall be taught of the Lord, and great shall be the peace of your children." What a wonderful promise in an age of anxiety! Why not take some time to read, talk, and pray over kids today, dads? Their righteous justice, judgment, and peace will be released through your impartation of faith. If you feel like you've displaced the proper affection and attachment to your family, which will rob you of your ability to influence the next generation, it's time to take back the reigns. The next generation needs active, engaged mothers and fathers to lead them to greatness. The future is family.

And that's really the mindset I want to return us to here—family. The future is family. The future of the church is family. The future of the city, the nation, the planet is family. If we live under a mindset of narcissism or me-ism, we will be so focused on our own little world that we will miss the great and glorious multigenerational work that God wants to do in us and through us. One of the most beautiful aspects of the parent-directed education movement, and something we are seeing coming alive across the county of San Diego, is this Luke 1:17 model of the restoring of hearts between parents and children. Parents are beginning to feel a relational shift and a thawing of their hearts (which they didn't even know were frozen). God is turning hearts of stone into hearts of clay.

This is a miraculous work, friend, for as we look at the fruits of the current generation, the data is sobering. Parents have willingly outsourced their offspring to indoctrination centers that are imposing on their freedoms. One of the most distressing arenas where we see this captive mindset unfolding is in the realm of mental health. Depression has reached epidemic proportions in our nation's young. The National Institute for Mental Health (NIMH) defines depression as by at least a two-week period of time where there is a loss of interest or pleasure in daily activities and problems with sleep, eating, energy, concentration, or self-worth. The NIMH says that 17.3 million are affected, with the majority of those being 18-25 year olds. According to the CDC, 3.2% of 3-17 year olds have been diagnosed with depression in the US. About 13% of those ages 12 and over in US take antidepressants, and according to the Citizens Commission on Human Rights, that includes 30,000 children aged 2-5 years old. That stat represents a total jump of 65% in just 15 years (and, as a side note, a total of $17 billion in revenue globally).

Among other causes, depression can be exacerbated by hormones impacted from poor diet and a lack of exercise. Read Barbara Reed Stitt's research on the foods that are supplied to public schools (and prisons) and how behaviors change when children eat healthy, whole foods. Depression can also be influenced by soul ties, by friends who like to ruminate (focus on the negative), and even by constantly dishonoring ourselves by not keeping our promises or commitments to ourselves. Significantly, perhaps most significantly for the youngest generations, we see a correlation between social media usage and depression: More time on social media correlates with higher rates of depression, especially for teenage girls. The total screen usage per day should be no more than 2 hours for ages 2 to adult.

The most common emotion experienced by our youngest generations today, according to the National Institute for Mental Health, is anxiety. Anxiety is a feeling of worry, nervousness or unease about an imminent event or uncertain outcome. This can include panic, phobias, or obsessive-compulsive thoughts and behaviors. The NIMH says 23% of females and 14% of males are affected, with 31% of US adults having an anxiety "disorder" at some point. According to the CDC, 7% of US children ages 3 to 17 have been diagnosed with anxiety, and a whopping total of 1.5 million 0-17 year olds in America take anti-anxiety medication. Anxiety is also the most prevalent mental disorders among college students (61% according to the American Psychological Association, 2017).

As we begin to orient to a biblical worldview, we see the importance of rightly navigating the surfeit of human emotions, for allowing them to take their rightful place: Emotions are to be informants, not masters. They draw us closer in relationships, they illuminate situations, and they enhance spiritual gifts like discernment, but emotions were not created to rule over us. Proverbs 17:22 tells us, "A joyful heart is good medicine, but a crushed spirit dries up the bones. The word "merry" here is translated gleeful, joyful, glad, and the word medicine means a cure. In other words, a joyful heart is curative, cathartic. Romans 14:16 tells us that the kingdom of God is "righteousness, peace, and joy in the Holy Spirit."

These emotional states are vastly distinct from the emo-driven, turbulent teenager of today. Parents often ask me if it's normal that their two year old is a monster and their teenager a brat. No, friends, this is not normal in the biblical worldview. Normal in the world system is not normal in the kingdom of God. The psalmist declared in Psalm 16:11, "You make known to me the path of life; in your presence there is fullness of joy; at your right hand are pleasures forevermore." Whatever your teen or toddler (or their parent) is trying to find perfect happiness and fulfillment in, it will never be enough, Only God's presence can bring perfect peace and joy. The longer a child has been severed from God's presence, starved from it in the public system, the longer it will take to recalibrate. Be patient. The healing of relational attachments will produce a dramatic shift in emotional regulation and mastery.

Stanford University professors have coined the term

"duck syndrome" for this anxiety in our youngest citizens. The visual describes a duck gliding gracefully across the pond, akin to the GenZ and Alpha image protection, but underneath the surface, the creature's legs are paddling frantically just to stay afloat. Every GenZ I have shared this visual with has said they relate, that it is an accurate descriptor of teen life today. As with depression, we can also become more anxious when we are not caring for our bodies: Dr. Daniel Amen and Dr. Josh Axe stress the importance of certain minerals like magnesium for regulating the central nervous system. Parents must recognize the importance of a healthy diet (a healthy physical and mental diet), exercise, fresh air, and minimized screen time.

Dr. Amen, the world's leading brain researcher, has scanned over 46,000 human brains, the largest database of this nature in the world. He emphasizes the importance of practical techniques for overcoming anxiety. One such technique is stomping out ANTs, automatic negative thoughts. Like the process of taking thoughts captive, Amen says to recognize that a thought is negative and confront it by mentally stomping it out. Philippians 4:6 says, "Do not be anxious about anything but in everything by prayer and supplication with thanksgiving let your requests be known to God. And the peace of God which surpasses all understanding, will guard your hearts and your minds in Christ Jesus." The word anxious, *merimnao,* translates worry, and to worry means to give way to anxiety or unease, to allow our mind to dwell on difficulty or troubles. A few synonyms of the word are brood, agonize, and panic. The word *guard* denotes someone trained to give his life to keep intruders out. Philippians says that peace is that guard, iron bars that are designed to protect your heart and your mind from torment. "Great peace have they that love your law, and nothing shall offend them," Psalm 119:165 says. "All your children shall be taught of the Lord," Isaiah 54:13 reminds us, "and great shall be the peace of your children." We can't dissect the teachings of the Bible from our entire scholastic foundations and then wonder why anxiety is on the rise.

I understand anxiety and depression on a very personal level. I used to be completely tormented by memories of abuse. I was constantly reliving past experiences, especially right before I would fall asleep. It was, in a word, torturous. I'd tell myself over and over, "I'm taking that thought captive. I'm not letting it in," but to no avail. The image would burst through my neural circuitry and embed my past in my present. Anyone who's struggled with PTSD will understand the battle. I was striving and stressing on my own strength for years. But one day, it shifted. I can't mark a specific calendar day, but in a reflective conversation, I looked back in the rearview mirror of my life and suddenly realized that I rarely ever have that experience anymore. Instead, that Philippians 4:6 peace became a protective guard stationed over my mind. Now, I can literally feel a thought coming up against me, and before the details are unpacked, the toxic thought is stopped at the door and denied entry.

If you've stood outside Buckingham Palace and seen the Queen's guard (men who are secure enough in their own manhood to wear those massive, furry bearskin hats), then you get the visual. Those guards will do whatever it takes to keep a visitor with ill intent out of that castle in order to protect and preserve their country's most prized possession. In the same way, I can feel it. That thought sweeps into my sphere, but it's as if there's a Buckingham Palace guard keeping the thought with ill intent out of my mind. It's a surreal experience; it's nothing I can do it my own strength. It's supernatural, living evidence of Philippians 4:6. This same protection is available for you too, friend.

Our children need this peace, this freedom. Parents, we need this peace, this freedom. It's time for us to wake up, to rise up, to speak up, to step up. It's our responsibility as believers to make the needed sacrifices right now to rescue the next generation from the indoctrination of the public system. If we are honest, we can see that we've willingly exchanged our freedom for convenience. Instead of being trapped in a mindset of captivity, beholden to the big yellow prison bus, let's charge up the chariots and join Moses in the anthem of freedom, "Let my people go." We can't look back at the statistical tragedies of the youngest generations without seeing the thread of influence from the public school system. Freedom is just a prayer away. Truly, as John 8:36 reminds us, he whom the son has set free is free indeed.

CHAPTER EIGHTEEN

Defining the Terms:
The Heart of Home Education

Since we've been dropping hints about this concept of the parent-directed education model for 17 chapters, I thought we might want to spend a little time in this chapter unpacking the construct. What, precisely, is home education? There are several different types of educational systems recognized by the Department of Education including traditional public school, homeschooling public school, traditional private school, and traditional homeschooling. And, of course, there are also multiple variations of each of these models. The focus of our attention in this chapter is home education, also known as homeschooling or the parent-directed model of education. In my terms, home education is a system of family discipleship where parents take on the responsibility of educating their children at home through a variety of methodologies and systems. As NHERI founder Dr. Brian Ray points out, this doesn't have to mean educating solely at home, only that the parent is directing the process of education, which means the parent is making the primary decisions about what's taught, who teaches it, and how it will be taught.

Before 2020, home education was already the fastest

growing movement in education with about 2 million students nationwide being homeschooled. But after the scholastic debacle of 2020, parents began to see even more clearly the harm that traditional education was having on the minds, emotions, and bodies of the next generation. By late 2021, just 15 months later, the numbers of families who identified as homeschoolers had jumped to astronomical proportions, over 11% of the general population—5 million students!

People homeschool for a variety of reasons, including concerns with the public school's safety, bullying, negative role models, peer pressure, academic failure, and morally bankrupt curricula. The vast majority of families who decide to homeschool in America do so because of two primary reasons, unsafe school environments and morally-bankrupt curricula. With our 2020-2021 homeschool recruits, the most common reasons for leaving public school were the increasing pressures of masks and medical mandates. For Christian families whose objective is training children in a biblical worldview, homeschooling centers not only on academics but on providing a Bible-based education that provides for spiritual formation. Homeschooling is a purposeful and powerful methodology for ensuring the transmission of the faith from one generation to the next. Again, home education doesn't have to be at home, and it doesn't have to mean that the parent teaches all the subjects. The key is who is taking the reins and who is calling the shots, the secular government or the parent? Who is teaching the children, and what are they being taught? These foundational influences have shaped human history, driven the trajectory of civilizations. Future generations are in training right now under these two constructs, the who and the what, and the answer to the questions will determine the eventual outcome of the nation. Ideas have consequences.

Homeschooling, then, is less of a specific methodology and more of a mindset. Parent-directed education means the parent makes the who and what decisions, and though mom or dad may certainly contract out some of that teaching, the difference in the parent-directed model is that parents are the ones who choose the person who will be pouring into the student via the subject of math or biology or dance. Parents choose the person who will tutor or coach the student in a specific class or subject. When we have the freedom to choose those influences, and when we have the margin outside of the rat race to make intentional, fully conscious decisions about what, how, where, when, and with whom our children will learn, we are the ones driving education, not the state. These influences shape the trajectory, the outcome.

For parents just starting out, there are hundreds of curricular options for home education. In the next chapter, I provide some resources that will help you get started on your journey. But it's important to know that you're not alone, and home education is not some weird cult that you're joining, as I once thought when I first heard the term "homeschool" 20 years ago. Home education is not a new concept. By comparison, school is actually the new concept! The vast majority of our forefathers learned in homeschool-like environments. Prior to the Industrial Era, education was organic, familial. As Teri Ann Berg Olsen (2004) explains in *Learning for Life: Educational Words of Wisdom*, many historical leaders, authors, university presidents, and creative geniuses had the benefit of being homeschooled for all or part of their educational career: Benjamin Franklin, George Mason, James Madison, George Washington, Andrew Jackson, Thomas Jefferson, Abraham Lincoln, Theodore Roosevelt, Winston Churchill, Alexander Hamilton, Patrick Henry, Albert Einstein, William Blake, Claude Monet, Leonardo da Vinci, Alexander Graham Bell, Thomas Edison, Orville and Wilbur Wright, Wolfgang Amadeus Mozart, Hans Christian Anderson,Charles Dickens, Robert Frost, C.S. Lewis, Beatrix Potter, Walt Whitman, and Laura Ingalls Wilder, just to name a few. Let this list inspire you to see the potential within your student! As Denise Mira says, this is no ordinary child! Our kids were born for such a time as this!

One of the common worries we get from parents who are just starting out on the journey is the concern about viability, the model's capacity for producing academic success. Even though they know full well that the public school is a colossal failure, parents still assess themselves by this humanistic measuring tape. They wonder nervously how their children will fare in the homeschool model, and the answer is almost always that they will excel! I encourage parents to take the state tests just for fun and see how much better their homeschooled students do when compared to their traditionally-schooled counterparts. The longer students homeschool, the higher their scores rise. When parents see the fruit of the homeschool model, where children are more influenced by adults than their peers, where their vocabularies and critical thinking skills are activated by being in the company of those who are more mature, wise, and solution-oriented, they begin to place their trust in the model.

As studies by Dr. Brian Ray of the National Home Education Research Institute show, homeschoolers consistently outperform their traditionally-schooled counterparts on standardized tests by 37 points on average, regardless of the level of education achieved by the parent doing the homeschooling. Yes, there's that pesky little stat again, the one that confounds teachers and enrages administrators: A parent who didn't even graduate from high school gets better results from her students than a teacher certified by the state! Let me say that again. The level of education carried by the parents bears no negative impact on the academic success of the child. Isn't that wonderfully ironic, even oxymoronic? Furthermore, in addition to outperforming traditionally educated students in academics, homeschoolers are also more involved in their community, and despite the unfounded rumors to the contrary, they are far better socialized than their public school counterparts. That doesn't mean there aren't exceptions, but we don't judge a program's success by its outliers; we judge it on the wide swath, the majority result. To hear more on those statistics, listen to my interview with Dr. Brian Ray on The Communication Architect podcast or visit his site, NHERI.org.

As Drs. Nabor and Mate point out in their book *Hold on to Your Kids: Why Parents Need to Matter More than Peers,* healthy socialization is not developed through spending all of one's time with a peer group, despite this pattern being constantly reinforced in the age-segregation of the public system. Instead, healthy socialization requires connection with those outside of one's peer group, which is a pattern that is regularly reinforced in home education. Humans of all ages need ongoing connection to both mentors and protégés to develop to our fullest academic, moral, and spiritual capacity.

And more important than the academic success is the character growth that is modeled in a typical homeschool environment, where children are primarily mentored by their parents rather than by their peers. Deuteronomy 6:6-9 instructs parents to impress God's laws upon the hearts of their children, to talk about them as they travel on the highways and the byways. In traditional educational environments, unreasonable schedules dictate much of the home life: students attend class for 7-8 hours a day, and then they have another two to three hours of homework each night, not to mention sports, music, or ballet lessons. Frantic, overfilled schedules significantly limit the opportunities for family discipleship.

Ken Ham and Josh McDowell have documented the tragic and rapid decline of the faith in today's generation. According to their research, 85% of teenagers who grow up in Christian homes but attend public schools walk away from the faith by the time they graduate. Conversely, only 5% of Christian homeschoolers walk away from the faith—a staggering contrast and a remarkable ROI! Be sure to check out Ken Ham's latest book, *Ready to Return,* the fundamental need for a shift in church culture for more support and data on this topic. As Barna's 2016 State of the Church research demonstrated, only 20% of Christian families read the Bible together at home outside of church, and only 10% worship together. Clearly, the majority of Christian homes in America are not functioning in an effective discipleship modality. However, as we see homeschool rates rise in the current socio-political climate, we are also seeing discipleship rates rise. The homeschool model creates an intentional opportunity for parents to invest daily into the lives of their children and train them up in the way they should go. We can expect a good harvest from a good investment.

This construct is opposite to the pathway of the modern culture. For example, many people in modern culture believe that the teen years are "destined" to be full of turmoil and relational distress, but this idea is both historically inaccurate and non-Scriptural. Social scientists didn't even identify an onset of teen rebellion until researcher James Coleman first noted a shift in behavior in 1966 (a notably tumultuous time of rebellion in the United States). Coleman said that a perceptible behavioral shift was taking place, and teens were "beginning to care more about what their peers thought than about what their parents thought." Ironically, Coleman's contemporaries mocked the observation, saying that "a disassociated teen culture" would never, could never exist in America. But indeed, it was the beginning of a social shift where teens started to pull away from the biblical model of family discipleship and relationship and instead orient themselves toward a "modern teen," peer-centric mentality.

The Bible does not delineate individuals as teens (the word "teen" didn't even become a separate category of adulthood until the 1950s). Instead, the Bible teaches a multigenerational system of discipleship as shown in Titus 2:3: "Teach the older women…to teach what is good. Then they can urge the younger women to love their husbands and children, to be self-controlled and pure, to be busy at home, to be kind, and to be subject to their husbands, so that no one will malign the word of God." This generational transmission of the faith does not happen by accident; it requires an intentionality that is fostered through the system of home education.

In the last four decades, the public sector has become increasingly and overtly anti-Christian in nature. The Department of Education now forbids the teaching of "sectarian" viewpoints during the school day, and California schools are now prohibited from allowing prayer, Bible study, creationism, or abstinence-only education. The 51 million students who attend public schools in the United States are taught from a perspective of secular humanism. Not only is God overlooked from the educational system, he is purposefully dissected from the heart of the educational process. This stands in stark contrast to the Bible's viewpoint on the development of wisdom: "The fear of the Lord is the beginning of wisdom," Proverbs 9:10 tells us, "and knowledge of the holy one is understanding."

By age 7, most boys in traditional educational institutions say that they "hate" school. Taught in largely feminist environments, public school students are rewarded for traditional "girl behaviors" like sitting still and listening quietly, and they are punished for traditional "boy behaviors" such as being physically active, talkative, or competitive. Classroom management absorbs 65% of the school day, which means teaching hours are stretched out from three hours (the actual time it takes to teach the subjects) to seven hours. These stifling approaches limit students' creativity and their love of learning. Not surprisingly, we have seen a rapid decline in college enrollments for males, which dropped 10% over the last decade. Whereas men were once represented 90% of the college roster, today, they represent only 40%. Women are now outperforming men in the workplace, and more women than men are listed as the "head of household" on U.S. Census data than ever before in history. Instead of providing an academic system that nurtures individual styles of learning, the traditional sector of education has catered to a feminist approach that undermines male behavior and crushes the male spirit. Both boys and girls need individualized learning structures that cater to their needs and allow them to succeed—but not at the expense of one another.

Homeschooling provides parents with the option to direct what and how their children learn. Instead of an Industrial Era, one-size-fits-all approach, parents can tailor the coursework and the studies to their child's individual learning style. When it's done well, homeschooling creates a love of learning and a curiosity that fuels research and inquiry. My most successful college students are not necessarily those who are most gifted, but those who are most determined. Character plays a powerful role in success. Colleges and universities have been actively recruiting homeschoolers for over a decade because of their academic performance, their commitment to volunteerism, their social maturity, and their real-world experience. But again, it's more than that. It's bigger than that, bigger than us, bigger than this generation. In his book *Education for Human Flourishing,* Dr. Paul Spears gives this charge:

> If Christians do little to deflect the view that theological and ethical assertions are merely parts of a tradition...then they inadvertently contribute to the marginalization of Christianity precisely because they fail to rebut the contemporary tendency to rob it of the very thing that gives it the authority necessary to prevent that marginalization, namely, its legitimate claim to give us moral and religious knowledge. Both in and out of the Church, Jesus has been lost as an intellectual authority, and Christian intellectuals should carry out their academic vocation in light of this fact.

From a developmental science perspective, the homeschool model restores education to its healthiest and most spiritually productive location, the shoulders of the parents. The fruit of home education is irrefutable. Though it isn't always easy, and we certainly have to stretch and learn and grow along the way as parents, homeschooling gives us an opportunity to train up our children in the way that they should go, fostering a love of learning and a commitment to God and family that we would likely not have experienced in other academic settings.

When Harvard University opened its doors in 1636, the goal was straightforward: The Pilgrims wanted to found an educational institution that would ensure the clear and accurate transmission of the Bible to the next generation. In other words, they didn't want to pass along the tremendous responsibility of governing a new America to a biblically illiterate population. Oh, how far we've strayed. At the time of this writing, Christian colleges in the United States are facing rapidly surmounting pressure to succumb to an opposite appeal: Continue to accept government funding, and the government will tell you what you can and cannot believe, think, do, say. Homeschoolers have watched this same wave of scholastic slavery looming on the horizon for several years. We have faced many of the same decisions Christian colleges are facing today: accept government funding and you will be forced to submit to a law that cripples the Great Commission.

Michael Farris, United States constitutional lawyer and founder of Patrick Henry College, warned homeschoolers in 2010 that "a wave" was coming. He said at the time that there were over 180 documents on file written by powerful lawyers in pubic universities whose intentions were to turn all education into secular education, making it against the law to teach from a Christian worldview. At the time, it all seemed a little Huxleian— a *Brave New World* for the modern millennia. However, today, we see these talons digging in swiftly and deeply across the educational sector.

In the United States, it has become accepted and commonplace that students are not allowed to pray, to share the gospel, or to make any other overt displays of faith while on the grounds of a public school. Those who dare to break this anti-Great-Commission ruling receive cease and desist orders from the teacher, the principal, or even the local sheriff. Homeschoolers have known the ferocity and importance of this battle because many of us have chosen to homeschool so that we will not be subject to the anti-Christian laws of a secular government. As a case in point, let's return to the charter conversation from two chapters ago. Many homeschoolers were faced with a tempting decision when the government launched an offering they called 'free money' for homeschoolers: the charter system. Accept government funding for your homeschooling, they said, and we will provide your child with all the extras you probably can't afford on one income: art classes, music lessons, sports, theme park admissions, laptop computers, and free programs for your kids.

Some organizations, like CHEA, wisely warned homeschoolers to steer clear of the charter temptations, calling charters a Trojan Horse that would pull students back into the government system where they would once again lose the freedoms homeschoolers had fought for in the beginning. After all, charters operate under the same principle as the public schools, for they are indeed government institutions: If you take our money, you must follow our rules. As Proverbs 22:7 reminds us, the borrower is servant to the lender.

This is the number one reason that families (and schools!) must break free of the unequal yoke with a secular government. We can no longer afford to accept money from a government that requires us to eliminate prayer, to silence Scripture, and to ignore the Great Commission. Haven't we learned this lesson from watching the travesty in the public school sector since the Values

Clarification Movement swept through just 50 years ago? All traces of Christendom were swept out of the classroom, and multiple generations have now borne the impact. As research from Barna (2015), Hamm (2014), Focus on the Family (2016), and many other institutions show, the spiritual damage that has been done in just the last five decades is staggering.

So, where do we begin as a collective impetus for change? A three-pronged approach might look something like this. First, we must actually place our trust in the God that we profess, allowing him to guide and direct us as we follow him wholeheartedly. Matthew 6:24 reminds us that we cannot serve two masters. We will either serve God, or we will serve money. The current wake-up call on scholastic subversion is most certainly an opportunity for us to cease from wavering between those two alternatives. It is also an opportunity for us to stand firm, not to shrink back: In an era where the grace and truth of God could radically transform the tragic statistics of hopelessness and brokenness in our culture, we must be mindful of our singular mission as aliens in this world—to share boldly the good news of Christ.

Second, we need to find alternative sources of funding, including the support of churches, businesses, and alumni who will lend money and support to future generations without robbing them of their First Amendment rights. In our current funding structure, the public schools and colleges get all the tax money to support their causes while the private schooler or private homeschooler has to relay on bake sales and creative purchasing power to close that gap. If churches and businesses would step in to show support for Christian institutions in the way that the state shows financial support for state institutions, homeschoolers would be less tempted by the government handout.

Third, specifically for Christian colleges, we need to decrease the cost of education. We need to take a good, hard look at our internal structures and see where we are bleeding. Are there singular job loads that could be shared by other departments? Are there any non-degreed positions that could be run by junior and senior college students who have already proven themselves faithful by their performance in the classroom? Are there other internship opportunities that could decrease the cost of payroll and increase the work/study options for students? How much could these colleges (and other Christian businesses) save by partnering with other Christian organizations like Christian Healthcare Ministries, Medishare, or Samaritan's Purse?

These are some of the many reasons I started Chula Vista Christian University, and why I continue to help churches start homeschool academies across the nation. As innovators and visionaries, we don't have to remain stuck in an outdated, unfruitful method of doing life and school and work; we can be part of the solution, part of the transformation of education in this generation. The old model is broken—not just in content but in methodology. It's time for a new breed of education that honors God and partners with the learner-driven methodology of the youngest generations.

The dissection of moral absolutes from the public sphere has caused complete and utter anarchy throughout the system. Because we have removed the discussion of right and wrong from the public conversation, our young people have no moral compass to guide their decision-making process. As a nation, we have pulled funding and cultural support away from Christian institutions and poured it instead into abortion providers, morally deficient schools, and bastions of secular humanism. Then we find ourselves wondering why 1 in 5 students is cutting or burning themselves on purpose. We wonder why the leading cause of death for Black and Hispanic youth in America is homicide. We wonder why our country has one of the highest rates of abortion in the developed world. We wonder why our 15 to 24 year olds are both STD-ridden and oversexualized. We wonder why Christianity now seems irrelevant and bland to the young. There are psychological, emotional, and physiological dangers of living outside the protective boundaries that are inherent to the Christian worldview. Because the one voice that is continuously silenced in the public school classroom is the voice of truth, the word of God, the youngest generations have not had access to the wisdom they need to make informed decisions. They've been exposed only to rhetoric, not relationship.

Furthermore, as long as our financial systems continue to fund morally averse programming while punishing the Christian institutions that teach abstinence, value, human dignity, and personal worth—the foundational personal values that can actually protect against rampant promiscuity and violence in the first place—we will continue to witness this tragic moral decline. So maybe it's time we put our money where our mouth is. The wave that Farris predicted is now upon us. Instead of allowing ourselves to be swallowed up by this misguided malefaction, we must preserve the rights of the First Amendment and the call of the Great Commission in a once-Christian nation. The choice is clear. Homeschooling is not only a highly effective educational strategy; it is also a purposeful and powerful methodology for ensuring the transmission of the faith from one generation to the next. In the words of Psalm 102:18, "Let this be written for a future generation, that a people not yet created may praise the Lord."

The walls have crumbled all around us, and we are standing today in the midst of the rubble. The level of biblical illiteracy in the next generation has reached epidemic proportions. As I shared in the book *The Science of Social Influence,* our family was in a California history museum several summers ago, and our tour guide was highlighting facts and trivia about the many artifacts housed on the property. There were a few other families in the tour group, as well as a father and daughter. The girl was about nine years old and seemed to know every answer to the trivia questions, even regarding academically-obscure factoids like the history of ketchup. As we rounded the corner of one of the rooms, we saw a large book lying open on a stand. The host wanted to make a comparison to the importance, the relevance, of the book, so she said, "It's kind of like a Bible." The little 9-year-old ketchup expert turned to her dad and asked aloud, "Daddy, what's a Bible?" The man looked around at all of us, then back at her, and said, "You really don't know what a Bible is?" He was either incredulous or just personally embarrassed that he had never told his 9-year-old daughter about the greatest fount of literature in all of human history. "No," she said. "Okay," he whispered back. "I'll tell you later."

At the time of that observation a decade ago, I was shocked. It was difficult for me to fathom that an otherwise well-read American would not know what a Bible was! But today, that no longer surprises me. The Bible has been suppressed, revoked, buried, lied about, forcibly dissected, and outlawed in America's youth training ground, the public school system. Is it any wonder at all that today's youngest generations find the Bible irrelevant and archaic?

There was a similar time in history recorded in 2 Chronicles 34. King Josiah had inherited the throne of Judah at age eight. Even as a boy, the Bible says he walked "in the ways of David" and did what was right in the sight of the Lord. In the eighth year of his reign, at age 16, he began cutting off access to the false gods of the day, smashing the pagan altars that had been constructed all over the cities of Judah and Jerusalem. At age 26, Josiah employed a group of men to rebuild the ruins of the temple of the Lord. As the men were clearing the stones out of the dusty temple, a book catches the eye of Hilkiah the priest. Can you can picture the scene? I imagine Hilkiah pulling gently on the document lodged in the rubble, his heart racing as he anticipated the untold treasure of his archeological discovery. As he pulled it out of the darkness and into the light, his knees must have grown weak as he realized he was holding the ancient book of the law. The book (a scroll, really) had been buried and forgotten by the previous generations, much like the word of God has been lost today, its guiding wisdom suffocated by the darkened rubble of the temple ruins. When the words from the book were read aloud to King Josiah, he tore his robes and cried aloud, saying, "Great is the Lord's anger that is poured out on us because our fathers… have not acted in accordance with all that is within this book."

What strikes me most today about this reading is when Hilkiah the priest came across the book of the law in the temple, it had been 57 years since the book had been part of the common vernacular. He and his generation were bearing the consequences for the folly of the previous generations. But Josiah called the community to account for the actions of his forefathers.The Bible says that because Josiah humbled himself, tore his clothes, and wept before the Lord, God spared him from seeing the forthcoming disaster. I believe that there are modern-day Josiahs in our midst, young men and young women who will live right before the Lord, who will be unmoved by the false gods of the day, who will refuse to worship at the altar of convenience and comfort—young men and women who will speak up for the truth of God's word and his way. The nation had faced 57 years of apostasy, and King Josiah recognized that the generational disconnect from the wisdom of the past had created an anchorless present. Remarkably, the timeline parallels America's own state of apostasy. It has been 57 years since the Bible was forcibly removed from our nation's youth training centers, the public school system. In the spirit of Josiah's courageous leadership, it's time for our generation to rise up, shake the dust off the timeless word of God, and take back the culture.

Parents, let us not be guilty of the same crime that Josiah's forefathers grievously committed by refusing to obey or pass down the word of God to the next generation. Let us take seriously the mantle of authority God has placed on our shoulders to equip and empower our children. It's up to us to lay the faith foundation for the next generation. We can't wait around for the school system to get its act together. We can't wait around for the culture to catch up to the truths of God's word. Even as Jesus calls out to us to ask, seek, and knock, the government system turns a deaf ear, a blind eye to the only one who can solve the world's problems.

Homeschooling works. The parent-directed method of education results in tangible fruit: students who are confident but not cocky, who can connect with people across all generations, who are civically engaged, emotionally mature, and driven to learn for the sake of learning. They are heads and shoulders above their traditionally-educated peers in virtually every available measurable outcome. They are the academic Daniels of their day. The data is in. The only question now is, "What are you waiting for?" Parents, you are equipped. You are called. You are capable. It's time for a public school exit, and it's time to take up the mantle of educating our children morally, academically, relationally. We are the force of change that will transform the next generation, one heart, one home, one city at a time.

In the next chapter, we will look at some practical applications of the model that will help reset your family culture and begin building the foundation your children and your children's children will need for the road ahead.

CHAPTER NINETEEN

Relational Recalibration:
Bringing Home the Outsourced Generation

Carl Rogers, an early American psychologist, tells a story from his childhood that serves as a powerful metaphor for helping parents navigate the relational components of parenting and educational discipleship. Maybe you can relate to his observation. One winter day, Rogers went down into his cold, midwest basement, and he found a forgotten sack of potatoes slumped over in a corner. What happens when potatoes are left alone in the pantry or basement? They sprout. Despite the cold, dark environment, the potatoes were growing anemic little offshoots that pushed upward toward the only available source of light, a tiny basement window. Their heliotropic instincts drove them toward the light. The offshoots were shriveled and colorless, and Rogers was struck by the visual metaphor. He called the anemic offshoots "life's desperate attempts to become itself."

Like those forgotten potatoes, maybe you grew up in a cold, dark environment, whether through abuse or neglect. Maybe you lacked the basic ingredients needed for healthy emotional and spiritual development. Maybe the words spoken over you caused pain, fear, or hopelessness. If so, when you look closely at the outer shell of your life, you might see a few of those same anemic offshoots, attempts you've made throughout your life at reaching upward toward that tiny basement window and becoming the person you thought you were supposed to be. As adults, personal growth often requires pruning off the anemic offshoots to make room for positive transformation. It means cutting back the words, thoughts, and actions in our lives that aren't bearing good fruit. That's the renewed mindset of Romans 12:2. We are literally transformed by the renewing of our minds.

I can certainly relate to those anemic potato offshoots, having grown up in an environment devoid of the light of relationship, an environment lacking the essential nourishment children need for healthy development. Many of the self-protective habits I learned for survival in childhood had to be pruned off in adulthood. A mindset of fierce independence may help us survive abuse, for example, but that same skill set will undermine the trust and interdependence needed for healthy adult relationships later in life. Looking back on that era, I recognize the anemic offshoots of a "not enough" mindset that came from scarcity: the visceral sensation of not having enough love, hope, trust, food, freedom, peace—these overarching losses created a feedback loop, an anemic offshoot, a crippling fear of loss that persisted well into adulthood.

Growing up in that kind of environment, it was easy to focus on the lack rather than the provision, to set my eyes on the waves rather than on the master of the waves. For the first half of my young adult life, I didn't know how to navigate the profound sense of rejection, the indelible stamp of worthlessness, or the paralyzing fear of loss. When my husband and I first met in college, we were both very broken people. But God sent mentors and role models to help us break free of the mindset of scarcity, to help us learn to become victors instead of victims. He planted us in a church that taught us discipleship and connected us in strategic relationships where we could develop the tools we would need to renew our minds, to develop a spirit of unity, and to focus on kingdom objectives.

This is where many of our reluctant homeschool families find themselves today. With great regret, parents who woke up in the scholastic crisis of 2020 tell us they had inadvertently neglected their children. They found themselves subsisting in a robotic rhythm: daily donning their chauffeur's cap, grinding in the groove of the rat race myth, and shipping their kids out to be trained up by someone else. Sleep. Wake up. Repeat. But once these courageous parents recognized the insidiousness of the system, once they started spending more than 30 minutes a day getting to know their children, they began to see the fractures in the relationship, broken attachments that often manifest as attention-seeking misbehaviors. Now, many of these champion parents have acknowledged the brokenness of the traditional system, repented for their complicity, and are leading their families on a path to healing and hope. This is faith's redemptive work! Just like those heliotropic offshoots, 2020 was a floodlight of God's love and grace that drew families to the window of truth.

"Faith," as Hebrews 11:1 so poetically defines it, "is the substance of things hoped for, the evidence of things not seen." Faith is a mental scaffold, a lens that sharpens the picture of possibility and gives us the courage to take action. Sometimes we have to get out of the emotional fray in order to see the evidence-based objective, the end goal that has its roots in kingdom objectives. That's the big picture. We know a tree by its fruit. So, we want to be careful not to develop a mindset that will cause us to echo the narrative of a fallen world. As one of my pastors says, don't put your "amen" to that. Make sure you're planting the right seeds if you want to reap a harvest of peace, hope, joy, love, and unity in your family. This will require a relational reset, and homeschooling provides the perfect opportunity for this foundational shift.

It's helpful to understand a little bit about the science behind relationships as you build or rebuild the interpersonal connections in your home. Through his research in the field of communication, University of Texas professor Dr. Mark Knapp discovered a compelling model of relational development that can provide a deeper understanding for how relationships grow, develop, and, sometimes, how they end. It's important to locate where we are in these stages so we can create an intentional intervention if needed.

The first phase of relational development is initiation, a brief stage where we are focused on making a favorable impression. The second phase is experimentation, where people analyze the other person and look for common ground. Many new homeschool families find themselves here, in the place of superficial discussions and the search for common ground. It's okay. Start somewhere. The third phase, intensifying, is where self-protectiveness begin to drop away. People begin sharing more of their true selves and expecting a level of commitment from the relationship. The fourth phase is integration, where relationships grow closer than the surface level, resulting in an interconnectedness that is essential for healthy family identity. In the fifth phase, bonding, partnerships are evident. Durable relationships are formed, and there is a clear expectation of longevity and commitment. Many families we talk with today have not reached this level of commitment, but clearly, attachment relationships are vital. If you see your relationships clinging to the lower runs of Knapp's ladder, parents, begin the ascent today. Be patient. You can do this.

These first five phases are all segments of relational development, and healthy relationships will fluctuate between stage five and six, which we will talk about in a moment. If a child has not had the opportunity to spend enough time with his or her parent to develop past the third phase (which is increasingly common in homes where families spend less than an hour a day together), a specific strategy for the development of trust must be undertaken.

The next five steps are phases of "relational termination," and these indicate as disintegration of the relationship. In this phase, conflict and misunderstanding are evident. The first phase of relational termination is differentiation. In this phase, people begin to focus so much on their differences that they lose their connectedness to the whole. We often see this in the teen years in America, where a child "suddenly" decides his values are different from those of the family. Now, there is a balance here: one of the goals of identity achievement is recognizing how we are similar to and different from our family of origin, but without a secure base and an anchor in the stages of relational development, a teen will not have a sense of self in relationship to the family. A healthy family environment, like a healthy organizational environment, will allow for differences of thought while still supporting a connectedness to the values and vision of the whole. We are each unique as individuals, but we also share connective experiences that identify us as members of the same tribe. Sadly, for the vast majority of America teens who have come through traditional education, they lack connection to the family identity and instead feel more connected to and understood by their peers (or even to celebrities and songwriters). It will take intentional time, patience, and effort to rewire this misplaced affection and identification, but as Matthew 19:26 reminds us, with God all things are possible.

The second phase of relational termination is circumscribing. In this phase, individuals begin setting up new boundaries in their relationships. Personal space increases, and discussions about meaningful personal issues cease. Conversation is limited to superficial constructs. The third phase is stagnation. True to its name, this is the phase of deterioration where little to no progress is being made that moves the relationship forward. Communication becomes even more limited, and if the relationship does not improve in this phase, it will most likely terminate. In the family, this stage is normally marked by a communication gap or one person feeling neglected or less important than another.

This stage is closely followed by stage four, avoidance, which is easy to spot. Individuals stop communicating, and the awkwardness in the room may be palpable. When stage four relationships are both in the same room, the air is thick and awkward. In this phase, people are often allowing resentment or neglect that has developed on the inside to manifest on the outside. A much healthier and productive way to deal with conflict is to approach the topic personally right away and seek unity. If we deal with offenses right away, we are far less likely to reach this avoidance stage. The final stage of Knapp's relational development is the terminating stage. In this stage, the relationship ends. The signs will have all been present for some time, from differentiating to circumscribing, from stagnation to avoidance, and then to this final tragic phase of relational departure. Relationships are ended, and often, bridges are burned.

When parents bring me their icy-hearted 18-year-old children asking me to help them, students who have spent a lifetime in peer-oriented indoctrination centers, they often say at first that the change in demeanor and connectivity has been sudden. As they reflect honestly, though, they can see the signs in retrospect. The warning signs were there all along; they just chose not to see them. Parents, now is the time to trace the steps back to relational healing and connectedness in your family. Don't wait until your child is balancing on the tightrope between avoidance and termination to step in and change the trajectory.

The goal of healthy growth is actually a dialectical tension between integration and differentiation. If we fall into groupthink or familial cloning, we will find ourselves once again refusing to embrace the God-given distinctives, the wonderful uniqueness, between us and our children. Instead of being divided by differences, we must strive to live in a constant state of reflective action, where we are keenly aware of differences, and where we leverage those differences to create an ongoing synergistic exchange. As you approach your new role as a mentor and parent educator, think honestly about where your familial relationships lie on this timeline, and focus on the healing of attachment and trust if that's needed. True to form, the mentor model requires reaching up to someone ahead and back to someone behind you in the race. In addition to pulling your own kids off the big yellow prison bus, you can help other parents too. We can't look the other way when confused and hurting parents are stepping out to try to homeschool, even if we are secretly exasperated by their lack of family discipleship. Remember, this is the most anxious, depressed, atheistic, suicide ideation prone generation in the history of our nation. This is our mission field.

One of the most effective, agency-producing habits you can add to your life as a new homeschooling parent is the relational reset, in both your home and your circle of influence. This reset will rebuild the relational structure and organic systems of support within your household. Social science research tells us that relational support is tremendously beneficial, both physically and psychologically. An article in the *Journal of Psychiatry* (2016) notes a reduction in heart rate, blood pressure, cortisol levels, fewer incidences of disease, and even a longer lifespan for those with socially supportive relationships. We weren't created to be fiercely independent or codependent. We were created to be interdependent. We are already hearing phenomenal testimonies from new homeschool parents who are 6 months to a year into the process: the relational reset is turning the hearts of misattuned, disengaged, and disruptive children. Instead of constantly butting heads with their parents, they are starting to walk in stride. The more the relationship heals, the more you will walk in tune and in peace with your children.

When my daughter was little, I was in graduate school,

and she would often give me words of encouragement. I was still carrying a weight of anxiety (hear the full testimony on my podcast), and she would say sweet things like, "Mommy, remember you are never alone. Jesus is always with you." Once, when she was a teen, she heard part of my testimony and said, "Mom, I wish I could go back in time and be your friend when you were little." Her sense of agency and compassion have always been carriers of hope to those around her. In the same way, Jesus gave his disciples the gift of encouragement when he reminded them of the nature of their relationship with him. "You have not chosen me, but I have chosen you," Jesus said in John 15:16. "I no longer call you a servant, as the servant does not know what his master is doing, but I have called you friends." This friendship is beyond human understanding or design. Human friendships are not mutually exclusive, but worldly friendships are: James 4:4 says that friendship with the world is enmity, hatred, toward God. Just as he chose us, we too must choose him daily. And just as God chose us to be the parents for our children, we too must choose both them daily. This prioritization of family is a vital force to counteract the secular system of influence.

Many parents, though, have inadvertently trained a generation of children to befriend the world system, to live in it and of it, to mirror its methods, to sip from its cup of popularity. As a result, these students are dependent on the gold star dispersement of the world's system, the dopamine rush of likes, the slavery of the fear of man and living for the approval of others. It's time to snatch our children out of the bonds of captivity and restore their friendship with the creator. Jesus said if we love him, we will obey him. Our children need someone who will repair the foundations, a modern-day Nehemiah who will build up the wall of protection with a spear in one hand and a hammer in the other.

Parents often ask me how long it takes to see change in the family, how long it takes to bond with a child who has been physically or emotionally distant, where the parent relationship has been supplanted by peers or public school or even screen time. Though the rate varies depending on the child, the family makeup, and the length of time the student has been in the system, there are some rather formulaic supports we can rely on to help strengthen that bond. For example, the development of an attachment bond requires authentic presence. As Dr. Siegel notes in *The Developing Mind*, "Healthy, secure attachment requires that the caregiver have the capacity to perceive and respond to the child's mental state." Parents, this means we have to be present, both mentally and physically, in the child's life. We have to be watching and listening and responding to what our children are experiencing. If we don't bridge that gap from superficial to meaningful relational stages, we won't develop a lasting bond.

In their book *Attachments,* Clinton and Sibcy give eight steps to healing interpersonal relationships, and I think they apply beautifully to the healing of attachments for those coming out of the brokenness fostered by traditional scholastic environments. To bring the freedom of truth and authenticity into your home, the authors suggest the following: Remember your story, recognize your pain, reframe the meaning of your story, repair your story, and reconnect with others. These small steps can help parents and their students address wounds and heal relational attachments that will strengthen the core of their family bond and help them grow both individually and collectively. "Attachment injuries and soul wounds break the ties that bind...relationships together," the authors note. "They erode our willingness to trust others."

A key characteristic I've seen emerging in Millennials and GenZs in my research has been their inability to make deep, lasting friendships. They, like many Americans, are living in that "together but alone" culture where we are surrounded by other people but don't really feel connected to any of them. In addition to attachment wounds, many Millennials and GenZs are held back by their unwillingness to regularly place themselves in environments where healthy relationships can flourish: church, for example. My church does such a fantastic job of facilitating friendship—I've really never seen anything like it. The women of our church love each other, encourage each other, speak the truth in love, and believe the best about each other. We are not a gossip culture. But even in that environment of healthy soil, the seeds of friendship still require intentional care. If you're not in a healthy church, find one. That's step one. Connect to the body of Christ.

A lot of moms, too, tell me they are lonely, that they crave adult conversations. Like GenZ and Millennials, parents can follow the relatively formulaic process of friendship to step into victory in this arena. First, recognize that you can't gain emotional closeness with another person without proximity or self-disclosure, revealing something of yourself. In fact, God has actually designed a helper for facilitating friendship. It's that tiny but mighty neuropeptide oxytocin that helps increase the bond of trust when we peel back the veneer and share not just our triumphs, but our trials. Dr. Paul Zak, one of the leading authorities on oxytocin, the bonding hormone, says it decreases the sensation of stress, fear, and pain, and it increases trust, relational strength, and feelings of attachment, creating a rich sense of community and connectedness. We can clearly see God's fingerprints at work here.

This self-disclosure process should be reciprocal in nature. As the relationship grows, so should the level of trust. This is especially important to remember if parents are homeschooling teens who have been in the public sector their whole lives. It takes time and patience, qualities we aren't necessarily accustomed to in our microwave, Amazon-Prime culture. As George Washington once said, "Friendship is a plant of slow growth that must undergo and withstand the shocks of adversity before it is worthy of the appellation" (the name). A healthy relationship should also lead to a balanced level of individuation and differentiation. Our children are a "we," part of a family, but they are also an "I," an individual. They need time, space, and permission to be different from us. Families can still have shared values even if they have different personalities. One of my relatives tried to change the handedness of her son from right to left to match her own. This is an extreme example of trying to fashion our children into little mini-me versions of their parents. That's not the goal of parenting. As we guide arrows, we are training them up in what God has destined for them, not living out vicariously through them our own failed hopes and dreams.

The time you spend with your children over the next few weeks will play a powerful role in their overall development, so don't worry that your student will fall behind or that she won't get into that college you've been dreaming of if you don't check off every single academic box. In fact, the more time you spend being involved in your child's education, the better his or her chance of scholastic success will actually be in the end! Remember, Harvard University's Family Involved Network of Educators program has shown over and over that the number one predictor of a child's socio-academic success from kindergarten to college is an involved parent. So, you are actually increasing your child's chances of success just by investing this time, energy, and focus into your child. How amazing is that?

No matter how many children you have or how far apart their ages are, you can make homeschooling work for your family. As someone who's been part of the homeschool movement for two decades, I've known parents that homeschooled with one child, with five kids under the age of eight, with five teenage boys (my friend Denise Mira—check out her book *No Ordinary Child*), and even with ten kids of all ages all homeschooling at the same time. Wherever you fall in that mix, you can do this. There are many creative ways to partner together as parents and to leverage our individual gifts and talents for the betterment of our offspring. For most of our homeschool journey, my husband and have I shared responsibilities, with him teaching classes like music and math, and me covering classes like literature, history, and the sciences. Not only did this distribute the load more evenly, but it gave us individual time with our kids to nurture their own gifts and talents, and it provided us the opportunity for influence outside of the home as well. It's not that parents can't do both, work inside and outside of the home: It's just that it needs to be in the right order, and we have to be realistic about our own limits, our personal capacity. If we expend all of our emotional and physical energy on temporal, ego-enhancing ventures outside the home and then have nothing left to give to our children or our spouse, then our home life is structured in the wrong order. We need a domestic adjustment. It's that simple.

A few helpful tips will guide you in maintaining sanity and establishing new levels of relational health in your home. First, keep it all in perspective. Don't panic. This is an incredible opportunity to spend time with your children and to discover and sharpen their gifts and talents. You will be amazed at how smart your children are and how much they already know! Focus on the benefits of being able to educate your children at home, to see God work in and through them. The season of childhood passes by so quickly! Get a vision for the character growth and development you want to see in your children during the fleeting span of time between 0 and 18.

Second, know your strengths. Recognize that you know a lot more than you think. Moms tell me all the time that they don't feel qualified to teach their kids anything. When I remind them that they've already taught their children to clap, to speak, to walk, to read, to write, to color, to dance, to use table manners, to play nicely with other children, and to interact appropriately with other human beings in general, they remember that they are indeed teachers by nature! And if you haven't yet taught your children those last two skills, playing nicely and interacting appropriately, these are great starting points that will help you get through your week much more effectively and efficiently.

Third, plan ahead. Set a schedule the night before or at the beginning of the week, recognizing that school won't take 7 hours a day at home. In the traditional sector, 65% of the school day is spent on what we call classroom management (sit down/ get out your books/stop throwing spitballs, etc.). Plan for 2 hours in elementary and about 3 hours in junior high to high school. I also recommend not starting your official school day before 9am. As I mentioned in a previous chapter, the 7:30am start times at traditional schools were not established for the emotional or physical health of children. Numerous studies show that kids do better in school when they start later rather than earlier. So, let them sleep in a little! Don't worry. They will still get their work done—and they will be less moody and more focused during the day. Sleep deprivation is a very real concern for children, and you have the privilege of being the solution to that problem right now! And as you're planning out your curricula, don't forget the arts! Children need a place to express and explore their creativity, even if it's as simple as handing them a mini canvas and turning on a Bob Ross video for art class (which was my personal secret of success as a non-artist). You might even discover you have a budding painter or sculptor on your hands!

Fourth, begin well. Before you start your homeschool journey, take some time to talk with your children about the adventure, what they can expect, and what you are excited about. Start your homeschool day with a time of conversation and devotion. Read a chapter of the Bible to your kids, discuss what it means and how it applies, and pray together as a family. Even very small children can understand the Bible and learn how to pray. Again, you'll be amazed at how much your children know and how much they remember! As you move through the day, work in short bursts of time, depending on your student's attention span. For little children, this may only be 10-20 minutes per subject area at a time, but even for high schoolers, avoid planning lengthy, non-interactive blocks for each subject. Discuss the learning together. Ask them questions. Have conversations. Remember the model of reading and relationship Jesus set for us.

Fifth, keep it real. Have realistic expectations. It's okay if you don't get through everything you planned—that doesn't mean deep learning didn't take place! And be realistic about academic expectations too. Your seven-year-old will not perform at peak efficiency if you require him or her (but especially him!) to sit quietly for two hours without a physical break. Kids (and adults) need outdoor time, mental rest time (especially boys, whose brains experience regularly occurring patterns of what neuroscience calls a "neural rest state"), and physical activity. Make rests and PE part of your daily plan. Take a walk together. Go outside and watch the rain, the snow, the ocean, the sunset, the sunrise. Collect leaves, listen to birds, watch ants, and enjoy the beauty of the natural world around you. Some of our sweetest family homeschool memories were walking through the neighborhood collecting leaves for classification as deciduous or coniferous, softwood or hardwood, finding little forest paths that led to unexpected blackberry picking and the discovery of robins' nests. Human beings need times of reflection and connection to grow and develop in a healthy manner. Build opportunities for both into your daily schedule. As you step out of the rat race of traditional education, resist the urge to recreate a homeschool version of the failed methodology of public education in your own living room.

Sixth, focus on what's really important: relationship. Spend intentional time and energy on personal development and enjoying your time together. Children of every age need guidance and direction, the scaffolding that will help them reach their full capacity. They need to be socialized by trusted adults, which is of far greater importance than being socialized by their peers. Integrate your kids into the real world instead of doing everything for them. Help them watch, learn, and imitate how you cook, clean, plan, run a household. I remember how empowered our daughter felt when she was allowed to take over her own laundry duties. Laundry literally became her favorite chore (and I found myself wondering why I didn't turn that over to her earlier). You may even find your own "chores" growing a little lighter as you integrate your children into the household as participants rather than just spectators. We do a disservice to our kids when we cater to their every whim, expecting nothing from them. For 20 years, I taught college students who were totally stressed out because they never learned to cook, clean, do laundry, create a budget, or care for themselves. Raising successful citizens of tomorrow means teaching them how to be adults today.

Finally, avoid perfectionism. You don't have to know all the answers. Even as a college professor, I knew that I couldn't teach my students everything they needed to know. Instead, my goal was to teach them how to learn, developing in them patterns of life-long knowledge acquisition that will help them succeed in the world of work. The same is true for homeschooling. Our goal is teaching children how to learn, how to interact with others, how to develop social and emotional intelligence, how to find information, and how to process information. This last one is a vital skill in the "information" age: our children need to know how to filter through what is real and what is false at every level of culture.

As we reclaim education for the kingdom across the county, we need to be sure that we aren't just recreating mini public schools in our homes. Remember, it's not just the content of public education that's broken; it's the methodology. One challenges new homeschoolers often face is the ban on fun. They get so focused on the task and the imaginary checklist that they suddenly morph from fun-loving mom to screaming schoolmarm. Needless to say, this does not create the most effective learning environment for our children. Harvard professor Dr. Shawn Achor has shown that knowledge is more actively retained when teachers are positive communicators. As Proverbs 16:21 puts it, "Pleasant words promote instruction." Our students actually learn more effectively when we are optimistic and encouraging in our feedback. Find small things to praise throughout the day instead of focusing only on weaknesses or mistakes. And have some fun! Incorporate games or puzzles throughout the day. Pick up some inspiring historical biographies at the library and read them aloud together. When kids are young, they typically love being read to, but somewhere along the way, we often stop that habit, and as a result, they (and we) forget how special reading really is. Reading fuels the imagination, strengthens our visual creativity, and even helps children learn to quiet themselves and practice self-discipline. These will be powerful tools that will serve them well in adulthood too. Stoke the literary fire and keep those reading skills alive! As the saying goes, "Leaders are readers."

As you consider what you will teach, know that there are numerous online and on-ground resources for making home education successful. Some of these include math games, puzzles, and simple support books for reading and language skills as well as online support centers. You are not alone. Many people have gone before you on this journey. Prior to the Industrial Era, family life was built around the context of transmitting the values and the craft of the family name to the next generation. In the Industrial Era, however, we developed a "factory model" of education. This one-size-fits-all modality of academic instruction became the norm, and this trend has continued to the present day. Right now, though, you have the opportunity to offer an individualized learning approach to your child.

If you're new to the parent-directed approach, the freedom can be a little daunting. I've been an educator my whole life, and I will say in potential bubble-bursting fashion that there is no one simple one-size-fits-all model of curricular selection. But, there is a process, even a scientific process, that will help you bring out the best in your student. Begin, as Steven Covey said, with the end in mind. Start with your educational philosophy, your goal. What do you want to accomplish? Ask God to show you the gaps and the gifting. What harvest do you want to see in your children? What fruit do you want to nurture and develop? Your educational philosophy and personal mission will help guide our decision making process. Think about the values of your home, your family. What fruit do you want to see in your children? Maybe you want them to be confident in their calling. Maybe you want them to step up to the next level in their academic abilities. Maybe you just want them to stop arguing and get along. If you can't think of any other fruits, start with the fruit of the spirit!

Do we want kids who bubble over with love, joy, peace, patience, kindness, goodness, faithfulness, gentleness, and self-control? Then we create an environment where these characteristics will be cultivated, nurtured. So many parents today complain about the frightening levels of anxiety, depression, abortion, and suicide ideation in the current generation, and yet they send their kids off to the wolves every day, forcing them to navigate school environments where they are taught there is no God, they have no purpose, and there is absolutely no reason to hope. Why would we be surprised to see this fruit in GenZ when it has been cultivated daily in the public school system? Let's create an environment that nurtures Christian principles. We have to be intentional.

Dr. Howard Gardner is a Harvard professor who was launching into a career in law when he came across the works of Jean Piaget and Erik Erikson. He became fascinated with the way people think and learn. Through this, he developed nine different kinds of intelligence, known as Multiple Intelligence Theory. This is highly beneficial data to you as an educator: Knowing your student's learning abilities and personality traits will help you teach more effectively. My children loved taking personality tests together at home, and the tests facilitated great differ conversation. The Multiple Intelligence test will give you a profile with sample activities to facilitate learning. If you have a kinesthetic learner, for example, let him draw or color while you're reading aloud. If you have a verbal linguistic learner, choose a classical method of education and flood the table and the day with books and read-alouds. Kinesthetics learners need physiological engagement when they learn.   Your student can rock back and forth in a chair (non-maniacally, of course), jump on a mini trampoline, or walk on a treadmill while reading, listening to an audio book, or reciting facts.

Kids whose intelligences center on interpersonal or interpersonal intelligence learn best with knowledge linked to faith-based, self-improvement, or personal growth studies. Explain how a topic affects your child personally to make the content relatable. Children with musical intelligence learn through jingles, clapping rhythms, and listening to music. They also learn better when music is playing. Children with natural intelligence like hiking, outdoor activities, gardening, and learning cause and effect impacts of the world around them. They also enjoy being outdoors while learning. In our family, we read outside on the swing way more than we read inside on the couch.

Finally, children with linguistic intelligence love talking about and hearing about concepts. They are often auditory learners and can learn through reading and talking. Verbal processors do best when you can spend quality time in conversation before launching into schoolwork. Parents, it's important to remember that we will tend to teach through our own learning style, so be aware of that tendency and redirect your style to best meet the needs of your students. Verbal linguistic learners were common in the Boomer and GenX eras, whereas we see more visual learners in the Millennial generation and more kinesthetic learners in GenZ. Knowing your children's learning styles and natural intelligences will help you create an individualized learning style that makes the most of of your homeschool environment. Some of our favorite curricula are Sunlight, Apologia Science, Apologia Worldview, Institute for Excellence in Writing, Master Books, and the new Tuttle Twins history series. Every day, new resources are being added to that list, so do your homework, and don't be afraid of a little trial-and-error experimentation. If you find a curriculum that ends up not working for your student, stop and try something else. You are the captain! You choose how you will direct the course of education in your home, and you have the freedom to monitor, adjust, and to teach to your child's individual learning style. Accept and embrace that freedom!

This focus on learning style is vital, as it has a significant effect on our children's motivation. Human motivation is a whole scope of study on its own, but two emerging ideals in neuroscience are the important distinctions between intrinsic and extrinsic motivation. If we are constantly rewarding students extrinsically for their scholastic actions, bribing them, the data shows that they are less likely to develop their own fire, their own passion for education. In fact, two neuroscientists at Australian Catholic University found that the two most important supports for intrinsic motivation were competence (feeling effective) and autonomy (volition/decisions of their own will). Couple these with topics and margin that inspires creativity, and we have a motivated learner! This is why when Andrew Pudewa came to speak to our Awaken Academy faculty, he emphasized the importance of helping students feel successful in their efforts, even if it was just putting a period correctly at the end of the sentence. This idea goes back to the quote from William Butler

Yeats, that education is not the filling of a pail but the lighting of a flame. Once we find the way our students learn best, once we help them find a pathway to success in learning, and discover their (and your) "why" in the process, motivation is rarely an issue. If your child is obsessed with horses, center your study of science, writing, art, and reading around that topic. She will eventually be ready to take off the training wheels and learn about something else, but this is a great starting point for intrinsic motivation!

Homeschooling is an opportunity to re-educate yourself and to rekindle the relationships that are most important to you. Many times, the majority of our homeschool days as a family were spent reading and talking to each other. Even at 17, my daughter needed at least a 30-minute conversation before we could start our studies. That was not wasted time. In fact, I would argue that this is the heart of educational discipleship. Today, as I hear her giving her friends advice as they contemplate life choices in the absence of parental influence, I hear her drawing from the depths of our conversations, discipling her friends as I discipled her. What could be more beautiful?

One pressing question for new homeschool parents is the question I hear regularly, "How do I know if it's working?" Parents who are new to the methodology often doubt the efficacy of the organic model of homeschooling. This is because they have been trained in the culture of the expert, which attempts to undermine the intrinsic gifts, talents, and naturally didactic drive of the parent. How do you know if your students are learning? Test for fruit! What were the goals you set for your family? Did you meet or exceed them? What evidence exists? In our family, the first difference we noticed in our annual tests and our observations of their improvement was in vocabulary development. Our kids knew multisyllabic words we hadn't intentionally taught them. How did this happen? They were raised by parents instead of peers! The ceiling of maturity and intergenerational connectivity cannot be lifted when a child's most regular influence is a classroom full of immature peers. Children need adult mentors and role models—parent orientation instead of peer orientation—to reach their full potential. A kid who hangs out with other seven year olds for eight hours a day will be limited by the ceiling of maturity and knowledge acquisition in that environment.

For our family, homeschooling was one of the most incredibly rewarding journeys of our parenting lives. Your relationship with your children will be strengthened and deepened as a result of your time together during this season. As parents, we bear the mantle, the responsibility for training and discipling our kids to be self-governing, productive, followers of Jesus. It's going to take intentionality and time. Remember that old saying, "Only one life, twill soon be past. Only what's done for Christ will last."

Early on in our homeschool journey, my husband and I realized that our children would benefit from having a healthy community around them would provide the best of both worlds, the educational and spiritual direction of a parent mixed with the balanced interaction of peers who could sharpen them and provide benchmarking opportunities. Like Thoreau, who "went into the woods to live deliberately" and alone, some homeschooling parents mistakenly believe that their children should have no external interaction, no connection to the outside world. But this is an artificial laboratory. It's easy to feel strong about our gifting when we have no competitors. For example, when I'm out running intervals on our neighborhood trail by myself, I feel fast. But when an Olympic runner zips by (as is frequently the case), I am reminded that the perception of "fast" is relative. I've met children who were told all their lives they were leaders or great writers only to get to college and realize that their skills were subpar. If they had been sharpened by healthy community influences, they would have been able to benchmark, to see reality, and to hone their craft. That, in essence, is the ingredient for greatness. We all the need the sharpening of community to bring out what's broken and expose what's weak to the possibility of transformation, of betterment, to raise our ceiling on what's possible. The balance just needs to be in the right order: parent-directed and peer-enhanced.

When I first met my husband Adrian in England, I was struck by the central presence of houses of worship. Everywhere we walked in virtually every city, we could see a church and hear a church bell. In America, churches had been marginalized. Yet, these sleeping giants were sitting empty all week long, housing the untapped potential of cultural influence. We knew if pastors could embrace the vision, they could dedicate their empty classrooms to the training up of the next generation, opening their doors to the homeschool community and reconstructing the spiritual blueprint of the city: The church would once again be the center point of culture.

Adrian and I just knew there had to be a way to bring these elements of parent directed, peer enhancing, church-supported systems together. So we prayed. We met with our pastoral team, and they believed in the vision. Thus, in 2009, we started launching homeschool academies in local churches, offering a variety of core and elective classes that brought together homeschooling parents and students in the centralized venue of the local church. The vision quickly grew into a multi-denominational outreach that has influenced parents and students across the state of California and beyond. We knew if pastors could embrace the vision, they could dedicate their empty classrooms to the training up of the next generation, opening their doors to the homeschool community and reconstructing the spiritual blueprint of the city. We saw a day when the church would once again be the center point of culture. Parents and pastors, if we can restore the church and the family to the central position of influence in the culture, we will not only save both entities from extinction, we will radically transform our nation.

Homeschooling builds stronger, more resilient homes and provides a "secure base" for attachment and confidence. And stronger homes strengthen the fabric of our society, so that's a win-win for everyone. As a professor, a parent, and a Ph.D., I say unapologetically and with great conviction that homeschooling is by far the superior method of socio-academic training. Homeschooling produces smart kids, kids that are more civically engaged, more academically equipped, more mature (5-10 grades by many analyses). And we know that their character growth is exponential when they have a parent discipling them daily. To the survival point of Christendom, homeschooling is a purposeful and powerful methodology for ensuring the transmission of the faith from one generation to the next. As Psalm 102:18 says, "Let this be written for the next generation, that a people not yet created may praise the Lord."

When we look at the tragic fruit, the socio-emotional, spiritual, and academic harvest of our today's youngest citizens, we must admit that we can't afford look the other way. We know the time to act is now. We can work together to create the rescue mission America's kids desperately need. It's our responsibility as believers to make the needed sacrifices today that will steward and guide the next generation of champions for the kingdom of God tomorrow. If every church in our city, our state, and our nation stepped up to be part of the solution, we would flip the tragic statistics of our nation's students in just one single generation! Learn more about our journey to relational recalibration and why we need every church active in this mission by visiting CVCU.us and clicking the Start a Homeschool Academy tab. Listen to stories of homeschool inspiration on my weekly radio show on KPraise Radio or my weekly podcast, The Communication Architect, where you'll find tools for support, community, and encouragement. Search out your state's private homeschooling support agency, reach out, and plug in. We all need the benefit of community in its rightful place in our lives. And from that vantage point of relational health and wholeness, we can overflow into the streets of our cities like the mighty rushing river of life that we are intended to be as the body of Christ.

Carl Rogers, whose potato offshoot story opens this chapter, is a case in point for the needed community these church-based centers can provide. As a child, Rogers felt called to the ministry. He was a voracious reader and displayed great scientific prowess from a young age. But his studies led him further from community and away from his denominational roots. In his teen years, he was known as an isolated, independent, and disciplined person, which is often the dialectical tension experienced by scholars—an imbalance of two vital ingredients, reflection and connection. At age 20, as he considered his path of ministry, he began to doubt his faith. He attended a seminar titled "Why Am I Entering the Ministry" to help him codify his questions, and shortly thereafter, he announced his change of beliefs from Christian to atheist (which he later modified to agnostic). Had there been more connection to community, more discipleship over reading or lecturing, perhaps the young Rogers may have held fast to his faith and found its roots beautifully intertwining with his beloved field of science.

In the brief season of our parenting years, while we still hold the power of influence in our children's lives, let's make disciples. In the final chapter, we will look at some broad steps we can take to be difference-makers, culture-shapers, and industry-disruptors in the field of education. Wherever we are in the journey, we can be part of the change. We are not of those who shrink back and are destroyed, Hebrews 10:39 reminds us, but of those who stand firm to the preservation of the soul. Parents, the season for change is upon us. The harvest is ready. It's time to bring home the outsourced generation.

CHAPTER TWENTY

I'm Awake: So Now What?

In my small, southern Illinois hometown of 2,100 people, one gas station, and one stop light, gossip was an everyday part of the school culture. As a child, I always carried the piercing perception that the whole school, the whole city even, was whispering about my tragic family life, pitying the obvious pain, hopelessness, and dysfunction. Certainly some of this mental anguish was the result of adolescent egocentrism, but that didn't nullify the fact that I felt intrinsically different from everyone else. As a result, I carried a persistent mental burden, feeling like I was personally deficient, that there was something inherently wrong with me. I spent a lot of years trying in vain to disprove this underlying sense of worthlessness, to quell the sense of inadequacy. However, anyone who has been through a similar journey knows that no amount of external victories can alter our mental landscape until our sense of identity is rightly rooted. As Gary Chapman once said, "You haven't lost your self-esteem; you've just been looking for it in the wrong place."

The same sense of fear and inadequacy is profoundly exemplified in the current generation of parents who feel ill-equipped for the journey of child-rearing, let alone the journey of homeschooling. If you relate to any of these fears, let me encourage you to create community. Look around your extended social circle for someone you admire, someone you'd like to emulate. Reach up to someone 10 years older than you and out to someone 10 years younger than you. Mentor and be mentored. These healthy adult attachments will help refuel you for the hard days, because the reality is that there are mountains and valleys, easy days and tough days. There are hard days in marriage and hard days at work and hard days in parenting and hard days in homeschooling, but we don't shrink back. We stand up, step up, and rise to the battle.

Throughout the pages of this book, we've come face to face with the tragic situation facing our nation's youth. We've assessed the brokenness of America's education system. We've witnessed the tragic fallout from the lack of attachment in parental relationships. We've seen the concerted attack on the minds, hearts, and relationships of the next generation. We know that America's kids are in desperate need of an education revolution, a rescue mission. Thankfully, a generation of courageous parents are awake and ready to take action. So now what do we do?

First, the bad news. The fallout is severe. One of my favorite cultural analysts, George Barna, recently released his updated "Millennials in America" report, and the findings are, to put it lightly, rather stinging. Barna, the most quoted living Christian researcher, offers a finality of data that is at once sobering (hence the bad news warning) and, given the context of influence, truly unsurprising. As Frederick Buechner once said, the gospel is bad news before it is good news. And it is with this same assertion that we come to the closing chapter of this book in order to bear the weight of reality in this generation, the haunting harvest of America's outsourced children. Buckle your seat belt as we review some of the highlights (or rather, lowlights) of 18-25 year olds in America today according to Barna's latest findings:

- Only 1/3 claim to believe in God
- Only 19% say human life is sacred (a drop from 50% over just two generations)
- Almost 30% report having a mental disorder
- Almost 50% report having a mental illness
- Almost 50% prefer socialism to capitalism
- Only 19% of 18-24 year old born-again believers have a biblical worldview
- Only 2% of the general 18-24 population holds a biblical worldview
- 39% identify as LGBTQ, lifestyles that have been pushed daily in the public school system
- Only 28% trust the Bible as the inerrant word of God, down 16% from older adults, 44% of whom trust the Bible as inerrant

All is not well on the American home front, friends. As we saw in the first chapter of this book and every telling point in between, the youngest generation is in great need of a rescue mission. Their unfortunate harvest is largely the result of their generational inheritance, much like King Josiah inherited a rebellious city because of his forefathers' unwillingness to pass along the faith baton. In the same way, as Barna notes, America's youngest generations are "largely the product of the unaddressed dysfunctions of the generations that came before them...a generation that has inherited a cultural war zone but not the tools to bring peace to that war." Parents, our youngest citizens are standing in the cultural war zone without being equipped for battle. Their safe spaces, play dough parties, and puppy petting rooms have left them ill prepared for the rough terrain of adulthood. But listen carefully to this remaining point of influence: though only 26% of 18-25 year olds say they would trust a pastor, Barna found that a full 46% say that they still trust their parents to influence their lives. Parents, that means this is our time to shine.

How will we respond? In Matthew 8, when the residents of Gadara saw two ruffians' lives turned around in an instant, we would have expected the citizens to cheer, to rejoice, to celebrate the work of God in their midst. But they didn't. In fact, Matthew records that the Gadarenes actually kicked the miracle worker out of the city. Yes, the transference of demonic presence from man to beast was probably a bit frightening. And yes, the loss of their pork-based livelihood probably made them angry, as their treasure (and thus their heart) was more inclined toward profit than prophet. But the Gadarenes had probably also normalized the behavior of the demoniacs, who were "so fierce that no one could pass that way." These tomb-dwellers likely met and tormented visitors to the region, as they did when Jesus and his crew landed on the shore, and yet the Gadarenes lived amongst them and either ignored or accepted their behavior. This is such a powerful parallel to modern parenting!

Parents so often look the other way when they hear the stats on the next generation: Not my child. Not my school. Not my state. But the reality is that an entire generation has been affected. The roots of socio-cultural conditioning run deep. We can no longer afford to look the other way or to accept as "normal" the status of today's angst-filled American teenager or "terrible two" toddler. Believers have a responsibility not to normalize the behavior of the culture, not to look the other way when the demoniacs are flooding the streets, not to allow the miracle-worker to be driven out. We are called to see and think and believe at a different level, desiring the eternal over the temporal. Instead of normalizing the accepted behaviors of the day in parenting and education, let's see through the lens of the biblical worldview, stepping up and speaking out so that our city, our state, our nation can experience the great and glorious awakening that will lead us down the pathway to revival.

What if you're a parent who's just now waking up to

these realities about your own children for the first time? First, recognize that you are not alone. There is a radical restoration in parenting and family happening all across the nation in this very moment, and there are many tremendous resources available for you. The first step is getting your children out of the public school system, and this includes "free" charters that masquerade as beacons of hope to desperate families who falsely believe that charters will offer academic freedom. Remember, a charter is a government school, and its strings are attached to the same system of confusion and control as the traditional neighborhood public school is. As Gatto said, "Government monopoly schools are structurally unreformable." They are doing exactly what they are designed to do, creating cogs in a machine through both their content and their methodology.

The second step is to begin assessing—and where needed, healing—the relational attachments that may have been fractured by the public, peer-driven, family-segregating system. By all external accounts, many of our new homeschooling families tell us they felt like they were good, solid, churchgoing families before this season of parental awakening. They chauffeured their kids to school, to games, to practices, to youth group. They provided food and shelter and clothing. They truly believed they were checking all the boxes, but when the world shut down in 2020, they were forced to reevaluate their family's health, and what they saw was not pretty. The X-ray left them concerned about their relational attachments and the longterm impact of the educational methodology to which their children had been exposed. The slow release of this radioactive poisoning meant that the longer their kids were in the system, the more parents saw the predictable fruit of the system: in the way their kids thought, spoke, and interacted with the rest of the family. Like the parents in Barna's studies, many moms and dads suddenly realized their families were spiritually anemic, relationally malnourished: they weren't reading the Bible with their kids, engaging in meaningful conversations, directing the content or structure of their studies, helping them unlearn what the school culture was pouring out daily, mentoring them, investing in them, or discipling them. Like most American parents, they realized they were simply outsourcing their children to the lowest bidder, the neighborhood public school.

And this is perhaps the biggest wake-up call for many families entering the home education movement today. Some parents were shocked into reality when they found themselves panicking over what, in retrospect, they realized was a marker of their lack of connection with their kids. Virtually every academic homeschool resource was delayed by several weeks in August 2020, when millions of parents stepped into the parent-directed movement for the first time. This meant they didn't get the books they were counting on for structure, for content, for comfort. Many panicked. "What do I do with my kids if we don't have books yet? What do we talk about? What do we do all day?" Even as they asked the questions aloud, they recognized instinctively that something was off. What was causing such discomfort in the presence of their children? Why did they feel the need to pad the time with activities instead of authentic discussion, relationship? Many parents began to recognize that they had lost something of the heart connection that they had with their children before their potty-training milestone, the point where they were conditioned to believe their parental purpose had reached its end.

We hear this alarming awakening from new homeschooling families all the time. Because they had outsourced their children for two years, five years, ten years, they had gradually begun to lose touch with the intuitive connection, the mom instinct, the dad directive, to know how to lead them well in every area. Parents had been so focused on academics or sports or chauffeuring their kids through life that they realized they had never stopped to think about what it truly means to disciple their own children. Their kids were so deeply oriented to peers and others outside the home that parents felt uncomfortable, even awkward, in a supervisory role with their own child. And this discomfort created an awareness of the misattunement, the misalignment. Parents could feel it. Something was off.

One of our new homeschool parents described the experience as one of awakening. As she sat around the table with her children, she felt her heart begin to thaw toward them. Before that moment, she had no sense of awareness that an icy obstacle existed between her and her children. As the saying goes, we don't know what we don't know. But once she saw it, she couldn't unsee it. As she remained faithful and patient in the process of growth, this mom began to see a tremendous turnaround in her family: good relationships became great relationships, academic potential developed into academic curiosity that fueled inquiry, reason, new levels of courage and creativity. Now she mentors other young moms in the model, helping them detox from the traditional system and refocus on a relational reset. The first year out of the system is a time to reconfigure family priorities and define values. Listen to some of my interviews on The Communication Architect podcast, where new homeschooling parents recount how they saw God move in their relationships through a few simple additions and deletions to the family schedule.

Jack Hayford once said that it's easier to build a man than to rebuild him. The youngest generations are leaving the church in droves only to come back, if they ever do come back, hurting and broken. That isn't what we want for the next generation. The best testimony for our kids is not that they were chewed up and spit out by the world and then came crawling back to the church dragging their mangled baggage behind them. A more desirable testimony would be that they followed hard after God all the days of their lives, shining like stars in a darkened universe, that their actions have brought him glory from childhood to adulthood. If we want a different outcome from the world's model, then we need a different methodology from the world's model. In 20 years of teaching college students—whose lives exemplify the cumulative impact of parental, peer, and scholastic influence—I have made this unwavering observation: The return-on-investment, the ROI, for the parent-driven model of educational discipleship is beyond comparison. There is simply no more effective model or methodology for producing spiritual giants and academic champions than homeschooling.

In *Parenting from the Inside Out,* one of my favorite books to buy for new moms, Dr. Dan Siegel emphasizes the importance of attachments, which is the foundational element of stability and support we see in healthy homeschooling families. Babies are born completely dependent. The world system teaches that they are innocent, but anyone who has raised a child can clearly see the sin nature evident within even very young children. We are born sons and daughters of Adam but must be redeemed into our positional authority as sons and daughters of the King. It is his righteousness that changes us, and our children, from sinners to saints.

Healthy attachments are vital to the health and well-being of the next generation. Having a primary adult dedicated to perceiving and responding to the child's needs gives the child a sense of safety, a secure base. No teacher, however excellent, can carry that mantle for a lifetime. The parent-child attachment is pervasive in its influence. As Dr. Siegel notes, parental attachments play a significant role in children's relationships with others, their sense of security, their resilience, their emotion regulation, and their interpersonal relationships. When kids are out of the home all day, raised in the peer-centric environments of the public system where many feel a constant undercurrent of danger from bullying peers, attachments are often damaged. Sadly, it's a subversive, surreptitious process. Many parents I talk with don't realize it until it's too late, when they suddenly come face-to-face with a calcified anti-faith worldview, a crusty heart, an emotionally distant teen who is now more attached to peers than to parents. It's one of the great heartbreaks of working with families who are leaving the system later in their child's scholastic career, seeing the despair in their eyes when they realize that years of daily distancing themselves from their children has borne a fatal fruit: The relationship between parent and child has slowly, tragically, and fully dissipated.

Today's youth lack the trust and security that comes from a secure base. They have significantly low resilience levels (hence the snowflake moniker), and they have low emotion regulation levels. Many of these generational shortcomings could be turned around with the healing of attachment. And even though we can't re-pour the foundational concrete of childhood, Drs. Neborsky and Solomon have shown that healthy adult attachments can help heal wounded childhood attachments. It's never too late. God is the father of redemption, the ultimate source of hope. He doesn't leave us stranded and victimized, hopelessly awaiting the exit lane of life. Through his marvelous design of neural plasticity, he gives us the opportunity to grow, change, develop, and heal throughout our lifetimes. Remember, Romans 12:2 tells us that we are not to conform to the patterns of this world but to be transformed by the renewing of our minds. This is true for both parents and children.

As a parent, taking responsibility for a lack of attachment in your children is not an easy step, but it's a vital one. It might begin as a jovial family conversation, a time of shared repentance, or a quiet commitment to change. The pattern will be unique to you and your family dynamic. I remember once in my twenties when I tried to confront my now-late father about our relationship. At the time, I was in counseling, attempting to make sense of my painful past. I had wholeheartedly decided I was going to forgive my dad, as Jesus clearly commands us to do, so that I could be free of bitterness from the scars of childhood. In my naiveté and exuberance, I called him on the phone from five states away and said, rather flippantly, "I just wanted you to know that I forgive you." I somehow imagined this one call would be a magical gateway through which our wounded relationship would be propelled into an idyllic process of healing. But he was less than enthusiastic.

Instead, his voice belied a sobering and calculated iciness, which I'm sure in retrospect was probably shock, both at the personal nature of the conversation (we had never spoken about anything beyond a surface level) and at the insinuation that he committed any wrongdoing. "You forgive me for what?" Speechless, I stammered on in an attempt to recount for him all my childhood traumas. He stopped me mid-sentence. "You turned out okay," he said, "so I must have done something right." Everything inside me wanted to scream, "I turned out okay *in spite* of you not *because* of you," but I knew there was no upward spiral to that conversation. I should have let it go right there.

However, in my stubbornness, I tried to force a connection with him later that year, sending him a letter with a Christmas picture of our family. But he was clearly not ready for authenticity, and my pursuit of that imaginary ideal of relational restoration was again halted in dramatic fashion. He tore my family picture into tiny pieces and mailed those pieces back to me, reminding me in a very clear, fatal-attraction-like visual that he did not desire to talk with me on any personal level whatsoever. When his sister passed away shortly thereafter and willed her estate to me instead of him, he did not respond well. That's another book in its own right, but suffice it to say that the traumas of his own childhood were once again stirred up and unleashed on those who should have been the closest in the circle: his family.

In his brokenness, my father pushed away many people, not only the multiple wives and family members, but also friends. Tragically, at the end of his life, when he died of a heart attack, his body lay on the kitchen floor for almost two weeks before anyone noticed he was gone, a piercing and painful example of how the lack of attachment and an inability to deal with one's own wounded past can create such deep isolation, both internally and externally. Parents, we must preserve and protect our relationships with our children while there is time, while they're tender, receptive. A day will come when they no longer call on you to comfort them when they have a bad dream, when they no longer run to you when they scrape their knee. While there is time, make every effort to protect the parent-child attachment.

If you're a young adult healing from a childhood trauma, going back to a broken person and expecting him or her to take responsibility for that behavior, to acknowledge and accept your forgiveness, is not always the most relationally productive of moves. More often than not, it's better to work out the forgiveness in your own heart. Jesus doesn't give us the option of forgiving only the worthy. We are called to forgive all who wound us. No caveats. No exceptions. Bitterness, as the saying goes, is like drinking poison and hoping it kills the other person. As believers, we are called to walk in positional honor of our parents, so we must release the trauma of the past in order to move forward in health and healing. As I learned too late, some parents may not be capable of accepting or processing the reality of the past. In retrospect, I should have allowed forgiveness to reign in my heart without requiring it to leave my lips. "I forgive you" can sound a whole lot like "I blame you" to someone not capable of processing their own trauma. I wish I had known that before my father passed away.

Maybe you're a parent recognizing that your own relationship with your children is not what you'd like it to be. Maybe you see yourself in some of the earlier topics we've addressed: feeling embarrassed of your children's public behavior, caring more about what your peers think about you than what your children think about you, exchanging the worship of other gods for time with your family, or chasing after endless goals and accolades that only leave you feeling empty in the end. Or maybe you've just realized that you've been the chauffeur and the chef for the whole span of your children's lives, but you've never been the mentor, the trainer, the coach, the disciple-maker. Friend, it's not too late.

Moms, especially, this is a vital word for us. In his work *Separation, Anxiety, and Anger* (1973), Bowlby, the founder of attachment theory, was struck by the powerful impact of maternal deprivation. The mother-child relationship, he believed "was capable of generating responses and processes that are of the greatest interest to psychopathology." I was fascinated with this topic in graduate school, obviously, because I had grown up without a mother, and despite neighbors not allowing me to babysit because they said I would never be "warm" without maternal influence, I beat the statistic. I found healing in adult relationships and developed the attachments in adulthood that I was deprived of in childhood. Rest assured, if God did it for me, he can do it for you.

Bowlby wrote in 1979 that adults who become suicidal, delinquent, and unable to maintain a stable bond of affection often share in common a childhood with "prolonged deprivation of maternal care during the earliest years of life, usually combined with later rejection and/or threats of rejection by parents or foster parents." This adult behavior is born of childhood pain, Bowlby surmised, because "models of attachment figures and of self an individual builds during his childhood and adolescence tend to persist relatively unchanged into and throughout adult life." Like the saying "hurt people, hurt people," Bowlby says that we are "apt to do unto others as we have been done by."

Again, as believers, we have the hope of redemption in Jesus, but the pattern of multi-generational sin is clearly outlined in these early studies. For parents of young children who have found those attachments replaced by someone or something else as a result of the systematic rat race, this is the hour to tap out and step in. Because the pain of self-reflection runs deep, and because Bowlby made his most striking observations at the height of feminism's rise, many cultural leaders discounted his works. In their eyes, having to spend time with one's child meant "missing out" on something of greater importance, some higher honor. The siren song of feminism shifted a cultural mindset, downgrading parenting to a lesser calling. But this tragic exchange has had profound implications for the next generation. How do we navigate our way out of this cultural parenting maze?

Bowlby outlines a reflective checklist for what he calls a "pathogenic parent." This list is a great cautionary tale as we evaluate our parenting processes and step into a new level of educational discipleship with our children. Pathogenic parents, Bowlby says, are persistently unresponsive to the child's attempts to elicit care. Their parenting is isolated, lacking in continuity, and they often use threats of taking away love or abandoning the family as a means of control, discipline, or coercion. Pathogenic parents threaten to leave, kill their spouse, or commit suicide. And pathogenic parents try to make children feel by saying that the child's behavior is the reason or cause for the parent's illness or death. Now, some of these are rather dramatic, but the lack of responsivity and continuity, as well as the presence of blame, are common parenting "techniques" we hear regularly from parents and their GenZ children. Of these three, the lack of responsivity is perhaps most pronounced today because parents' affections are often divided. There is an ongoing battle between the rush of dopamine from a string of likes on social media versus the perceived daily drudgery and thanklessness of childrearing. Parents desperately need to find in their children the joy and the treasure that God has entrusted them with to sharpen and guide, to be propelled into a future that we will never see ourselves. Psalm 127:3 says that our children are a gift to us, a reward, arrows in the hand of a warrior. Through our influence, they become a blessing or a curse to the generation to follow. To paraphrase Titus, our children are our resumé. Not remarkably, children who have grown up with pathogenic parents exhibit insecurity. They have a low threshold for attachment in adult relationships if they do not heal. Of the top three most common maladies of GenZ—anxiety, depression, and suicide ideation—anxiety is the most prevalent. As Mel Levine once looked out over the landscape of Millennial children and saw what they would become as adults, we too are now looking out over the landscape of an anxious, malattuned and misattached generation with great concern for their future families. It's time for action.

One of my all-time favorite culture-shapers, Pastor Leanne Matthesius, gave a compelling message recently where she talked about the parable of the ten virgins in Matthew 25. All ten virgins were waiting for the bridegroom, but only half of them took flasks of oil with their lamps. She wondered aloud what those lacking oil had exchanged for the oil that was supposed to gain them entrance into the chamber of the bridegroom, representing the return of the King of Kings. In the same way, we must ask ourselves, as parents, as leaders, as culture-shapers, what are we personally exchanging for the mental, social, emotional, and academic health of the next generation? We will trade something for our time with our children. The question is, will that exchange be worth the investment?

Secure attachments, Siegel writes, require "consistent, emotionally attuned, contingent communication" between parent and child. These are built on what Siegel and Hartzell call the ABCs of attachment: attunement (A = aligning your internal state with that of your child), balance (B = being aware that we are the thermostats, and children regulate body, emotion, and mental states by being attuned to us), and coherence (C = our relationship with our children should fuel their internal integration and interpersonal connections).

Maybe you doubt you have what it takes to be that kind of a parent. The Bible tells us otherwise. In the book of 2 Peter, Paul says that God's divine power has given us everything we need for life and godliness through the knowledge of him who called us to his own glory and excellence. And we have discussed over and over throughout the last several chapters, the mantle God has placed on parents is to disciple their children, to train them up. So the first step, parents, is to make sure that we ourselves are leaning on his divine power, on his knowledge, on his wisdom, as we train up our children. It will require sacrifice, consecration, setting apart. It will mean choosing family over other events, choosing great things over good things. But over time, out of the overflow of your heart and then your home, you will begin to see a shift, a new day dawning. This is why homeschooling is so important. It slows down the clock, checks us out of the proverbial rat race, and gives us the treasure of time to invest into our children. And out of those interconnected relationships come rich opportunities for teaching, training, and discipling.

If we want our relationships to flourish, we can't be afraid to feel, to take risks. We have to face the reality that hurt is a possibility. As C.S. Lewis wrote in *The Four Loves,* "To love at all is to be vulnerable." We can protect the heart, Lewis says, by giving it to no one, by distracting ourselves with luxuries or hobbies. But, he says, the end result will be tragic: "Lock (your heart) up safe in the casket or coffin of your selfishness. But in that casket, safe, dark, motionless, airless, it will change. It will not be broken; it will become unbreakable, impenetrable, irredeemable." Relationship involves risk. Parenting involves risk. Marriage involves risk. Anything worthwhile in life will cost you something.

In what is perhaps one of the most chilling paragraphs in the New Testament, Jesus tells his disciples in Matthew 7:21,

"Not everyone who says to me, 'Lord, Lord' will enter the kingdom of heaven, but the one who does the will of my father who is in heaven. On that day many will say to me, 'Lord, Lord, did we not prophesy in your name, and cast out demons in your name, and do mighty works in your name?' And then will I declare to them, 'I never knew you. Depart from me, you workers of lawlessness.'" Clearly, there will be people who look like they are followers, who call Jesus Lord, who even believe in their own hearts that they are followers, but are ultimately deceived. A verbal confession does not necessarily guarantee a repentant heart. How do we know the real from the counterfeit? Jesus says we know them by their fruits, by whether they build their lives on the bedrock of his word, regardless of shifting cultural traditions. One great benefit to the darkness of our day is that the light of true followers shines ever brighter in contrast to the darkness and folly of the world system. We are to enter "by the narrow gate," to swim upstream, to push against the current of the culture in pursuit of the way, the truth, and the life. While the rest of the culture promotes an educational methodology that is not only broken but also harmful, we must step out of the flow and look at the fruit. Rather than being trapped in the lens of cultural traditions (we've always done it this way; everyone in our family went to this school), we need to envision new methods, new practices, new strategies that are grounded in the word of God.

Let's go back once more to Gatto's power quote: "Over the years of wrestling with the obstacles that stand between child and education, I have come to believe that government monopoly schools are structurally unreformable. They cannot function if their central myths are exposed and abandoned." Parents, it's time that we exposed the central myths of traditional education and left them behind for a healthier, happier, more effective method. My platform as the president of Chula Vista Christian University is this: I want to encourage every Bible-believing church in America to launch a Christian education program that will provide parents the support they need to sever their ungodly yoke with the public sector.

At the end of his sobering study, Barna calls parents to account: "Although the Bible exhorts parents to embrace the primary responsibility for teaching their children biblical content, most of them don't," he says. "What would happen to the United States as a nation of influence if parents loved their children enough that they owned that responsibility? How many lives would be changed if parents were dedicated to ensuring that their children knew biblical principles and applied them to all of the decisions they make?"

We've seen the fruit of today's youngest generations: anxiety, depression, suicide ideation, atheism. We've seen the lack of attachments between parent and child and the tragic fallout that has been evidenced in the last two generations of increasingly outsourced offspring. But as I said at the beginning of this chapter, the gospel is bad news before it is good news. The bad news is that we are broken. The good news is that we have a Great Physician who can help put us back together again!! We've heard the problem. We've seen the solution. What remains is action. By engaging our hearts anew in the training and discipleship process of home education, you will see your parent-directed model of education increase in flow and function every semester, and you will begin to reap a great harvest in your children's lives. Most importantly, you will create a rich network of multigenerational connectivity that will help transmit the faith from one generation to the next.

Let hope arise.

At the closing moment of this book, the US Census Bureau records an example of the ground shaking beneath our feet, the cultural curtains tearing open to allow in that great disinfectant, the light of truth. For the last 20 years, I've watched the numbers climbing in public schools: 52 million students, 56 million students, in 2019, 57 million students. But as I checked the numbers this week, I saw the miracle in our midst. Public school enrollment across the United States has fallen from 57 million last year to just over 50 million this year. Almost seven million children are fueling a public school exit across the nation. And for good cause. Let's recall the track record. Public schools have failed the American public. Students are performing lower academically, socially, emotionally, and, certainly, spiritually. They are less engaged politically. They are more engaged sexually. They are less participatory in the culture and more observers, spectators. They are numb, disengaged, detached, depressed, and anxious about their present and their future.

The two most important questions, the social, spiritual, and academic queries that have shaped entire civilizations, must be answered. We must give account for them: Who is teaching the children, and what are they being taught? At the end of the day, a system that trains us to seek the approval of man, even inadvertently, is not a healthy system. A system that drives a wedge between parents and children is not a healthy system. A system that crushes critical thinking and innovation in favor of conformity is not a healthy system. Human beings are not cogs in a machine. We are not robots. We are innovators, dreamers, creators, made in the image of our loving God who has both a plan and a purpose for our lives.

It's time to stop outsourcing our children to the lowest bidder, the government school system. We have everything we need right here in our parental arsenal to train up well-rounded, well-read, emotionally-resilient, critical-thinking, industry-disrupting citizens who will turn the trajectory of this great nation. As Gatto, said, "Government monopoly schools are structurally unreformable." Let's not mend them, parents; let's end them. It's time for a new day, a new era, a new breed of education for the next generation.

Parents, can I give you some homework? *Read Dumbing Us Down, Hold On to Your Kids, No Ordinary Child, Abolition,* and *The End of Education.* Make time every day to read the Bible to and with your kids. Discuss it. Activate it in your lives. Write down verses and memorize them as a family. Help your children to write the word of God on their hearts. Deuteronomy 4:11 says that we are to take care to share what our eyes have seen with our children and grandchildren so that the next generation will have an eternal hope—even in the midst of a national or global crisis.

As we reflect on the social, physical, academic, familial, and spiritual status of the day, let's end with a few action steps. Create community. Care for yourself physically, emotionally, and spiritually. Be aware of your emotional state. Squash the ants. Create scaffolding and opportunities for intergenerational mentoring, reaching up 10 years for mentorship and down 10 years for influence. Remember the acronym GIGO (garbage in, garbage out). Guard your heart, the wellspring of life. Read the Bible every day. Study it like you're about to take a test (you are). Forgive often: Jesus was and wasn't exaggerating when he told us to forgive 70 x 7 times a day. Build up your courage muscle, your gratitude muscle, and your peace muscle through ongoing practice. And remember that everything we experience, every name or label of all that was or is or is to come, it all bows to the name of Jesus. This time next year, you'll look in the rearview mirror of your life and see a new harvest: the fruit of peace, hope, joy, purpose, and relational recalibration in your home.

I echo the words of Colonel Raymond Moore, founder of the Exodus Mandate: "Unless we change education, we will lose the next generation." Our personal and national liberties can be protected and preserved through the multi-generational model of home-based education centered around the church community. You can be part of the solution by joining the rescue mission and starting homeschool academies in your church, turning the trajectory of anxiety, depression, and hopelessness in this generation and preserving the transmission of the faith from one generation to the next. As Ken Ham writes in *Ready to Return,*

"Unless we reverse course and return to the bedrock, foundational Judeo-Christian beliefs in the Creator and his unchanging morality, we too will fail. And the experiment that once was America will have failed, having lasted only a few centuries," he says. "The cracks in our foundation are openly visible, though some try to deny it. The truth is that we are rapidly crumbling and soon to collapse unless Christians take action." It's up to us friends. We are the church, the hope of the world. Jesus gave us a mission of discipleship, and it begins first in our own homes. All we need is a vision and a plan.

Recently, a pair of brand new homeschool moms in our community wanted to be part of the solution to our county's public school crisis. They threw together some simple ads on social media and advertised a homeschool expo. They didn't have a location, connections, or any experience, but what they did have was passion. And guess what? The word spread like wildfire, and within just a couple of weeks, 1400 people from all walks of life all across the county had signed up for the expo saying, "I want out of the system, and I need help." Another 90 people stepped up and said, "Here am I; send me," and they put out tables and flyers to share with the newbies how they could best support them. Let's go! This is a grassroots movement at its finest! If we have even a hazy vision and an ounce of passion, we can turn this trajectory around.

In one of our homeschool academies this year, a child's father passed away suddenly. Not only were we as a homeschool community able to meet some of the practical needs of the widowed family, we were able to attend the funeral and be there to hold up the arms of his mom as her 6-year-old son gave the eulogy for his father. It was both tragic and touching to see the impact of authentic community. Teachers are an anemic substitution for parents, though they can offer support when they have the right positioning of influence. And peers will always be a shallow, hollow substitute for the nurture and approval we naturally seek from our parents. The homeschool academy method promises the best of both worlds, reflection and connection, parent-direction and peer-support.

When I think back to my own experience in a sterile, relation-less classroom where I was unknown and underdeveloped, misguided and miserable, I recognize God's hand of provision and purpose reaching into my brokenness and creating a transgenerational pathway toward hope and healing. The level of confidence and courage and identity that my own children carry as a result of being parented and discipled rallies me to stand in awe at the miraculous work that God has done, turning my ashes to beauty and my mourning to dancing so that the next generation in my bloodline could walk in freedom.

What about you? What's in your hand right now? What creative skills and strategies can you stir up within you to help us turn the tide for the next generation? As my friend Dr. John Jackson writes in his book *The Prevailing Church*, "The bride of Christ was never meant to be a retiring and reticent creature of comfort." We were meant to prevail, he says, to push back the realms of darkness and take our place as agents of change, bearers of light, and beacons of hope. Parents, it's our time to shine. "Store up for yourselves treasures in heaven," Matthew tells us. "Where your treasure is there your heart will be also." If some other lesser God has absolved you of your rightful focus on your children, it's time to shake the dust off. The gift of God to us as parents, our reward, our training ground, is the next generation.

I am greatly heartened by the movement I see happening across the nation right now. The realm of impact is not simply temporal; we are truly making an eternal difference. The potential for a cultural shift, a great awakening, is within our grasp like never before. Let's examine the practicality of the vision: In the state of California, for example, there are 23,558 churches and 6,002,523 kindergarten to 12th grade public schools students. If just 75% of the state's churches would be willing to step up and give their empty children's church classrooms and auditoriums to parents during the week, we could open 17,668 homeschool academies of 340 students each—and we could empty every public school classroom in the state of California tomorrow. Boom. Mic drop. Let's go, parents.

The visual that comes to mind when I consider the power of parents stepping into the ring to take back education is an unforgettable scene from the book of I Samuel, where the ark of the covenant has been captured by the Philistines, who foolishly bring the ark into the temple of their god, Dagon. The ark of the covenant represents the living presence of the Lord, and if you remember the story, the Philistines come back to the temple the next morning only to find their false god lying prone on the floor in front of the ark. They prop the idol back up, only to find the next day that it has fallen again—this time completely dismembered before the ark of the covenant, the presence of the living God. This is what's happening in our culture today. As the carriers of the presence of God come in contact with the false idols of the day, we are seeing the walls crumble, the foundations crack, the idols destroyed. Parents, the false idols of the day can't contend when they attempt to stand in the presence of the living God within us.

This book is about education, yes. But more importantly, this book is about parents stepping into their rightful, ordained role as a leader of the home, as captain of the scholastic ship. Your children do not belong to the government. They don't belong to a teacher or a coach or a well-intentioned youth director. The mantel for leadership and discipleship of the next generation begins and end with us, parents.

The time is now. Our youngest citizens are ready for an infusion of hope, joy, and purpose that can only flow freely when parents rise up and take their rightful place on the battle line. Scholastically and experientially, the data clearly points in one direction: The most effective educational methodology is the parent-directed model, and a church-based homeschool academy provides the perfect catalyst for relational sharpening that will help students and their parents thrive. Mom, dad, pastor, artist, business owner, visionary, we need you. Won't you join us on the rescue mission? Instead of ignoring the problem, we can play a powerful role in the living solution that turns the trajectory for the next generation. The harvest is ripe, and we need all hands on deck: every church, every city, every parent across America. Our nation's students are facing a socio-academic crisis of epidemic proportions, and the responsibility for relational restoration rests squarely on our shoulders. It's time for courage. It's time for vision. Parents, let's take back America. The harvest is ready. It's time for an education revolution.

ACKNOWLEDGEMENTS

As a parent and a professor for almost 20 years, and now as a college president, I am deeply committed to the success of the next generation. I saw the brokenness and anxiety in my students' conversations, in their actions, in their relationships, in their journals. These outpourings were ultimately the impetus for the launch of Chula Vista Christian University as well as a number of homeschool support academies.

The goal of this book is to help launch a grassroots cultural shift that will turn the tide of anxiety, depression, and atheism in the next generation. Yes, it's about education, for we must change that. But it's also about attachment. It's about parenting. Children need the influence, support, connectivity, and correction of their parents. Children need to be discipled, and there is no one more equipped to disciple a child than the child's parents.

This book is the result of many years of both experiential and scholastic reflections. I am grateful to my graduate school professors at Regent University and Fielding University, who taught me to think critically, to reason, and to become an agent of change. I am thankful to the courageous, alert parents across California whose stories have been shared on my Communication Architect podcast and MindsetMatters radio show as a complement to this book. And I am grateful to my students at Chula Vista Christian University and Awaken Academy for providing a living laboratory that brought textbook research to life. It's one thing to read a statistic on a stark page and quite another to see that statistic transforming in the classroom.

Thank you to our courageous lead pastors at Awaken Church, Pastors Jurgen and Leanne Mattheseus, for believing in the mission and vision of a homeschool academy. The academy took root at an exponential pace that neither they nor I saw coming, rescuing hundreds of families from the state's indoctrination centers in its first 18 month alone. It takes an army of laborers to carry out an education revolution, and I am grateful for their trust in me as we have begun to make a significant impact on our county. At the time of this writing, Awaken Academy is the largest Christian private homeschooling group in Southern California, and it is an immeasurable joy to see the lives of families in our midst transforming before our eyes.

Thank you to the many kind friends who offered their thoughtful endorsements in the introduction to this book: Dr. Jackson, Dr. Garlow, Dr. Yeager, Brian Reiswig, Christine Gail, David Ewing, Ebey Sorenson, Corie Di Matteo, Brittni De La Mora, David Baldwin,

Rebecca Kocsis; and thank you to Andrew Pudewa for writing such a powerful foreword. I first met Andrew years ago at a Christian Home Educators Association conference, and I have been an Institute for Excellence in Writing fan ever since. Though Andrew is accustomed to speaking to sold-out crowds across the nation, he graciously and humbly flew to San Diego to speak to a handful of parents and faculty at one of our academies even before any of them knew who he was or the wisdom he carried.

I worked with many parents in researching this book. One in particular, Corie Di Matteo, stands out to me because she not only caught the vision for the homeschool model right away, but also because she quickly stepped up to the call with a blazing fire and an all-in mentality. She displayed the tenacity it takes to launch an education revolution. Within months of her public-school-to-homeschool conversion, she began voluntarily mentoring other parents and joining me on the road as I shared the vision with other churches. She also dedicated considerable time to editing and sharpening this book, enduring my many rewrites of entire pages as well as my hours of deliberation over singular words. E.B. White once said he rewrote the last page of *Charlotte's Web* eight times. Corie stayed the course with each of my many rewrites, offering invaluable generational insights.

Thank you to my mom, Carolyn Rollberg, who is an example of God's power of transformation. Though we grew up separated from one another, in her latter years, she became a follower of Christ and made many noteworthy and admirable strides in her life and in her walk with the Lord. Today, we enjoy a relationship of mutual encouragement and prayer support, and as I've written in these pages, I am grateful for her willingness to persevere through life's storms.

Last but certainly not least, I am thankful for my amazing family. My British husband, Adrian, has been my best friend and business partner for the last 31 years. I am deeply appreciative of the weight he shoulders in our home, especially during my book writing seasons. In a household where everyone is juggling multiple roles and responsibilities, this is no small undertaking. One of his many skill sets is the ability to turn perceived disaster into humor, so on the frequent occasions where I take myself and my writing far too seriously, he helps me keep life in the proper perspective. For three decades now, he has been a tremendous source of strength, support, and encouragement in my life. He's also the fabulous designer of my very best book covers, so his creative vision is felt in the visual as well as linguistic elements of this book.

Thank you my children for the many ways they intentionally and unintentionally bless me. I am thankful for the incredible fruit they bear, personally, professionally, and relationally. They both carry the gift of servitude, and it is a joy to see them using their remarkable talents to further the kingdom of God, especially when the majority of their generation is MIA from the modern church. Ethan and Cymone have taught me unconditional love, unbounded creativity, and, as all well-loved children teach their parents, the power of mentorship. The social science literature is replete with examples of the capacity for healing from trauma through adult relationships, and I have personally experienced new levels of healing from my past wounds in every season of my life with these two precious gift from God. As the scholastic specimens in my living academic laboratory, my children have also taught me that homeschooling works. I am extraordinarily grateful for each one of them and impact they have had on my life.

Friends, I hope you find this book to be a source of encouragement, despite the painful realities presented herein. There will be times when you are tempted to go back to Egypt, where the allure of alone time at Starbucks—that modern equivalent of Israel's cucumber craving—might make desertion seem alluring. I pray that you will resist the seductive siren song of the world's temporal system, follow hard after God, and train up children who will protect and honor their families, their faith, and their freedom. May we all labor together with a finger on the pulse of the culture, a hand on the plow, and an eye toward the realm of possibility. As Psalm 102:18 says,"Let this be written for a future generation, that a people not yet created may praise the Lord."

Dr. Lisa Dunne
March 2022

REFERENCES

Amen, Daniel (2015). *Change Your Brain, Change Your Life.* Harmony Books.

Anfuso, Francis and Lisa Dunne (2011). *Numb.* The Rock of Roseville: California.

Barna, George (2018). *GenZ: The Culture, Beliefs, and Motivations Shaping the Next Generation.* Barna Group.

Barna, George (2010). *Revolutionary Parenting: What the Research Shows Really Works.* Tyndale Momentum.

Barna, George (2020). State of the Church in 2020. "Signs of Decline & Hope Among Key Metrics of Faith." *Faith and Christianity.* Ventura: Barna Group.

Blankenhorn, David (1985). *Fatherless America: Confronting Our Most Urgent Social Problem.* New York: Basic Books.

Brooks, Robert and Goldstein, Sam (2004). *The Power of Resilience: Achieving Balance, Confidence, and Personal Strength in Your Life.* New York: McGraw Hill.

Bowlby, John (1988). *A Secure Base: Parent-child Attachment and Healthy Human Development.* New York: Basic Books.

Bowlby, John (1989). *The Making and Breaking of Affectional Bonds.* London: Routledge.

Cain, Susan (2013). *Quiet: The Power of Introverts in a World That Can't Stop Talking.* New York: Broadway Paperbacks.

Clear, James (2018). *Atomic Habits: An Easy and Proven Way to Build Good Habits and Break Bad Ones.* New York: Random House.

Clinton, Timothy and Gary Sibcy (2002). *Attachments: Why You Love, Feel, and Act the Way You Do.* Nashville. Integrity Publishers.

Collins, Jim (2001). *Good to Great: Why Some Companies Make the Leap...and Others Don't.* Random House Business Books.

DeMille, Oliver (2006). *A Thomas Jefferson Education. Teaching a Generation of Leaders for the Twenty-first Century.* George Wythe College Press, 2nd Edition.

Dreher, Rod (2020). *Live Not by Lies: A Manual for Christian Dissidents.* New York, New York: Sentinel Press.

Dunne, Lisa (2017). *The Multigenerational Marketplace: Eight Communication Competencies for Creating a Culture of Value that Attracts, Retains, and Engages the Next Generation of Employees.* Waco: Book Ripple.

Dunne, Lisa. *The Science of Social Influence: How the Culture of Media Shapes Our Identity.* Waco: Book Ripple.

Dweck, Carol (2006). *Mindset: The New Psychology of Success.* New York: Random House.

Erikson, Erik (1994). *Identity and the Life Cycle.* W.W. Norton.

The English Standard Version Study Bible (2008). Crossway Books.

Family in America, The: *A Journal of Public Policy* (2014). The Quarterly of the Howard Center for Family, Religion, and Society. Cambridge University Press.

Gatto, John Taylor (1992). *Dumbing Us Down: The Hidden Curriculum of Compulsory Schooling*: Philadelphia: New Society Publishers.

Ham, Ken and Britt Beemer (2009). *Already Gone: Why Your Kids Will Quit Church and What You Can Do to Stop It.* Master Books.

Ham, Ken and Greg Hall (2011). *Already Compromised: Christian Colleges Took a Test on the State of Their Faith and the Final Exam Is In.* Master Books.

Ham, Ken and Jeff Kinney (2015). *Ready to Return: The Need for a Fundamental Shift in Church Culture to Save a Generation.* Master Books.

Jackson, John (2021). *The Prevailing Power of the Church: Confronting the Five Giants of Culture.* Jessup University Press. Rocklin, CA.

Loehr, James and Tony Schwartz (2003). *The Power of Full Engagement: Managing Energy, Not Time, is the Key to High Performance and Personal Renewal.* New York: Free Press.

Lukianoff, Greg and Jonathan Haidt (2018). *The Coddling of the American Mind: How Good Intentions and Bad Ideas are Setting up a Generation for Failure.* New York: Penguin Press.

Mendoza, Kimberlee (2021). *Teaching Squirrels. How to Reach Generation Z and Create Lasting Engagement.*

Mira, Denise (2006). *No Ordinary Child: Unlocking the Leader within Your Child.* Winepress Publishing.

Neufeld, Gordon and Mate, Gabor (2004). *Hold on to Your Kids: Why Parents Need to Matter More than Peers.* Toronto: A.A. Knopf Canada.

Novak, Kevin (2016). *Abolition: Overcoming the Christian Establishment on Education.* Deconstructing the Coliseum, LLC.

Peterson, Jordan (2018). *12 Rules for Life: An Antidote to Chaos.* London: Allen Lane.

Postman, Neil and Weingartner, Charles (1969). *Teaching as a Subversive Activity.* New York: Dell Publishing Company.

Postman, Neil (1992). *Conscientious Objections: Stirring up Trouble about Language, Technology, and Education.* 1st Vintage Books.

Postman, Neil (1982). *The Disappearance of Childhood.* New York: Delacorte Press.

Postman, Neil (1995). *The End of Education: Redefining the Value of School.* New York: Knopf.

Siegel, Dan and Mary Hartzel (2014). *Parenting from the Inside Out: How a Deeper Self-understanding Can Help You Raise Children Who Thrive.* New York: Penguin Group.

Sinek, Simon (2009). *Start with Why: How Great Leaders Inspire Everyone to Take Action.* New York: Portfolio.

Siegel, Dan (2012). *The Developing Mind: How Relationships and the Brain Interact to Shape Who We Are.* New York: Guilford Press.

Van Der Kolk, Besser (2015). *The Body Keeps the Score.* New York, New York: Penguin Books.

Young, Ed (2004). *Kid CEO: How to Keep Your Children from Running Your Life.* FaithWords.

Zak, Paul (2013). *The Moral Molecule: How Trust Works.* Corgi Books.